Building Time

Praise for *Building Time*

"*Building Time* is a graceful, timely, and purposeful walk through a garden of architectural knowledge, offering an account—in all, a theory—not just of human spatial experience through time (first we go here, then we go there...), but of the world experiencing itself through the medium of buildings, especially buildings which, in having long-term ethical projects as well as complexities of their own, are works of architecture. With Proustian intimacy and often dizzying insight, Leatherbarrow enlarges the very language we use to understand architecture. Buildings are indifferent only apparently. In marking time, in accommodating the fleeting, in witnessing and in suffering, they bring up the future."

MICHAEL BENEDIKT, *The University of Texas at Austin, USA*

"Leatherbarrow focuses his meditative attention on lasting works of art and architecture. Discussing paintings and projects with particular sensitivity to light and material, he perceptively reveals changes wrought by three kinds of time. Working like a clockmaker, patiently disassembling architectural mechanisms into their component parts, he explains how buildings operate in time."

JOHN TUOMEY, *O'Donnell + Tuomey Architects, Ireland*

"When Leatherbarrow writes about time he is also writing about the slow and then ever faster passage of our own lives. Even as we visit the Pantheon to watch time literally move before our eyes and we are reminded that it also measures the span of our own existence. This is a dense, lyrical, and heartbreaking book about our lives and our buildings."

BILLIE TSIEN, *Tod Williams Billie Tsien Architects, USA*

"Linger, return, and remember rhythm this meditation on the interactions of time, space and place for both author and reader. Not since the romantic writers of the early 19th century has the temporal dimension of architecture been viewed patiently from so many facets."

BARRY BERGDOLL, *Meyer Schapiro Professor of Art History, Columbia University, USA*

"*Building Time* suggests that architecture matters partly because architecture weathers orienting and grounding us: by keeping its identity amidst contextual change, inevitable decay, and eventual renewal, as well as recording its own creation and survival. The world stage, the active body and the project script frame the close reading of chosen modern masterpieces in time and as time. Sound, serviceable, and delightful."

CARLOS EDUARDO COMAS, *Federal University of Rio Grande do Sul, Brazil*

Building Time

Architecture, Event, and Experience

David Leatherbarrow

BLOOMSBURY VISUAL ARTS
LONDON · NEW YORK · OXFORD · NEW DELHI · SYDNEY

BLOOMSBURY VISUAL ARTS
Bloomsbury Publishing Plc, 50 Bedford Square, London, WC1B 3DP, UK
Bloomsbury Publishing Inc, 1359 Broadway, New York, NY 10018, USA
Bloomsbury Publishing Ireland, 29 Earlsfort Terrace, Dublin 2, D02 AY28, Ireland

BLOOMSBURY, BLOOMSBURY VISUAL ARTS and the Diana logo are trademarks
of Bloomsbury Publishing Plc

First published in Great Britain 2021
Reprinted 2022, 2023, 2025

Copyright © David Leatherbarrow, 2021

David Leatherbarrow has asserted his right under the Copyright, Designs and Patents
Act, 1988, to be identified as Author of this work.

For legal purposes the Acknowledgments on p. xv constitute an extension
of this copyright page.

Cover design by Eleanor Rose
Cover image © Sverre Fehn, Villa Busk, 1987–1990, Bamble, Norway; detail of
external concrete. Photo by David Leatherbarrow

All rights reserved. No part of this publication may be: i) reproduced or transmitted in any form, electronic or mechanical, including photocopying, recording or by means of any information storage or retrieval system without prior permission in writing from the publishers; or ii) used or reproduced in any way for the training, development or operation of artificial intelligence (AI) technologies, including generative AI technologies. The rights holders expressly reserve this publication from the text and data mining exception as per Article 4(3) of the Digital Single Market Directive (EU) 2019/790.

Bloomsbury Publishing Plc does not have any control over, or responsibility for, any third-party websites referred to or in this book. All internet addresses given in this book were correct at the time of going to press. The author and publisher regret any inconvenience caused if addresses have changed or sites have ceased to exist, but can accept no responsibility for any such changes.

A catalogue record for this book is available from the British Library.

A catalog record for this book is available from the Library of Congress.

ISBN:	HB:	978-1-3501-6519-9
	PB:	978-1-3501-6518-2
	ePDF:	978-1-3501-6520-5
	eBook:	978-1-3501-6521-2

Typeset by Integra Software Services Pvt. Ltd.
Printed and bound in Great Britain

For product safety related questions contact productsafety@bloomsbury.com.

To find out more about our authors and books visit www.bloomsbury.com
and sign up for our newsletters.

*Dedicated to the memory of my father,
whose time was entirely full of life.*

Contents

List of Illustrations x
Acknowledgments xv
About the Author xvi

Part One Introduction 1

1.1 Making Space for Time 3
  The Time of the World 12
  The Time of the Body 14
  The Time of the Project 16
  Structure and Approach 17

Part Two The Time of the World 21

2.1 Day Time: Adolph Menzel's *Balcony Room* 23
  Forces at Play 25
  Changing Circumstances 29

2.2 Well-Timed Openings: Eileen Gray's Tempe à Pailla 31
  In the Blink of an Eye 31
  A Solar-Site-Plan 34
  Scheduling Plan Positions 38
  Timely Adjustments 41
  Good Timing 46

2.3 Tempered Terrain: Sverre Fehn's Villa Busk 49
  Vestiges as Clues 51
  Past as Prologue 52

Lasting Impressions 64
Pre-Recordings and Recordings 70

2.4 World Rhythms: Álvaro Siza's Swimming Pools at Leça da Palmeira 75
The Vocation of Construction Materials 80
Potentialities 82

Part Three The Time of the Body 91

3.1 Taking Steps: Nicolaes Maes' *The Eavesdropper* 93
One Moment among Many 95
Again and Again 98

3.2 Pacing and Spacing: Bo and Wohlert's *Louisiana Museum of Modern Art* 101
A Museum without Walls 105
Landscape Configuration 108
Landscape Movement 110
Viewing Distance and Angle 111

3.3 Wandering Sites: Wang Shu's Hangzhou Guest House 123
The Time of Spatial Passage 131
Non-synchronic Passage 135
Distances and Depth 138
Depth and Duration 140

3.4 Pedestrian Rhythms: Álvaro Siza's Swimming Pools at Leça da Palmeira 149
Pacing 152
Opportune Beginnings 157
Still There 161

Part Four The Time of the Project 167

4.1 Past and Present Possibilities: Leonardo da Vinci's *Adoration of the Magi* 169

The Time of Given Conditions 170
Project vs. Product 171
Project Making Prospects 172
Anachronisms 173

4.2 Proposing Precedents: Rafael Moneo's *Museo Nacional de Arte Romano de Mérida* 181
Converging Parallels 187
Time and Again 194
No Longer and Not Yet 201

4.3 Recalling Future Projects: Pezo von Ellrichshausen's Poli House 203
From Time to Time 204
Bloodlines 210
Intentions 215
Two as One 218
Recollection Forward 223

4.4 Project Rhythms: Álvaro Siza's Swimming Pools at Leça da Palmeira 227
Before the Beginning 229
Is That How Projects Begin, Destructively? 235

Notes 243
Bibliography 261
Index 268

Illustrations

1.1.1 Álvaro Siza, *Leça da Palmeira Pools,* view from shore to city 4
1.1.2 *Wells Cathedral,* Chapter House steps 7
1.1.3 Louis I. Kahn, *Salk Institute* 8
1.1.4 Kengo Kuma, *Hiroshige Museum* 8
1.1.5 Marcel Breuer, *De Bijenkorf Department Store* 9
1.1.6 *Ferrara Cathedral* 11
1.1.7 Oscar Niemeyer, et al., *Ministry of Education* 13
1.1.8 Le Corbusier, *Swiss Pavilion* 15
1.1.9 Louis I. Kahn, *Dominican Mother House*, collage plan 17
2.1.1 Adolph Menzel, *Balcony Room*, 1845 24
2.2.1 Eileen Gray, *Tempe à Pailla*, Castellar, France, ceiling oculus 32
2.2.2 Eileen Gray, *Tempe à Pailla*, Castellar, France, bedroom plan and section 33
2.2.3 Eileen Gray, *Tempe à Pailla*, Castellar, France, solar site plan 35
2.2.4 Eileen Gray, *Tempe à Pailla*, Castellar, France, topographical site plan 39
2.2.5 Eileen Gray, *Tempe à Pailla*, Castellar, France, ground plan 40
2.2.6 Eileen Gray, *Tempe à Pailla*, Castellar, France, sliding shutter 42
2.2.7 Eileen Gray, *Tempe à Pailla*, Castellar, France, terrace 45
2.3.1 Sverre Fehn, *Archbishopric Museum*, Hamar, Norway 50
2.3.2 Sverre Fehn, *National Museum of Architecture*, Oslo 52
2.3.3 Sverre Fehn, *Villa Busk*, Bamble, Norway, entry walkway 53
2.3.4 Sverre Fehn, *Villa Busk*, Bamble, Norway, ground plan 56
2.3.5 Sverre Fehn, *Villa Busk*, Bamble, Norway, location plan 57
2.3.6 Sverre Fehn, *Villa Busk*, Bamble, Norway, bath 58
2.3.7 Sverre Fehn, *Villa Busk*, Bamble, Norway, outdoor terrace 59
2.3.8 Sverre Fehn, *Villa Busk*, Bamble, Norway, exterior columns 61
2.3.9 Sverre Fehn, *Villa Busk*, Bamble, Norway, rear wall meeting terrain 62

2.3.10	Sverre Fehn, *Villa Busk*, Bamble, Norway, half-height column bracket 63
2.3.11	Sverre Fehn, *Villa Busk*, Bamble, Norway, concrete stain 66
2.3.12	Sverre Fehn, *Villa Busk*, Bamble, Norway, column base 66
2.3.13	Sverre Fehn, *Villa Busk*, Bamble, Norway, stair treads 69
2.3.14	Sverre Fehn, *Villa Busk*, Bamble, Norway, threshold 70
2.3.15	Sverre Fehn, *Villa Busk,* Bamble, Norway, plaster finishing 71
2.3.16	Sverre Fehn, *Villa Busk*, Bamble, Norway, fireplace 72
2.4.1	Álvaro Siza, *Leça da Palmeira Pools,* Porto, shore 76
2.4.2	Álvaro Siza, *Leça da Palmeira Pools*, Porto, rock depressions 79
2.4.3	Álvaro Siza, *Leça da Palmeira Pools*, Porto, rear walk and stair 81
2.4.4	Myron of Eleutherae, *Discus Thrower* 85
2.4.5	Álvaro Siza, *Leça da Palmeira Pools*, Porto, sink and mirror 86
2.4.6	Álvaro Siza, *Leça da Palmeira Pools*, Porto, entry ramp 87
2.4.7	Álvaro Siza, *Leça da Palmeira Pools*, Porto, area plan 87
2.4.8	Álvaro Siza, *Leça da Palmeira Pools*, Porto, front lawn and roofs 88
3.1.1	Nicolaes Maes, *The Eavesdropper* 94
3.2.1	Bo and Wohlert, *Louisiana Museum*, Copenhagen, view toward the Sound 102
3.2.2	Bo and Wohlert, *Louisiana Museum*, Copenhagen, entry 106
3.2.3	Bo and Wohlert, *Louisiana Museum*, Copenhagen, general plan 107
3.2.4	Ole and Edith Nørgård, *Louisiana Museum*, Copenhagen, garden rooms, view 108
3.2.5	Ole and Edith Nørgård, *Louisiana Museum*, Copenhagen, garden rooms, plan 109
3.2.6	Bo and Wohlert, *Louisiana Museum*, Copenhagen, gallery corridor elevation 110
3.2.7	Bo and Wohlert, *Louisiana Museum*, Copenhagen, gallery mezzanine 113
3.2.8	Bo and Wohlert, *Louisiana Museum*, Copenhagen, stepping stone walk 114
3.2.9	Bo and Wohlert, *Louisiana Museum*, Copenhagen, fireplace and dining room 115
3.2.10	Bo and Wohlert, *Louisiana Museum*, Copenhagen, dining room catalogue wall 116
3.2.11	Henry Moore, *Three Piece Reclining Figure-Draped*, *Louisiana Museum*, Copenhagen 117
3.2.12	Joan Miró, *Personage*, *Louisiana Museum*, Copenhagen 118
3.2.13	Bo and Wohlert, *Louisiana Museum*, Copenhagen, gallery 119

3.2.14   Bo and Wohlert, *Louisiana Museum*, Copenhagen, Giacometti room 120
3.2.15   Bo and Wohlert, *Louisiana Museum*, Copenhagen, Giacometti room 121
3.3.1   Wang Shu, *China Academy of Art*, Hangzhou, mountain and river 124
3.3.2   Wang Shu, Wenzheng College, Suzhou, rear elevation 127
3.3.3   Wang Shu, Wenzheng College, Suzhou, entry 128
3.3.4   Wang Shu, Wenzheng College, Suzhou, interior 129
3.3.5   Wang Shu, *China Academy of Art*, Hangzhou, preliminary sketch 130
3.3.6   Wang Shu, *China Academy of Art*, Hangzhou, gardens 131
3.3.7   Wang Shu, *China Academy of Art*, Hangzhou, classroom building 132
3.3.8   Wang Shu, *China Academy of Art*, Hangzhou, courtyard and mountain 133
3.3.9   Wang Shu, *China Academy of Art, Guest House*, Hangzhou, interior stair and court 136
3.3.10   Wang Shu, *China Academy of Art*, Hangzhou, external walkways 141
3.3.11   Wang Shu, *China Academy of Art*, Hangzhou, classroom building plan 142
3.3.12   Wang Shu, *China Academy of Art*, Hangzhou, sketch 142
3.3.13   Wang Shu, *China Academy of Art, Guest House*, Hangzhou, pool and bridge 143
3.3.14   Wang Shu, *China Academy of Art, Guest House*, Hangzhou, roof landscape 145
3.3.15   Wang Shu, *China Academy of Art, Guest House*, Hangzhou, ground plan 146
3.3.16   Wang Shu, *China Academy of Art, Guest House*, Hangzhou, terraces 147
3.3.17   Wang Shu, *China Academy of Art, Guest House*, Hangzhou, interior 148
3.4.1   Álvaro Siza, *Leça da Palmeira*, Porto, showers and rear walk 150
3.4.2   Álvaro Siza, *Leça da Palmeira Pools*, Porto, preliminary site plan 153
3.4.3   Álvaro Siza, *Leça da Palmeira Pools*, Porto, preliminary plan 153
3.4.4   Álvaro Siza, *Leça da Palmeira Pools*, Porto, roofs and distant shore 154
3.4.5   Álvaro Siza, *Leça da Palmeira Pools*, Porto, partial plan 155
3.4.6   Álvaro Siza, *Leça da Palmeira Pools*, Porto, entry ramp 156
3.4.7   Álvaro Siza, *Leça da Palmeira Pools*, Porto, cantilevered roofs 158
3.4.8   Álvaro Siza, *Leça da Palmeira Pools*, Porto, showers 159
3.4.9   Álvaro Siza, *Leça da Palmeira Pools*, rear deck 160
3.4.10   Álvaro Siza, *Leça da Palmeira Pools*, children's pool 161
3.4.11   Álvaro Siza, *Leça da Palmeira Pools*, entry roofs 163
3.4.12   Álvaro Siza, *Leça da Palmeira Pools*, rear wall 164
3.4.13   Álvaro Siza, *Leça da Palmeira Pools*, horizontal openings 164
3.4.14   Álvaro Siza, *Leça da Palmeira Pools*, adult pool 166

4.1.1	Leonardo da Vinci, *Adoration of the Magi* 174	
4.2.1	Rafael Moneo, *National Museum of Roman Art*, Mérida, front court 182	
4.2.2	Rafael Moneo, *National Museum of Roman Art*, Mérida, interior 185	
4.2.3	Rafael Moneo, *National Museum of Roman Art*, Mérida, ancient Mérida, bronze relief plan 186	
4.2.4	Rafael Moneo, *National Museum of Roman Art*, Mérida, ground plan 186	
4.2.5	Rafael Moneo, *National Museum of Roman Art*, Mérida, partial basement plan 189	
4.2.6	Rafael Moneo, *National Museum of Roman Art*, Mérida, aerial view 190	
4.2.7	Rafael Moneo, *National Museum of Roman Art*, Mérida, bronze relief plan 191	
4.2.8	Rafael Moneo, *National Museum of Roman Art*, Mérida, museum interior 195	
4.2.9	Rafael Moneo, *National Museum of Roman Art*, Mérida, basement level 196	
4.2.10	Rafael Moneo, *National Museum of Roman Art*, Mérida, external buttresses 198	
4.2.11	Rafael Moneo, *National Museum of Roman Art*, Mérida, terminal buttress and sunken court 199	
4.2.12	Rafael Moneo, *National Museum of Roman Art*, Mérida, basement stair, ruins and bridge 201	
4.3.1	Louis I. Kahn, *Study for a Mural Based on Egyptian Motifs,* no. 1, 1951 205	
4.3.2	Le Corbusier, *Parthenon*, sketch 207	
4.3.3	Pezo von Ellrichshausen, *Casa Guna*, San Pedro, Chile 211	
4.3.4	Pezo von Ellrichshausen, *Casa Solo*, Cretas, Spain 211	
4.3.5	Lina Bo Bardi, *Casa de Vidro*, São Paulo, Brazil 213	
4.3.6	Mies van der Rohe, *Villa Tugendhat*, Brno, Czech Republic 213	
4.3.7	Pezo von Ellrichshausen, *Poli House*, Coliumo, Chile, view from cliff 214	
4.3.8	Pezo von Ellrichshausen, *Poli House*, Coliumo, Chile, roof 215	
4.3.9	Pezo von Ellrichshausen, *Cien House*, Concepción, Chile, plan studies 216	
4.3.10	Pezo von Ellrichshausen, *Poli House*, Coliumo, Chile, double wall 219	
4.3.11	Pezo von Ellrichshausen, *Poli House*, Coliumo, Chile, plans 221	
4.3.12	Pezo von Ellrichshausen, *Poli House*, Coliumo, Chile, interior 221	
4.3.13	Pezo von Ellrichshausen, *Poli House*, Coliumo, Chile, concrete detail 224	
4.3.14	Pezo von Ellrichshausen, *Poli House*, Coliumo, Chile, detail of steps 225	
4.4.1	Álvaro Siza, *Leça da Palmeira Pools*, Porto, preliminary sketch 228	
4.4.2	Álvaro Siza, *Leça da Palmeira Pools*, Porto, aerial view 232	
4.4.3	Álvaro Siza, *Le Thoronet*, survey sketch 234	

4.4.4 Álvaro Siza, *Leça da Palmeira Pools*, Porto, preliminary sketch 235
4.4.5 Álvaro Siza, Macchu Picchu travel sketch 237
4.4.6 Álvaro Siza, *Leça da Palmeira Pools*, Porto, sketch of site 239
4.4.7 Álvaro Siza, travel sketch 241

Acknowledgments

Building time has been on my mind for many years, since my first books. Although I've often lectured on this subject elsewhere, most of my work on the buildings and themes addressed in this book developed out of my teaching at the University of Pennsylvania. The roles of student and teacher were frequently reversed, particularly in my Ph.D. classes. Current and former students whose research contributed to my thinking on the topics addressed in this book include: Stephen Anderson, Jin Baek, Liyang Ding, Rumiko Handa, Duffy Half, Linfan Liu, and Tonkao Panin. One of my current students, Zhengyang Hua, was especially helpful as my research assistant.

As this study presents close readings of a number of buildings, conversations with their architects, when possible, were very important to me. I'd like to thank each of them for their time, their explanations, and their patience with my observations and arguments: Rafael Moneo, Mauricio Pezo, Sofia von Ellrichshausen, and Wang Shu.

I also want to acknowledge the many benefits I've received from colleagues who have read parts or the whole of the text: Michael Benedikt, Carlos Eduardo Comas, Juan Manuel Heredia, and Franca Trubiano. I'm very grateful for the time they devoted to my work, instead of theirs, and also for their insights and suggestions.

While writing this book, I've had many productive conversations with friends and colleagues who share an interest in matters of building time: Per Olaf Fjeld, Stanislaus Fung, Michael Hensel, John Dixon Hunt, Mari Hvattum, Ada Karmi Melamede, Harry Mallgrave, Frank Matero, Anu Mathur, Michael Merrill, Quintas Miller, Yonggao Shi, Bruno Silvestre, and Richard Wesley.

Lastly, I'd like to warmly thank Lauren Leatherbarrow for her support, sharp eye, and sense of reality.

About the Author

David Leatherbarrow is Professor of Architecture at the University of Pennsylvania, where he has taught architectural design, history, and theory since 1984. In 2020, the AIA and ASCA awarded him the prestigious Topaz Medallion for excellence in architectural education. He lectures widely and holds guest professorships in Denmark and China. His previous publishing includes *20th Century Architecture, Architecture Oriented Otherwise, Topographical Stories, Surface Architecture* (with Mohsen Mostafavi), *Uncommon Ground, Roots of Architectural Invention*, and *On Weathering: The Life of Buildings in Time*.

Part One

Introduction

1.1
Making Space for Time

Forever—is composed of Nows—
'Tis not a different time—
EMILY DICKINSON, n. 624, *c.* 1860

Architecture, it is said, results from the thoughtful making of space.[1] But *time* is the dimension in which buildings actually come to life: how their shadows and steel engage the days and seasons of the world, how they guide the movements of people and things, and how they project the past into the future, the once-was into the could-be. Time is not a contingent attribute of the places intended in design and realized through construction but a key dimension of their structure and significance.

Perhaps it's no surprise that time gets little direct attention in an art dedicated to permanence. Once they're built, we expect rooms, houses, and offices to remain as they were, as if time hadn't passed or didn't matter—*here they are*, still ready for use, available now as before, rather like one's body. Although much in life changes, buildings seem not to. When we stop to think about it, probably some differences between appearances then and now will be allowed, changes that result from deterioration, refinishing, alterations, and so on. These are of course changes of state, not position. Even so, when compared to the aspects of furnishings and rooms that are *presently* apparent, qualities that once were and will be, former and future phases hardly matter—and that's by design. An architectural work is complete when what's meant to remain has been realized. As months fade into years, the once-was and the now stand shoulder to shoulder, as if concurrent, no matter if the floor, walls, and roof are a little worse-for-wear, having suffered the effects of inhabitation and environmental influence. Endurance is a building's most basic task and chief ambition.

Uncontroversial as these truisms might seem, they are contradicted by the fact that the building's "photo-ready" or "move-in" condition never lasts very long, hardly more

Figure 1.1.1 Álvaro Siza, *Leça da Palmeira Pools,* view from shore to city. Photograph David Leatherbarrow.

than a season, certainly not through the years and decades of its use, well after the builders have left the site. The first hour of inhabitation inaugurates a history of modifications that only ends when the building falls to ruin or is demolished. Even then traces remain, and thereby supply memory with a secure foothold, not only for one's own recollection, but more importantly for collective memory: traces of the Wall in Berlin, for example, or that same city's Memorial Church on Kurfürstendamm. Famous examples aside, the beginnings of the end are often trivial. First come scuffs on the floor and marks on the walls, then re-painting and re-furnishing, leading to the insertion of new doors, windows, or partitions, and the still more significant subtractions and additions that will come later. Succession follows on the heels of inception; new appearances supplant old, veiling the initial conception, although their appearance rarely attracts notice. Retrospective views of resemblance do not overcome; they reaffirm these differences. My thesis is that a key task of design is making space for this kind of time, the time of continual change, without, however, disavowing the desire for permanence.

Everyone likes landscapes of newly fallen snow, before they're spoiled when the day begins. Pristine buildings have a similar appeal, before the residents move in. When trying to describe the settings in which we actually live our lives, however, there is no good reason to privilege a work's first over its later appearances, nor to judge any present condition as necessarily superior to those that preceded and will follow it. The tendency among professionals, professors, and critics to concentrate on the qualities of the work that display the designer's intentions is a disciplinary prejudice that neglects the reality of a building's post-professional life. I realize this observation runs against the grain of most building restoration campaigns, no matter whether they are undertaken by preservationists, historians, or the designers themselves. The target of their efforts is normally the work's uninhabited condition, before its years of suffering began.

The truth of the matter is that many buildings improve over time. Maintenance doesn't always wind the building's clock backwards.[2] Improvements can result from modifications that compensate for inadequate foresight or faulty execution on the construction site. Positive changes can also result from the installation and operation of manual instruments or digital devices that improve a work's usefulness. They alter its appearance as well. Today, buildings that incorporate some of these devices are said to be "intelligent." A smart façade, for example, is one that incorporates instruments that moderate climate, accepting or rejecting free energy from the external environment, while reducing the amount of artificial energy required to achieve comfortable internal conditions. Materials, too, can be smart, which is to say endowed with their own manner of intelligence, more or less successfully and reliably.

But design is not required for changes to occur; alterations can also result from a work's natural tendency to settle into its location, absorbing into its physical body qualifications that can render it more congenial to ambient conditions, including light, air, and temperature together with patterns of use and, more broadly, cultural norms. Here the intelligence expressed by the work has its source in the world, not the design. Taking the long view, it would seem that buildings have no choice but to submit themselves to re-qualifications of this kind, for though they are often unforeseen they are also unavoidable. Cumulatively, they would seem to be fateful. Georg Simmel, speaking of material change in his essay on ruins, said that in every instance of building nature eventually reclaims what was taken from it.[3] Progress toward that end takes many forms. Considering surface alterations, for example, the spectrum ranges very widely, from bleaching, absorption, saturation, and staining, to polishing and abrasion. One of the most well-known instances of abrasion—not from natural but human forces—is the dishing of stairway treads that occurs over years of use, a re-profiling to which thousands of anonymous individuals contribute unknowingly. The result is not only prominently visible, but also usefully legible, showing the path most have preferred. Another eloquent example is the festive or seasonal whitewashing of vernacular buildings.[4] Obviously, this practice is subtended by extra-architectural ideas and traditions—on the Christian calendar Easter renewal, for example.

Forces at play in the ambient environment also remake architectural appearances: a building's sun and shade sides show different degrees of both chromatic intensity and variation—likewise, the alternately prominent and recessed parts of a single façade, such as the wooden panels on Kahn's Salk Institute. The power of light and shadow to animate an architectural surface is similarly obvious. Recently, Kengo Kuma developed a theory of "particles" that elaborates this basic fact of building under the sun.[5] Alterations that result from the sedimentation of air-borne particles are also familiar. Surface marks sometimes enrich, sometimes stain.[6] Although soiled often means spoiled, stains on buildings don't always suggest someone or something was at fault. In the case of Marcel Breuer's De Bijenkorf Department Store, a radically different façade has resulted from this type of alteration. One doubts he anticipated the improbable pattern but suspects he liked it.

Changes that are unforeseen, resulting from non-professional "agencies," interest me the most because they often enrich works in ways that exceed what design intended. Even if we postpone judgments about the merit of modifications that were never envisaged,

Figure 1.1.2 *Wells Cathedral*, Chapter House steps. Photograph David Leatherbarrow.

Figure 1.1.3 Louis I. Kahn, *Salk Institute*. Photograph David Leatherbarrow.

Figure 1.1.4 Kengo Kuma, *Hiroshige Museum*. Photograph David Leatherbarrow.

Figure 1.1.5 Marcel Breuer, *De Bijenkorf Department Store*. Photograph David Leatherbarrow.

I think we must admit that unforeseen changes are inescapable in works that last and therefore should be taken into consideration in any account of their concrete reality, as well as in initial designs that did not clearly foresee but permitted them. Might that be a measure of the project's intelligence: its capacity to absorb unanticipated effects and benefit from the result?

Nevertheless, when given just a little thought, the temporality that is peculiar to architecture seems contradictory. In architecture, time *maintains* what it has brought into being while it simultaneously *schedules the work's transformation*, ultimately its disintegration. How can the two—sameness and difference—occur concurrently?

By virtue of its physicality, suitability, and familiarity, every work keeps its past present; now, like then, the walls of this room are still plaster, timber, and glass; its apertures and furnishings continue to allow one to use it as others have and will; *in time* it will still be *this room*. During any of these uses, the distinction between what the setting once was and now is has no real force. The only aspects of settings that show themselves to be "of the past" are the few that have lost their tacit relevance. In a larger sense, this is the difference between living tradition and history. Practical involvements abrogate the distinction between now and then, particularly when that difference has been hardened into a categorical separation. The chief impediment to grasping the reality of change is our uncritical dedication to objective or clock time, as opposed to the time of events, examples of which would include any instance of residing—talking with friends in your apartment, or working in your office, or watching a movie in your hotel room. On this point, William Faulkner offered a blunt observation: "Time is dead as long as it is being clicked off by little wheels; only when the clock stops does time come to life."[7]

Thanks to the qualities I have just mentioned (physicality, suitability, and familiarity) every built setting not only recalls its past, but it also pre-figures its future. In the case of a lecture room, pre-figuration would anticipate the time when the next speaker or conference will begin, or more prosaically when the floor will be cleaned, the lighting repaired, or the overall appearance renewed. In other words, the room's present state continually outruns itself toward its yesterday and tomorrow, impinging on each of them simultaneously. Here is the key point: temporality is not only nor always moment-by-moment succession. The chronology of regular intervals, clock time, is not lived time, as Faulkner said. The past lingers into the present, just as the future prolongs it; every now is also a former future and every future is at the same time a present yet to come.[8] Current times in the living reality of an architectural work reassert the presence of a history which they also supersede, while they concurrently anticipate what is yet to come, though incompletely. My general point is that past and future define essential dimensions of the work's present reality, albeit as conditions that are no longer and not yet present in the way they once were and will be. Accordingly, we need to reconsider what is conventionally meant by the "completion" of the design and construction processes. Building materials are *pre-qualified* in the quarry or factory—that's how they recommend themselves for use—then they are *qualified* through the labors of construction, and lastly are *re-qualified* through patterns of practical use and environmental influence. This means the labor of finishing precedes itself and never comes to an end.[9] Can we think of built works as necessarily unfinished? More importantly, can or should we design them with this in mind?

Finally, the temporal order that seems to be contradictory—now plus then—unfolds at several levels. Every built work, and by that I mean every room, building, garden, and urban setting, has a stratified temporal horizon, from which it obtains definition and in which it renews itself. I will explain the levels or kinds of building time below.

But here I'd like to propose a more compact version of my opening thesis: *architectural permanence realizes itself in time*. I say *in time*, not *through time*, not diachronically, as the philosophers say or, pathologically, as Aldo Rossi once said, but synchronically, or, in

Making Space for Time 11

Rossi's terms, a propelling sort of permanence that allows adaptations and alterations.[10] To exemplify propelling permanence he mentioned the Palazzo Ragione at Padova. An even more vivid and eloquent case, I think, is the Cathedral in Ferrara, particularly the additions and alternations to the flanking walls of the nave, coupling in a fascinating way external shops with the side chapels within the church.

A thesis that may be more controversial is implied in this image of the past remaining present in works of architecture; namely, that buildings exist not only *in* but *as* time, that as buildings stubbornly hold their ground for days, months, and years they construct and render legible the persisting and predicting dimensions of the present—the sleepless nights in a friend's house, the sidewalk café lunch that passes too quickly, the dreary winters that make the apartment so confining, and so on. Rossi's

Figure 1.1.6 *Ferrara Cathedral*. Photograph David Leatherbarrow.

principle of propelling permanence has two corollaries: continuance without change is impossible in architecture, and individual buildings like places are co-defined by the once was and might be of their history. Although condensed, these observations should indicate the limitations of the conventional view of architectural permanence, poignantly stated by the great German theorist August Schmarsow, whose writings show sensitivity to social and historical change. "Architecture," he observed, "prepares a place for all that is lasting and established in the beliefs of a people and of an age; often, in a period of forceful change, when everything else threatens to sway, will the solemn language of its stones speak of support."[11] Despite the fact that it contradicts all that I have said, Schmarsow seems right: well-designed buildings defy transience, because they abide, they assure. What land is to sea, architecture is to worldly change, its polar opposite and fix. Moreover, this conceit encourages designers to pursue essences in their work—to dream of infinitely durable form—just as it allows a satisfying sense of cultural authority. But obvious notions are not necessarily true. I have argued, and now want to explain more concretely, that architectural reality appears *in* time, which is also, paradoxically perhaps, organized by it, *as* time. Works last because they change, according to chronologies they render visible and sometimes even legible.

We can take the next step in understanding how architecture makes space for time by distinguishing the *kinds* that are embodied in the buildings. I believe there are at least three distinct chronologies that co-exist, non-synchronically yet indivisibly in all built works. Contemporary discussions of architecture allude to one or another of these kinds with some frequency, but they are rarely described clearly, nor have they been shown to be equally important in significant buildings, landscapes, and urban areas. I shall outline these types briefly here, for they are considered more fully in the three major sections of this book that follow this Introduction.

The Time of the World

All manners of ambient phenomena and influences—weather, use, accidents, and additions and alterations—saturate the built work's surfaces with traces of what happened in the past. These marks also serve as indications and invitations to comparable events in future. When you approach an old building and walk up its entry steps, for example, you can plainly see that for centuries others have followed the same path, thanks to the "dishing" mentioned already, up the center of the stairway, short-cutting the width of the landing, pausing on the arrival step. Not only have the steps of hundreds of others polished the stone, they've reshaped its profiles. Traces of this kind testify to movement and therefore time. Implied in that record are human interests, orientation, and desires. As ages pass and the temporal horizon widens, the work functions less like a clock or calendar than a chronicle. In this case, we do not have evidences of my movement or yours, but ours; the past to which the building's physical body refers is a public or shared history. Traces also outline future patterns of use, as I observed earlier. These steps, this table, and all the other surfaces that we encounter in our practical lives have authored a book whose later chapters are still to be written.

The building, I implied in passing, can be understood as a clock. Still today we can tell the time of day by noticing the shadows cast on an architectural surface. Obviously, this was common before the age of mechanical time pieces. But even now we look to buildings for a sense of natural time. All the equipment installed into buildings to respond to changes in weather, seasons, and climate serves both practical and

Figure 1.1.7 Oscar Niemeyer, et al., *Ministry of Education*. Photograph David Leatherbarrow.

representational functions. Apertures, for example, together with their hoods, shutters, blinds, vents, screens, glazings, and curtains, can reveal the position and path of the sun. Also apparent in these elements are patterns of occupation, as they follow schedules of greater or less privacy for example, or occur in diurnal or seasonal cycles. Insofar as this equipment is adjustable, the building shows the advent and end of hours, days, and seasons. Architecture's task is to provide our lives with a clear sense of not only *where* we are, but also *when* we are.

The Time of the Body

Passage through works of architecture paces itself in various types of movement and at different speeds. The types include goal-oriented passage, which is sometimes ritualized, as well as wandering or strolling.[12] The speeds vary not only from fast to slow, or hurried to leisurely, but also various lingerings in the flow of movement that articulate its beginning, pause, or end. Spatial movements include phases of circulation, of course, the accelerations and delays that occur between and within a building's several settings, but also, and more importantly, the schedules of residing. Apprehension of spatial order thus requires the grasp of temporal structures: the settings *behind* the one we now see were experienced some time *before* this moment, while those *beyond* this one are yet to be experienced. At any given instant, places and times have linkages to distended conditions that are understood but unseen, which is to say tacitly recalled and secretly anticipated, *implied*.[13]

Take, for example, the meandering type of movement. Its time is just the opposite of passage along direct routes: not immediate, when what is yet to come is already apparent, but delayed, as a result of sequences of starts, pauses, and resumptions. Partial disclosures play a key role in this manner of phasing, for they slow the pace of apprehension, as do pauses which summarize or restart its rhythms. An entry sequence, for instance, might extend the meander of the approach, prolonging arrival, as if it were little more than a continuation or modulation of the initial impulse. Anyone who has visited Le Corbusier's Swiss Pavilion and taken note of the coordination between the building's immediate grounds and the wider campus landscape will have sensed this type of continuity. Alternatively, entry could introduce a different pace and schedule: a straight view from the doorway could bring the interior depth forward all at once, obediently one might say, no questions asked, even if there might be some uncertainties at the margins. Still another alternative would be the concentration of lateral opportunities into a single moment and vantage: those ahead, at the sides,

Figure 1.1.8 Le Corbusier, *Swiss Pavilion*. Photograph David Leatherbarrow.

and behind rendered available *now*, which is to say simultaneously. Passage into and through openings and concealings would then initiate and prolong spatial discovery, making content apparent, but keeping it out of reach, awareness excited but appreciation postponed. Spatial adumbration of this sort could make use of corner entries, diagonal movements, and divided pathways. Elements in such a temporal configuration would preserve their distinctness, as if the whole were governed by a principle of disconnection. The key point is that a work's recessive aspects allow it to *give more than it shows*, to yield content that exceeds what is seen at any moment, as well as what might be expected or remembered.

Commenting on his experience of Palladio's buildings, Goethe wrote:

> It might very well be thought that ... architecture works for the eye alone, but primarily it ought ... to work for the sense of movement in the human body. When, in dancing, we move according to certain rules, we feel a pleasant sensation, and we ought to be able to arouse similar sensations in a person whom we lead blindfold through a well-built house.[14]

Well-designed works structure sequences that stage the incremental and retrospective senses of its spaces, giving the ensemble its characteristic rhythms, which are apprehended by the body as much as the mind.

The Time of the Project

The first and most difficult distinction that must be made when considering this third dimension of architectural temporality is between project making and production. For production to occur, one must assume that much if not most of design development has been completed. Single-mindedly dedicated to its ends, production marginalizes all possibilities but one in order to arrive at the work's concluding stage. The term "fast track," used so commonly in construction management today, extends the metaphor locomotively. It is a process that draws the yet-to-come of the project back into the now, placing the future in the grasp of the present. And once products discard their preliminaries, the form they achieve bears little or no trace of its formation. Yet, when the outcome is assured at the beginning, unforeseen possibilities have a reduced role in project development, particularly those possibilities that cannot be described in the data sets that have been developed. The risk that attends to this aim is the reduction of the work to what the designer imagines it will be, ignoring or renouncing what I described earlier as the world's intelligence.

Projection, which I take to be the real core of project making, is different. Similar to probability in scientific discourse, projection in architecture remains within the limits of the likely. The basic idea here is that architecture—designed and built—never offers more than the conditions under which something is *likely* to occur: more than a possibility, less than a promise. Although project making is indeed forward looking, it is never more than a pre-figuration of a final product, a foreshadowing of an outcome. Far from being a deficiency, its partiality allows both self-correction and the participation of other agencies of formation—other people and things, living or not. But there is another apparent weakness compared to self-assured production: the advances of projective thinking are always coupled with delays, even retreats. Before it can anticipate anything final, let alone achieve it, the proposal must define its relationship to what exists, partly tearing itself away from the present, because its provisions no longer suit current needs, and partly remaining there, for that is where changes must be made and where their effects will be seen. A complete break is refused and adhesions are required. The difficulty for an uncritically progressive notion of design development is that these dimensions always overlap and intersect.

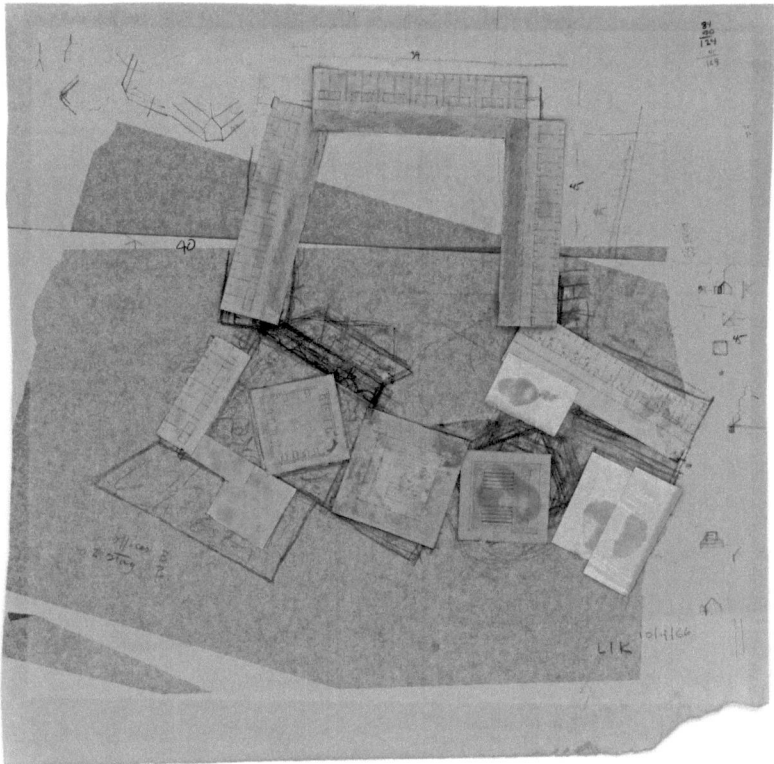

Figure 1.1.9 Louis I. Kahn, *Dominican Mother House*, collage plan. Courtesy of Louis I. Kahn Collection, University of Pennsylvania and Pennsylvania Historical and Museum Commission.

Three kinds of time, then, can be found in well-designed buildings: the time of the world, of the body, and of the project. The permanence that is proper to architecture realizes itself through each of them, even as they resist complete synchronization and full preconception. But as I have said, that apparent failing may also be the key to the building's potential richness.

Structure and Approach

Each of the chapters that follow focuses on a single work, a single painting in each of the initial chapters of the book's three major parts, then individual buildings in the subsequent chapters. I conclude each of the book's three major parts with a study of the same design: Álvaro Siza's swimming pools at Leça da Palmeira. Risking some redundancy, the aim is to show each kind of time in a single project. But why focus on a few paintings if the study is principally architectural? My premise is that paintings no less than buildings express the times I want to consider (world, body, project), but often with greater economy of means and immediacy. In that sense, the painting chapters introduce each of the book's three parts.

It is hardly unusual to interpret these two arts reciprocally. Some scholars have proposed an architectural equivalent to Horace's famous *ut pictura poesis* (as in painting so in poetry) for the art of building: *ut pictura architectura*. What's more, reading paintings and buildings together would seem to be natural when one recalls the fact that there have been many, many architects who saw themselves as painters, from the time of the Renaissance to the present, including the twentieth century's most famous architect, who described his painting studio as a "secret laboratory."[15] My concern is not, however, to discover and describe the transposition of elements or translation of forms from two to three dimensions, which is to say from pictorial surfaces to built spaces—even if many architectural works today are composed as pictures or designed to be camera-ready before anyone moves in. If anything is transposed in the cases I examine, it is kinds of organization or ways of composing and constructing. An example of this would be Wang Shu's understanding of movement expressed in the different kinds of depth in traditional Chinese landscape painting (the pace of strolling through a landscape as a key to analogous movement in architecture, the freedoms of both, and the roles they play in spatial and cultural recollection). Important for me are the *events* that are made visible in paintings: what occurred or is occurring in a particular setting, together with its timing or temporal structuring.

One could reasonably argue that buildings could serve this purpose equally well. In principle, I agree. Yet, the language and concepts that architects often invoke in their accounts of architecture's spatial and temporal order tend to impede access to precisely what I want to describe, how places persist through change. In some ways, the architectural blind spot with respect to change results from a disciplinary prejudice: buildings are made to last. An architect's basic concern is with durability. High rewards result from permanence. Hours pass, seasons change, people come and go, but buildings persist, and so on.

But *how* they last is what needs to be understood. How is it they stay as they were while taking part in conditions and events that continually change? I've found that a detour through the events that make up the subject matter of paintings helps one discover the temporality of architectural works that architects themselves typically overlook. The two arts can be used to illuminate one another because both render visible the ways people live in the world, in its spaces, situations, and events as they unfold through the course of days, seasons, years, and ages.

A second question on method must also be addressed: why are entire chapters devoted to single works, paintings or buildings? And why focus on works such as these—mostly well known and exemplary—not run-of-the-mill types of construction? Here, too, my way of proceeding is largely determined by the questions I want to ask. My aim is to ask questions that are infrequently posed, questions about the temporal structuring of space. The works I consider may be familiar, but the kind of inquiry I'm pursuing is not. The plain fact is that a-typical questions take time to develop and suffer when they are abbreviated or hurried. Developing useful vocabulary also takes time (definition, elaboration, and varied use), as does the identification of types, and associated concepts. I have selected examples that can be usefully reconsidered repeatedly—exemplary works—because of their density of content and evident attention to the full spectrum of issues I want to address.

My second reply to the question concerning this book's lengthy studies of single works is less practical than thematic. Broadly speaking, my interest is in the ways that works of architecture give themselves to human experience. Of course, buildings are seen and those that result from architectural design are composed to be viewed, but surely not only that. Many critics today complain there is far too much concentration on the work's visual appeal, to the neglect or detriment of a work's other aspects, its structural, environmental, or programmatic dimensions. Few would disagree, however, that just as much as they present themselves to the eye, works of architecture are apprehended by the active and ambulatory body, which is to say the perception of buildings is both visual and haptic: surfaces and furnishings that present themselves not only to the eye, but also to feet and hands, in their regular and daily commerce with things, rooms, and walkways that are meant to be seen, felt, and touched as they are alternately used and neglected. Textures play no less a part in architectural sense than shapes; soft- or hardnesses are no less significant than colors. Moreover, when the time of the work is one's concern, passage or movement through physical settings, as experienced in proprioceptive perception, is particularly relevant. Unhurried or "close" readings are necessary if the work's visual sense is to be complemented by an interpretation of its haptic meaning.

A slower, extended reading of architectural works also allows one to focus on a number of their most significant parts. This type of concentration seems sensible insofar a person's experience of a work is generally of one or another of its settings only, rarely, if ever, all of the rooms, in all of their aspects. Who would want that anyway—even if it were possible? Not every part attracts or merits attention. In what follows, I will view specific parts or details as clues, evidences, or keys to the nature or character of the project as a whole. My premise is that a single gesture, some local element or detail can reveal the work's general pattern or structure. Intellectual historians, such as Aby Warburg, or philologists like Leo Spitzer and Erich Auerbach, have shown how small gestures and casual expressions can reveal the character of an image, text, or figure. I believe the same is true for buildings, that parts can serve as keys to wholes, even parts that are typically overlooked.

The discovery of clues such as this requires patient and unhurried observation. I have in mind the work of a detective going over the grounds of a crime scene. The exemplary figure for this particular science is Sherlock Holmes, for whom a detail that would seem trivial to most passers-by initiates a chain of inferences that eventually explain exactly what has transpired. Police work, in both fact and fiction, practices precisely this method. Some historians see their work as directly analogous—the historian is a detective.[16] Hunters follow a similar procedure.[17] The signs they read are traces left by their prey. The animal is gone, but the imprint remains. The track in the soil or snow follows the contours of paws or feet, indicating precisely the animal's size and weight, and the direction it followed. The vestige is a form of *unwritten testimony*, fragmentary but factual, evidence of something that occurred in the past that has survived into the present. Surely traces of inhabitation are similar indications of the past keeping itself present: traces of a preferred path, stains on the wall behind a seat, "spoils" woven into the fabric of a new building, and so on.

Close readings, such as those included in this book, are commonly understood as preliminaries to analysis and interpretation. For my part, the two steps (reading and interpreting or describing and analyzing) are actually just one. Unlike elements of the natural world, works of art and architecture show what they have to give—or do so for those who take the time to really look at them. They intend sense and have been designed to communicate. Because each work has so much to say, one's aim is to let the work speak for itself. Sensible though it seems, I believe that ambition is often misconceived. No account of a built work or painting is wholly "objective," though a high degree of objectivity is sought, nor is any description "mere." Each invokes one's own sense of what merits description, decisions that tacitly assume a detail's, element's, or form's likely relevance to a possible interpretation. The arguments I shall make about *building time* could, perhaps, have been developed in consideration of other works, but insofar as architecture is my concern, I choose not to separate the ideas I want to explain from the things in which they appear.

Part Two

The Time of the World

2.1
Day Time: Adolph Menzel's *Balcony Room*

Let no part of the drapery be free from movement ... on the side struck by the wind the bodies will show a good part of their naked forms, and on the other side the draperies blown by the soft wind will flutter through the air.

LEON BATTISTA ALBERTI, *ON PAINTING*, SECT. 45

A setting's temporal character is apparent in different kinds of movements. The most obvious, perhaps, are those that pace patterns of occupation, the seated student's steady attention to the teacher, for example, or the bank clerk's unhurried, nearly mechanical handling of papers. But there are other kinds of movement in settings, some of which play themselves out more widely. Schedules of work, meals, and rest follow the rhythms of the day and the seasons. What is more, the settings in which these events take place are both quickened and qualified by diurnal and seasonal changes. Every afternoon the timber cladding on the building's south side is baked and bleached by the sun; every spring rainwater runoff from up the slope saturates its ground level masonry. By virtue of forces and effects such as these, buildings record times of different durations and the events or effects through which they are known and recalled, as if their various parts were clocks, calendars, or chronicles. In consideration of the last of these three—vestiges as testimonies—the late Paul Ricoeur once observed that the stories of our lives are given durable substance by the spaces of our lives.[1] Along similar lines, Peter Zumthor suggested that "if [the building's] body is sensitive enough, it can assume a quality that bears witness to the reality of past life."[2] In architecture, narrations of human history often articulate natural time, though sometimes un-authored inscriptions are erased or re-written.

Figure 2.1.1 Adolph Menzel, *Balcony Room*, 1845. Courtesy of bpk Bildagentur/ Bildarchiv Preußischer Kulturbesitz/Art Resource, New York.

To exemplify how the time of the world is rendered legible through architecture, I'd like to turn to a single setting, a window scene, not as it was built but rendered as the subject matter of a mid-nineteenth-century painting. The image I have in mind is titled *Balcony Room* (*Das Balkonzimmer*, Alte Nationalgalerie, Berlin), painted by Adolph Menzel in 1845. It shows a second-floor room inside an apartment building. The building, no longer standing because bombed in the Second World War, was located at Schöneberger Strasse 18 in Berlin and housed a set of rooms that Menzel and his mother had moved into just before this painting was executed. Many critics have said the painting appears to be unfinished. I doubt that. It is equally possible that house painters are still at work on the walls we see, for the patch of white between the window and sofa is hard to understand.[3]

Forces at Play

A recent authoritative study of the painting repeats an observation made in all those that preceded it: "The main incident in *Balcony Room* … is the implied movement, the gentle inward billowing, of the light-filled muslin curtains in the breeze entering the room through the open French windows."[4] Another historian not only offered a similar observation, but also measured the intensity and duration of the breeze: "An almost empty room in which just a few everyday items of furniture distributed according to a very equivocal law of chance arrest our gaze, the only event a slight puff of wind, and light the only protagonist: rays of light coming through the curtain … and shining on to the ground."[5] When applied to air currents, the adjective "slight" suggests something less than a breeze. Calling it a "puff" also indicates it has already had its effect on the curtain, and therefore the room, as puffs are rather short-lived in the range of wind patterns. The third and last critic I want to cite sees more than breeze or puff: the painting "brings the outside world bursting into the interior; as Fritz Laufer has rightly observed of this painting: 'The air and the light through the open window of the balcony takes possession of the space, to play over the walls and the floors, to stir the curtains, and to make the chairs set in front of the mirror cast shadows.'"[6] Even if one prefers breezing or puffing to bursting, this last version is useful because it accents the external source of the internal conditions: light and air have taken possession of the space, stirring the curtains and animating the floors and walls.

In contrast to the curtain, the figures in the mirror reflection are unstirred. Like the window, the reflecting glass is a vertical that illuminates part of the room. But the part it shows is very different in quality. Three figures appear in the reflection: a stretch of wall, a section of a sofa, and about half of a framed engraving. When compared to the elements spread out in the room, the "everyday items of furnishings"—chairs, carpet, sofa (or "easy-chair"), floor, walls, and cornice—those in the mirror seem more solid, more fully and finally shaped, more palpable and real. A number of critics have said that the non-reflected figures by contrast appear to be unfinished, sketched, light, phantom-like, and approximate. My view is that they are less approximate than congenial to the effects of ambient light and air. Their incompleteness—assuming completeness could be shown—is a result of their being co-determined by the forces of the natural world. Quickened by its enlivening power, their qualities are emerging before our eyes. The present Menzel has shown is one that is unfolding. This is clear when the elements of the room are contrasted with those shown in mirror reflection, which renders them static or still.

Although many questions have been asked of this painting, no one seems to have wondered about an issue that strikes me as fairly important: who opened the windows or French doors, as they are also called? Obviously, there can be no answer to this question. But raising it does help with the matter of the air and light, or their roles in the room's "animation." The position of the chairs has exercised the imagination of several critics. Recently Michael Fried has offered a gendered interpretation of their placement in the room; each chair, on his account, is attached to one of the verticals—to the muslin or the mirror, the soft curves or hard uprights, and so on—I will stop before listing the gender stereotypes he invokes. In any case, I'm not sure it makes sense to associate the foreground chair with the mirror. It is very unlikely that a room such as this had just one window. The spread of furniture suggests an interior of at least double the size of what we see, as does the room's height, for a width and length limited to what is shown would be disproportionate to the room's vertical reach. What is more, the symmetrical placement of wall lights on either side of the mirror probably concentrated a wider symmetry of apertures and substituted their supply of light after sunset. The chair in the foreground probably has a relationship to an (unseen) window that parallels that of the other one and its opening, possibly a corner window. So far as I can tell, the existence of such a window is the only plausible explanation for the patch of reflected light on the top corner of the foreground chair, particularly its front side (unreachable by the light of the window we do see). The same unseen source brightens the inside curve of the right-hand wall sconce. Keisch was more cautious than Fried in his interpretation of the chairs, seeing in their placement "a very equivocal law of chance." That really doesn't get us vary far. I cannot imagine Menzel placing anything in this room by chance, even if the concentration to the right seems something of a pile-up. One thing can be concluded without much doubt: the tense relationship between the window and "its" chair (to the left of the mirror) isn't much good for the use of either. Perhaps it was for this reason that Praz suggested the world has burst in on the room. Given its tangency to the window, my hunch is that the chair has stopped the inward swing of the frame. The "bursting into" reading is also suggested by the curtains. But their hang is strange. The fact that they remain closed, after the windows have been opened, is very odd. This oddity is particularly apparent in the tight squeeze between the window frame and seat of the chair. No less uncommon and unhappy is the way the top corner of each frame has been netted by the fabric. No tear is apparent, but clearly a pull. This pull—doubled, like so many elements in the painting—is a detail that most art historians have overlooked, perhaps because it contributes nothing to the setting's lightness and tranquility. In fact, it stands out as discordant.

Normally, curtains of this type are drawn apart or to one side or the other before windows such as these are opened. That is why they are hung on rings that slide along the top bar. Obviously, they could have been pulled back while the windows were still closed, and would be in winter, until night. The little riddle posed by this painting is why they haven't been pulled back on this summer's day. Anyone who has lived in a room with this kind of windows knows that some air can be let into the room without sacrificing privacy or suffering street noise through a simple rearrangement of the closing mechanism, that is, by swinging the latch in reverse and wedging it into the handle on the other window's frame. This fix works reasonably well until breezing air begins to gust. I can't say for certain that this is what has happened in this room, that the wind has blown the windows open, but something unexpected has pushed them inward, against the chair and "through" the curtains because they weren't drawn back. The *force* of the wind and the *play* of the light are what I'd like to stress and consider more fully.

Broadly speaking, architectural settings are *preparations*, readied through design, construction, and repeated use to respond to the likely actions of everyday life and the ambient environment. They react in two ways: allowing and resisting. Muslin, for example, allows light and resists views from the street or neighboring windows. All of the materials in the setting play their parts in this alternative: muslin, glass, and timber frames, as we've seen, but also woolen carpets, upholstered chairs, wooden floors, and plastered walls. Neither buildings nor their designers have any choice in the matter; the co-existence of finished surfaces and natural forces necessarily involves degrees of tolerating and opposing, depending on variations in desire (for a certain quality) and intensity (of external effects). Daylight is generally desired in architectural interiors.

But as soon as one progresses beyond that very broad statement, the whole question becomes a matter of degree and quality: more light is desired on the factory floor than on the shelves of a rare book room; light from the north works in a painter's studio, from the south in a greenhouse. On the other side of the equation, the supply side, conditions are just as uneven, depending on time of the day, the season, and the location. Those variables are subject to still greater qualification when the effects of a specific location are considered, when one side of the site is shrouded by the shadow of a tall tower, for example, or another is brightened by the light reflected off a nearby glass façade. And what is true for light is also true for air: ranging from a cooling breeze in the late afternoon to a gale force wind during the rainy season, the first welcome the second not. Insofar as the building's task is to suffer the influence of ambient conditions—sunshine, wind, and gravity, but also, and no less consequentially, behavior of people—there are two sorts of work that need to be performed by the building's parts: tolerating and resisting. Labor of this kind plays itself out over time, recorded in testimony of the most reliable kind, material.

If the building or its rooms can be seen as preparations for this sort of work, they can be seen as evidences of it too. A new building or a recent finish on an old one shows no signs of the labor of resistance. The surfaces of older buildings, by contrast, attest to their opposition in marks that qualify their surfaces. Any weathered wall is an eloquent example of this kind of silent testimony. By virtue of the sedimentation surfaces acquire over time, they chronicle their stand against so-called natural forces. To the traces of daily life that Rainer Maria Rilke saw on the recently exposed walls of a house were added

> much that had come from below, from the abyss of the street, which reeked, and more [could be seen on the walls] that had oozed down from above with the rain, which over cities is not clean. And much the feeble, tamed domestic winds, that always stay in the same street, had brought along; and much more was there, the source of which one did not know.[7]

The fact that the weather tends to follow patterns (Rilke's tamed winds and unclean rain) suggests that there might be some regularity to the building's labors, that every morning or spring the building faces tasks that are similar to those faced before—keeping warm and dry. Indeed, there is this regularity. The foresight essential to design is based on awareness of diurnal and seasonal patterns. But unexpected events also occur. Praz alluded to this in his account of Menzel's painting when he suggested that the wind and light burst into the room, uninvited and unexpected. The room's walls and surfaces chronicle both typical and unforeseen developments. The chapters of a building's history record both regular and singular events.

Changing Circumstances

Let me turn lastly to the ambiguous white patch on the far wall: curved at the top, stopping short of the floor, almost an archway, except for square shape cut out of its upper left side, as if a painting had once hung there. To its right, the shadow and shine on the floor of Menzel's *Balcony Room* disclose as much about the time of day and season as they do about the room itself. Rather like the tabletops in Cézanne's paintings, this surface tips forward to make a show of its contents. Consider first what the different times of this space say about the elements of the interior. At the base of the window chair, three patches of white mix with the brown of the floor: a particularly bright small rectangle between the window's bottom edge and the balcony; a slightly duller thin vertical that runs from its corner to the edge of the canvas; and a more intense, wider, and parallel patch that also gets cut off by the painting's frame. It seems to me plain that the un-brightened bit that joins these three together is where the wood of the window blocks the light. The light also catches the front corner of the chair, and parts of its back, just enough to show that its polish is brighter than that of the floor. The sunlight also reveals the qualities of the muslin, its translucency, lightness, floral pattern, and pliability. Despite all that has been said about the ambiguous patch on the far wall—about it indicating the incomplete character of the painting, for example—I think that it too is an evidence of the "natural world" taking possession of the space and bringing it to life.

Behind the base of the far window is a very dark patch of floor surface, nearly as dark as the bit at the base of the window chair. As shadows, both testify to the two-part makeup of the window, a solid panel on the lower third with glazing above, as well as the brightness of the day. A key point, I think, is that the edges of the second shadow do not reproduce the outline of the window that caused it, as do those of the first. Because nothing of the window has changed, when compared to its partner on the right, the difference in the shadows must result from the light source. A couple of alternatives come to mind: ambient light through the curtains and window glass, making its appearance on the wall, or light from the window we don't see but must exist to the right of the mirror. I would guess the "break" in the arched outline of white/

light patch on the wall also has an external source, whether the square shape projects from the face of the building, is part of the balcony or the street. The exact place of its projection is less important to me than its testimony to the externality of the cutout's external source. The ambiguous patch we see results from the influence of ambient conditions no less than the billowing, shining, and shadow casting.

If what I have inferred is true, the figure on the wall will not be there for long. Similarly short-lived will be the curtain's movements, the dark patches on the floor, and the bright spots on the chairs. Each of these—the wall, curtain, and chairs—can be seen as clocks because they record the time of the day. If we extend the temporal horizon, the opening and closing of apertures can be seen to calendar everyday life, measuring its seasonality. And finally, in view of even longer periods, the marks that particularize all the surfaces chronicle patterns of use, their typicalities, and exceptions. In coming months and years, the curtain "pull" will be a trace of the latter.

By allowing some movements and resisting others, rooms such as this one give voice to the time and history of their architectural service. In fact, one would not know that time has passed except for the evidences of its movements, forces, and effects on elements such as these. Time does not exist *elsewhere*, outside present circumstances. To accurately describe the ways settings give themselves to experience, we must try to catch the ways mornings, winters, and generations make themselves palpably present in the things around us. Rooms and buildings do not exist in time, but time in them, by virtue of the marks and invitations they offer to patterns of use, in the fluctuating and familiar qualities of their surfaces, and in their responsiveness to the movements of the natural world.

2.2
Well-Timed Openings: Eileen Gray's Tempe à Pailla

If the whole of rhetoric could be thus embodied in one compact code, it would be an easy task of little compass: but most rules are liable to be altered by the nature of the case, circumstances of time and place, and by hard necessity itself.
QUINTILIAN, *INSTITUTIO ORATORIA* II XIII 2

It's clear, at any rate, I think, that if one misses the right moment in anything, the work is spoiled.
PLATO, *REPUBLIC* II 370B

In the Blink of an Eye

Eileen Gray, in dialogue with Jean Badovici, once observed that a window without shutters is like an eye without eyelids.[1] Then as now, sight and light were decisive concerns in window design; she wanted to remind architects who had become fascinated with the potentials of larger and more perfectly made glazing that more light was necessarily good neither in all circumstances, nor at all times. She was also concerned with ventilation and fresh air. Not only did the windows in her buildings typically have shutters, their panels also had moveable louvers, which modulated breezes. Apparently, a reminder about the benefit of operable screens was required when the promises of fully air-conditioned interiors were first being made. Rendered in positive terms, her analogy argued that shutters attached to windows could not only block unwanted glare and heat but also regulate airflow, increasing comfort. She didn't say, but it seems clear they could also express a building's character.

The comparison between the eyelid and shutter was, nevertheless, still apposite when fresh air was not an issue, which is to say, when only light was to be admitted or excluded, sunlight mostly but also moonlight. Such was the case with the oculus Gray designed for the house she called Tempe à Pailla; its job was not to modulate wind or breeze but light and glare, in the morning, at midday, and in the late afternoon.

When the light that passed through the circular ceiling aperture in Gray's bedroom was too bright—too bright for an afternoon nap let's say—a thin metal disk could be shifted sideways to eclipse some or all of the unwanted intensity. At certain times of the day and year, the sun in southern France could be brutally bright. With this fact in mind, the oculus may be seen as an emblem of the region, an indicative device. Thanks to its carefully constructed geometry, the sunbeam's arrival was dramatic. Gray had her builders shift the circle cut into the plane of the roof southwest of the one in the ceiling so that the rays from the mid-afternoon summer sun passing through the tilted and truncated cone

Figure 2.2.1 Eileen Gray, *Tempe à Pailla,* Castellar, France, ceiling oculus. Courtesy of the Museum of Ireland.

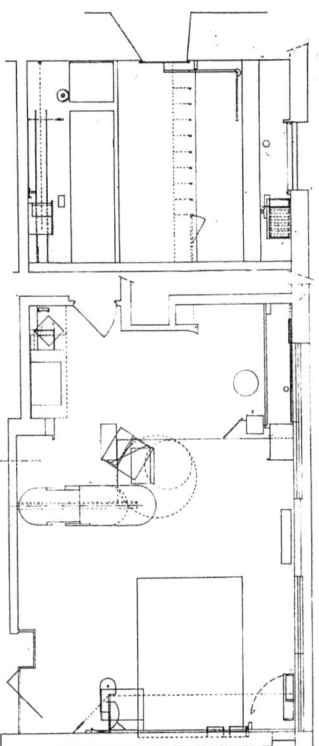

Figure 2.2.2 Eileen Gray, *Tempe à Pailla*, Castellar, France, bedroom plan and section. Courtesy of the Museum of Ireland.

could enter the room directly. Both the angles and the shifted circles can be seen on the cross-section of the bedroom ceiling. The tangency of the cutouts was indicated on the floor plan (the circles of dotted lines at the room's approximate center). This same spot was also marked, rather prominently, on Gray's solar-site-plan, to which I will refer shortly.

When the beam of mid-afternoon light hit the bedroom floor (covered with black tile on the raised rear part), the end wall, or the cosmetic countertop in the back corner, its outline would not be circular, of course, but elliptical, a Pantheon-like projection, but variable through the course of the day and the seasons of the year. Variable also was the location of the operable disk (*le disque occultant*) attached to the underside of the ceiling. It could be positioned directly over the oculus, completely obscuring the light, creating daytime darkness, or shifted to any other position along the arc of its possible transit. The mechanism was extremely simple, even primitive one can say: the center of the plate's underside was pinned to a horizontal bar that was in turn connected to a peg fixed to the ceiling, a swivel connection that allowed the arm to be easily rotated by a vertical handle within reach just overhead.

When put into operation, the oculus and its disk worked rather like the human eye and its lid, as Gray suggested, alternately opening, closing, or squinting. In this case, though, the eye emitted rather than received light—which is the way the ancients thought vision worked (an *active eye* capable of *emission*). Another obvious comparison is with a camera: the movements of its diaphragm, aperture, and shutter (receiving what moderns call *intromission*). Seen from below in the middle of the day, however, the plate would have looked something like the moon during a solar eclipse, apparently black, thanks to the strong contrast, but actually white, just like the ceiling. In any position other than the one that produced an eye-patch total eclipse, it would have reshaped the projected light's geometry, casting not an ellipse but part of one, a crescent. Gray's desire for some measure of daytime darkness would have determined the size of this crescent. Its intensity would result from the position of the sun and drift of the clouds.

Two factors operating in conjunction thus determined the plate's position along the arc of its possible orbit: Gray's preference for more or less light and the passage of the sun and clouds. Each had their patterns, but neither her habits nor the intensities were so definite or recurring that they could be predicted. Instances of *divergent schedules* would not have been rare—sleeping late, nighttime reading, afternoon storms, and so on—which is why the horizontal arm had no fixed positions or stops and could be rotated freely. No matter what its position, the eclipse-disk can, I think, be taken as an indication of *non-synchronicity* between the events of everyday life and the calendar of the climate. It was a type of representation that also had a practical purpose: to effect concurrency between the two schedules, temporary though that accord always was.

A Solar-Site-Plan

Of the site plans of Tempe à Pailla that survive, two are particularly relevant to my concern with the ways the house was occasionally synchronized with the times of its ambient environment. One of the plans positions the house in the midst of the local terrain, a terraced and cultivated slope outside the small village of Castellar, near the Mediterranean port of Menton. The other plan, a rather more abstract image, shows the house in the context of the sun's passage across the sky. Initially, I'll focus on the solar-site-plan.

Although its primary aim was to show the interplay between the parts of the house and the geometry and directions of the sky, terrestrial reference points were not entirely omitted from this drawing. City and sea locations are shown on one side, mountains on the other. Directions are thus indicated, but not distances. Maybe our conventional use of the word *directions* is incorrect in this case, for there is no north arrow on the drawing. Gray wrote *lever* and *couchant* (sunrise and sunset) not east and west, as if to emphasize temporal or diurnal events not spatial or geographical points of reference. That the sun's comings and goings had direct bearing on the house is plain from the plan's rather prominent center-point, the plan-position of the oculus just described (the ceiling not the roof circle, although the axis of that opening's southwest shift aligns precisely with one of the diagonals departing from the compass point). The implied vertical between the floor and ceiling circles recalls the fixed leg of Gray's compass when she traced the point and arcs that mark the sun's position and the spread of its effects.

Two diagonals extend from the compass point, one with a longer radius to the center of the disk marked sun (*soleil*) and another in the direction of the sunset (*couchant*), although more hours would have had to pass before the sun disappeared

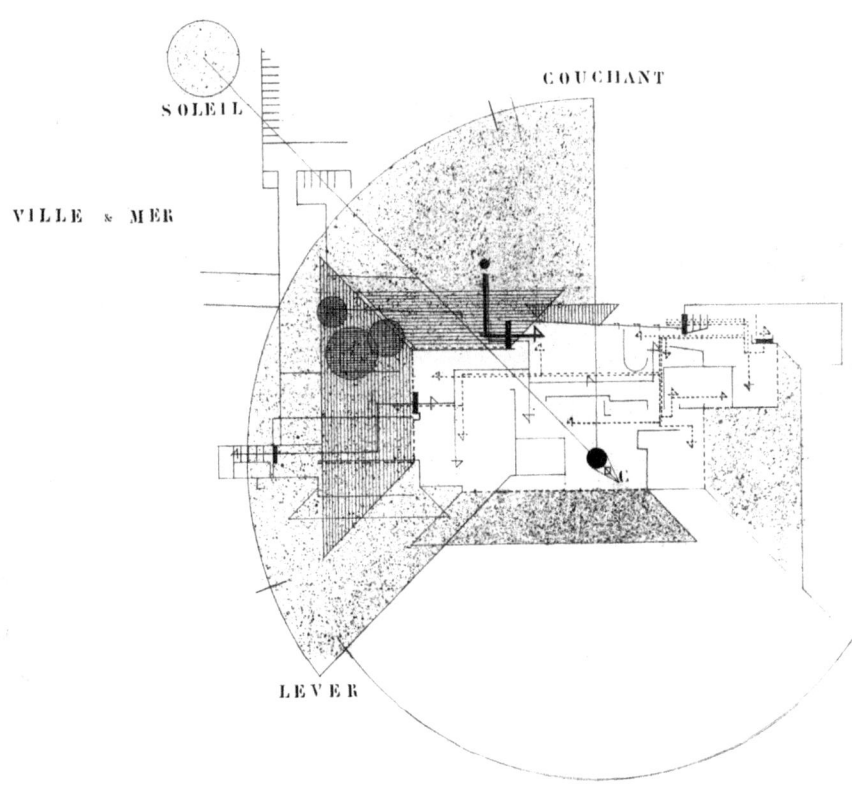

Figure 2.2.3 Eileen Gray, *Tempe à Pailla*, Castellar, France, solar-site-plan. Courtesy of the Museum of Ireland.

below the horizon. Sunrise was also marked with a diagonal, though that line departed not from the center of the oculus but the corner of the bed—more exactly the corner that linked together the bed, its headboard, a rotating shelf unit, and a small panel of light switches, but these details are not shown on this plan.[2] Morning light would have penetrated directly to this spot and been more effective than an alarm clock, at least when the operable shutters cut into the east façade were slid sideways or their louvers tilted open. Even with the eccentric departure of the morning diagonal, the oculus still appears to be the key reference point on the plan, for it not only joins two of the diagonals but connects the full sweep of the sun's daily effects. The places where their arcs stop and start show the limit of those effects, outside of which is nighttime.

Included within the sweep of effects, noted on the plan with a stippled surface, are a set of figures that extend the geometry of the principle apertures cut into the building's outside walls. Each of these openings is marked with a heavy dashed line. On the morning and night sides, the projections are simply outlined with lines that either parallel or are projected at 45-degree angles to the outer walls. Greater graphic weight was given to the projections on the afternoon and evening sides; they are not only outlined but inscribed with dark, closely spaced lines, again parallel to the outer walls. On a similar drawing of Gray and Badovici's E. 1027 villa, built a few years earlier, figures like these were labeled with the times of the day, which would also be degrees of brightness, heat, and glare. The key, however, is that each marginal condition was coordinated with one of the house's several settings, as a matter of solar and seasonal orientation. Perhaps a more appropriate term than orientation is *concurrency*, given Gray's evident concern for times of the day. Below I will discuss more fully the matter of *coordinated timing* in the positioning of rooms and their apertures.

When compared to a drawing of what was built, many walls are missing on this particular plan, and the walls that have been shown lack thickness. Still, the five points of arrival and departure are marked rather prominently, with thick, black verticals. Also shown are circulation paths, each with lines of movement and direction, the latter indicated with a terminal half-arrowhead. The abstraction of some and elaboration of other topics of design—stressing the movements of people and the sun—suggest their necessary complementarity, as if Gray found it impossible to position rooms and structure sequences without linking them to solar cycles.

The drawing's principal diagonals, two of which are radii, connect the limits of the two great arcs. Thus enclosed, the segments show the consequences or effects of what we assume to be the sun's path, none in the case of the pre-dawn sweep, several for the curve through the rest of the day, which is to say effects felt in the morning, afternoon, and evening. Three trees are rather prominent in this piece of the pie, sun blocks one assumes, therefore also shadow casters. As for the sun itself, its radial position is shown—at an angle that approximates mid-afternoon—but not its path. This doesn't mean it was fixed to this spot, only that its circuit (not an arc) was assumed to be self-evident. Methodologically speaking, I believe one shouldn't say anything definite about what Gray decided not to draw, the sun's movement especially. She could easily have shown its orbit but chose not to.[3] She tended to diagram the movements that interested her (generally with dotted lines) and did so much more creatively than most architects in the modern period, with the exception, perhaps, of Pierre Chareau, her near contemporary, who was equally concerned with diagram movements, mainly of interior furnishings and equipment. But in the case of this drawing, Gray did not map the sun's transit, only specified its direct relationship to the oculus, with which it shares a compass point. All she chose to show, all we can see are its effects: sunrise, sunset, pre-dawn approach, and localized intensities at the edges of a few rooms.

All of this raises a question: why does a pathless sun together with an arc circumscribe the spread of its effects? The key, I think, is a geometrical commonplace: arcs are not circles, only parts of them. Each has a starting and stopping point cut out of what is in principle a continuum, for the sun never ceases to spread its effects. Its (assumed) orbit implies unending influence; when not sensed here, it is felt elsewhere, alternately seen and unseen, thanks to movements that cannot in principle be followed and, therefore, in the case of this drawing, not shown. Gray's precision and fidelity to experience are as breathtaking as they are instructive. Instead of an unseen full orbit, she shows sub-divisions, fractions, or intervals that *imply* the over-arching cycle, fractions cut from it by the building and its parts, therefore limited in duration and effect, all of which is to say *temporalized*.

One of the etymological roots of the French word *temps*, derived from the Latin *tempus*, indicates "cut." The time to which the Latin *tem* (to cut) refers is not the unending sort, sky-time, but the kind made up of phases, seasons, or rhythms, each moment of which is in principle cut off from the others but in experience is nevertheless *assembled* and through design *composed*.[4] Perhaps the key term in this list of near equivalents is rhythm, not in the sense of flowing movement but in the rests, poses, or stops that indicate its potential, the much-discussed case of which in ancient art criticism was the pose of an athlete in which the moment of an arm's extreme backswing also showed the beginning of its forward swing—the simultaneity of ending and beginning—as in the comparable moment in a pendulum or metronome's movement.[5] Not any stop was thought to be significant, therefore, only the one that showed a unique style of movement, thus a particular life. The Greek word τέμνειν (*temnein*), meaning "to cut," is one of many Indo-European cognates; English words like template (used to make cutouts) and temple (a place cut off from) are among the derivatives.

In the case of Gray's site plan for Tempe à Pailla, the segmented effects of the sun's transit, occasional though they were, had direct bearing on the rooms of the house. They were represented by the depth and intensity of the projections linked to the apertures. The house's openings, then, proposed the coordination of separate and non-synchronous schedules. The drawing's task was not to solve the discrepancy between sky-time and house-time, but only to pose that very divergence (possible conjunction) as the project's basic problem.[6] The schematic lines and angles of rooms, terraces, and gardens indicate how the times of the settings would variably coincide with the hours and effects of the sun's movement.

Scheduling Plan Positions

Gray's topographical site plan brings the solar circuit down to earth and does so more elaborately than the segmented intervals of the sun's circuit. Once again, distances and directions were no more important than schedules. Plan configuration was certainly an expression of orientation, but toward occurrences and events, not just places. The topographical plan mapped the terrain's decisive characteristics. Its most prominent notations are the thick black bands that mark circulation routes: the roadway, at the side of which the house sits, and the footpath alongside the opposite face, which links the house's garden to other plots and fields, as well as farm buildings. Lighter lines show the subdivisions of those fields, most of which were terraced for agricultural purposes, an ancient practice in this part of France. The terraces marked "D," for example, supported the growth of lemon trees. Gray bought this land (and its trees) in order to prevent future building near her house. In time, she obtained other surrounding parcels for the same reason. Although both the drawing scale and the cardinal directions are shown on the drawing, Gray's primary concern seems to have been the ways that the nearby locations were put to use by cars, trucks, and pedestrians, for example, also by gardeners and farmers, even by plants and animals. Topography, thus, was not only terrain (the lay of the land) but the text or program of occupations that typically occurred there, equally earthbound and artificial.[7]

Gray's arrangement of domestic uses was installed into this topography in ways that took advantage of its opportunities and avoided its problems. We have seen already that the bedroom was situated to take advantage of the daily sunrise; its shuttered window was her alarm clock. When the louvers were closed, the timer was off; when open it was on. One suspects that street traffic also sounded a morning wake-up call, probably louder than she would have liked. The leaves of the lemon trees on the other side of the road would have had little smell through most months of the year, but the fragrance of their blossoms in spring would have been very strong indeed, no doubt wonderful, also of the ripened fruit months later.

The living room and its terrace absorbed the light and heat of the sun through much of the day and all four of the seasons. The eastern two-thirds of the terrace was shaded by a parasol-like covering, which greeted anyone entering from the stairway intended for guests (the steps started just inside the road-side gate, rose to the level of the guest rooms and then still higher to the terrace). Below this part of the deck and the rooms

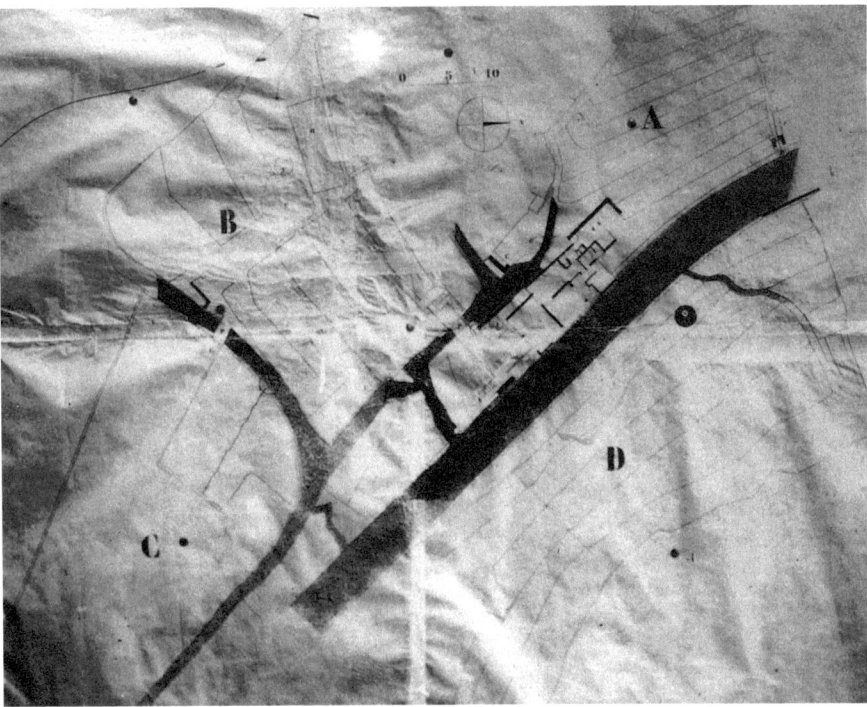

Figure 2.2.4 Eileen Gray, *Tempe à Pailla*, Castellar, France, topographical site plan. Courtesy of the Museum of Ireland.

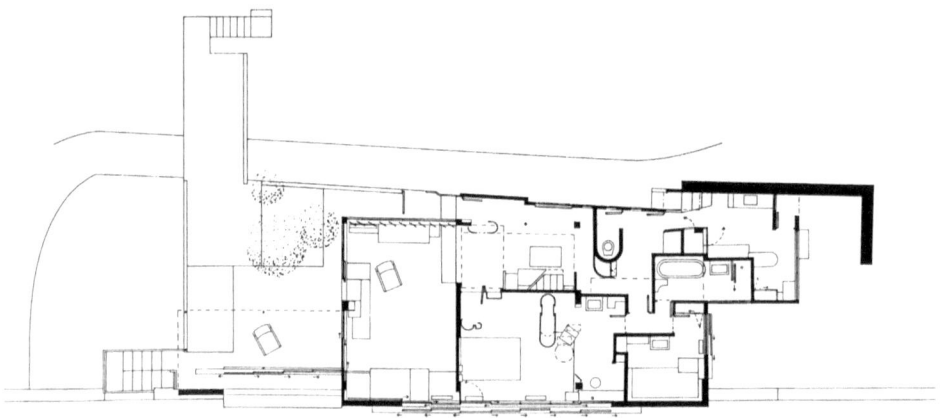

Figure 2.2.5 Eileen Gray, *Tempe à Pailla*, Castellar, France, ground plan. Courtesy of the Museum of Ireland.

provided for the guests was the garage, which was partly enclosed by remnants of the walls of a pre-existing cistern, one of three that had been on the site, each modified by Gray and reused for varying purposes. Similarly massive walls defined other edges of the plot, some from the old cisterns, others built anew at the time of the project. The land dropped off rather steeply on the afternoon side. Apart from the stairway with its landings, all that the tight space next to the garage wall would allow were a small planting bed and a few trees that were, nevertheless, tall enough to make the living room terrace enjoyable in the mid-afternoon. Another little grouping of trees was planted on the terrace's evening side. Their job was to block the sun later in the day. Raised as high as it was and sheltered by the two sets of trees, the terrace had a light, almost arboreal character, not only shaded but cooled by breezes, though Gray also said houses in this part of the country had to defend themselves against the *mistral*.

Because the dining room faced westward, it suffered the full intensity of the late afternoon and early evening sun. Perhaps this explains the small dimensions and horizontal shape of its only window. The same explanation could be offered for the little circular windows in the service area leading to the kitchen (enduring the sun and defensively equipped with small openings), as well as the louver-screened, wall-to-wall, raised window in the living room. No doubt the size and position of these garden-facing openings also expressed Gray's desire for visual and acoustic separation from the footpath just outside the house's enclosing wall. But as with the façade that faced the lemon trees, this one also benefited from nearby plantings—I mean the smells that would have arisen from the flowers and vegetables in the kitchen garden on the other side of the footpath.

Worktime, mealtime, and sleep time had their schedules, the result of which was the plan position of their settings, each coordinated with ambient cycles (sun, wind, agriculture, and traffic). Plan composition, I want to stress, was less a matter of geometrical configuration than of *scheduling a sequence of facings*—the bedroom facing the morning sun and traffic as well as the springtime blossoms, the living room terrace facing the afternoon shade and breeze, and so on. Gray could, of course, read a book anytime and anywhere in the house: at her desk below the louvered window facing the garden, on the terrace shaded by the entry court trees, or indeed in bed, morning, noon, or night. The plan position of one room or another took advantage of ambient events for the sake of habitual behaviors, but those habits could be broken. One imagines that occasional opportunities presented by the wider milieu may well have prompted unforeseen, entirely a-typical uses. With this possibility, perhaps likelihood in mind, one can reasonably infer that the schedules suggested by room positions represented but never insured synchronization.

Timely Adjustments

The quotation about eyelids referenced earlier contained a critique of the style of window design that had come to typify much of modern architecture. Aesthetic criticism was not suggested in what Gray and Badovici wrote, although it may well have existed; instead, the performance of openings without "eyelids." Here is the full quotation: "The problem, often neglected and thus very important, of shutters: a window without shutters is an *eye without eyelids*. Otherwise, all the current combinations lead to the same result: insufficient ventilation when the shutters are closed. Our method leaves a large area for the free passage of fresh air while blocking excess light."[8] *Resistance combined with allowance* was what this particular piece of architectural equipment was designed to achieve. Although they were writing about E. 1027, the same style of thought can be seen in Tempe à Pailla.

One of the most interesting, and indeed surprising, examples of such a device in Gray's Castellar house was installed on the southeastern edge of the living room terrace, exactly on line with the gap between the two halves of the stairway that rises from the level of the guest apartment, and just below the outer edge of the deck canopy.

Positioned in this way, this sliding shutter served two spatial functions: on one side, the afternoon and evening side, it oriented movement toward the center of the terrace and then still farther to the door into the living room, while on the opposite, morning, side it gave access to a rather unique balcony-like space, which faced the lemon trees in the foreground and the mountains in the distance. If the first can be seen to spread laterally across the width of the terrace, including the tree bed and prospect toward the kitchen garden beyond its reach, the second will appear to be compressed into the thickness of the façade, with the garage and street immediately below. Given these adjacencies and temporal indices, one can then say the lateral spread toward the garden had a delayed or rather slow pace of unfolding steps and views in several sequences, while the vertical drop from the balcony to the level of the lemon trees opened onto the quicker pace of the descending road. One of the sliding shutter's significant tasks was to bind these two

Figure 2.2.6 Eileen Gray, *Tempe à Pailla*, Castellar, France, sliding shutter. Courtesy of the Museum of Ireland.

types of time, these two speeds together. No less important was the shutter's role in modulating the light and air that had their origin on the building's morning side.

The element's adjustable parts moved in two directions, the first of which was horizontal. Each of the four shutters was built to slide sideways in tracks, three toward the outer corner of the living room and one toward the entry stair. The fact that the entry-side shutter could slide in the opposite direction means there could have been an unobstructed connection between the sunrise and sunset directions, the beginning and ending of the solar path. By connection I mean unimpeded passage of light and shadow, breezes, and views. A connection like this one was also significant at ground level. When one approached the terrace from the opposite direction, which is to say up from the kitchen garden and over the footpath on Gray's bridge, a very long and impressive prospect toward the mountains would have been visible. The point of arrival from the stair, just beyond the so-called sun-bed (attached to the south wall of the terrace), would have allowed views in these opposite directions. The breeze coming down from the mountains and the fragrances of the fields would also have been sensed there.

But the shutters moved in another direction, too, vertically; more exactly, the louvers rotated through nearly 180 degrees. When opened (rotated parallel to the terrace deck), they would offer no resistance to breeze Gray would have wanted to pass across the deck. One supposes some light was also allowed, and a largely filtered view from the street. The same was true for the identical shutters in the bedroom, variably allowing and resisting the passage of light, air, and views. Nevertheless, in-between the afternoon-side terrace and morning-side balcony, the louvers could regulate the airflow, depending on the ambient temperature and the force of the wind.

Speaking of the variability of such a site's ambient conditions, Gray wrote: "The fleeting patterns of sun and shadow play freely about, and the breeze flows in from the far horizon. It is a preferred location where one can, according to the hour and the mood of the weather, either hide from or stretch out in the full sun."[9] We've seen that the positioning of rooms is one way of acknowledging and taking advantage of environmental fluctuations. Adjustable equipment allowed the house to respond in an even more timely way. Occasional re-positionings could be described as instances in which the building *extemporizes* its performances. The premise of such operations is as follows: in this house two times are non-synchronous—the time of Gray's (any person's) variable desires (reading, sleeping, talking with a friend), and the time of the world (hours of the day and time of the year). She might have wanted to work at her drawing board a little longer than daylight allowed, or to remain in her terrace chair despite the afternoon sun, absence of a cooling breeze, or unexpected chill. Environmental schedules, seasons, and hours could also be out of sync, the smell of lemons preferred during the heat of the day, for example. Ambient expressions or environmental character also prompted adjustments: one day might be brighter than most—maybe the *mistral* had just blown through, clearing the air—another could be oppressively gloomy. Operable equipment acknowledged and represented these variations. And the adjustments and re-balancings would never end, for despite ambient and domestic patterns, interests and moods vary no less than the weather. Perhaps it is best to say of equipment such as this shutter that its task was not so much to achieve balance, harmony, or equilibrium, but to take advantage of favorable conditions of the moment (hour, day, or season), to adroitly respond to unforeseen opportunities and accept what gifts the local situation might have unexpectedly given.

The black-and-white floor tile we have seen in the bedroom of Tempe à Pailla was also used on the outdoor terrace. In this location too, Gray had resting in mind, not under the variable light of a ceiling oculus but beneath the shadows of trees she planted in the tiny street-level forecourt and the terrace garden. In the outdoor location, however, the black tiles covered not a raised floor but the top side of the raised bed. Why black tile in such a position?

The lower and larger expanse of the terrace was covered in white tile, rather like a square patch of sky brought down to earth. Its white grid stretched between the two points of arrival on the afternoon side (from the street-level stair on one side and the bridge that crossed the garden-side footpath on the other) and in the opposite direction toward the glazed wall of the living room. The parts of sky-patch that were not shaded by trees would have made the light of the afternoon very bright—as if Gray's aim had been to make what would be bright even brighter. A comparable case is the Van Nelle Factory in Rotterdam, where Brinkman and Van der Vlugt brightened interiors by adding quartz crystals to the mix of white stucco that covered the walls, as did Richard Neutra at the Desert House. Thanks to the living room's floor-to-ceiling glazing, reflections off the white tiles on Gray's terrace would have brightened the interior space too, particularly where she had positioned her drawing and writing table. The same kind of intensification would have occurred with black tile on the raised sun-bed, but to opposite effect: those tiles and that color would have darkened the darkness under the tall trees.

The thermal characteristics of the contrasting colors are not so straightforward—not so contrasting. The white would have reduced the potential buildup of daytime heat, even if what had been absorbed would have continued to radiate well into the evening. The

Figure 2.2.7 Eileen Gray, *Tempe à Pailla*, Castellar, France, terrace. Courtesy of the Museum of Ireland.

black would not have reduced but increased the heat from the sun that filtered through the leaves, making the raised bed warmer than it would have been otherwise, at least during the warm months of the year. Comparing the two, one can say the white intensified ambient conditions while the black *tempered* them—reducing glare while preserving some heat under cool shadows. That's the first part of an answer to the question: why black? So far as I know, Gray never commented on her use of black-and-white tile on the sun-bed and deck, but given their likely performance under those conditions one suspects a basic concern was to make the outdoor space "well-tempered."[10]

That the temperature of materials was also a matter of timing—as was siting, room layout, and shutter design—is suggested by the relevant etymology, even if the word origins are contested. The relationship typically assumed between words like temporary and temperature is still being argued by philologists. A recent study on the Greek term *kairós*, meaning *due time* or *well-timed*, summarizes the debate nicely.[11] The Latin *temperāre* is the stem for both temperament and temperature; both elaborate that root word's sense of proportioned or balanced—hence "losing one's temper," which is signified by the word distempered, a condition no one wants to last long. The Latin source generally conveyed a sense of the right mixture, or due measure, though that ideal is always only sought. Alternate conditions require alternating combinations. The word *temporary* takes us back to *tempus*, which has been related to one of the implications of *temperāre*, that is, doing something at the right time, during the suitable season, in a timely way, invoking, as we have already observed, a fractional sense of time (the original meaning of the cognate word *tempest* was period or season, good or bad).

The interdependence of these terms and ideas seems to be this: seasonal or hourly time, cut out of the yearly cycle, assumes the same types of divisions as the ingredients of the kind of mixture that makes a given situation well balanced or temperate. In the case of the Tempe à Pailla deck, black tiles are facing the afternoon sun under the shade of tall trees. At supper time, cooked food also wants warmth, which is why Gray installed a heated metal table at the foot of the black bed.

Good Timing

In none of the photographs of the interiors of this house, from either its first period or after the post-war restoration, can one see a clock. It is fair to say the walls are rather empty in the views of the first phase; observers have described it as spare or lean. For that reason, it is particularly significant that in a later view a rather large print filled one of the walls of the small dining space, a map of the ancient Mexican site Teotihuacan. Perhaps this is unsurprising given Gray's strong interest in the matter of solar orientation, not only as a key dimension of modern architecture but as an important aspect of ancient buildings.[12]

Gray traveled twice to Mexico, first in 1920, when she reportedly took a postal service flight between Acapulco and Mexico City, and again in the spring of 1934 with Badovici, when Tempe à Pailla was being finished. Her tours included not only Acapulco, Mexico City, and the ancient site of Teotihuacan, but also Oaxaca, where she would have seen Monte Albán, I strongly suspect. In Mexico City, she either met or resumed an acquaintance with Diego Rivera and Frida Kahlo (Rivera had been in Paris while she was there in early decades of the twentieth century, after his temporary stay in Spain). Although they were self-consciously and assertively modern artists, Rivera and Kahlo also had a strong interest in both traditional and pre-Columbian art and architecture. Although the great monuments of Teotihuacan—the temples of the sun and of the moon, for example—did not figure directly in their works, sensitivity to the interrelationships between the cycles of the natural world and rhythms of daily life and labor is evident in their paintings, as it is in Gray's designs. Solar rhythms measure time's movements, not mechanical clocks.

Something similar may have been intended by the house's name, *Tempe à Pailla*. In the early stages of the project, the house was locally known as the white boat (*Le Bateau Blanc*). Once it was finished, Gray renamed it. Why this name and what did she intend? Some interpreters say it derives from *le temps de bâiller* (time to yawn) in Menton dialect. If yawning is thought to result from boredom, that reading doesn't seem quite right. But time to think in a relaxed way may instead be what the term suggests. Others see it derived (with changed spellings) from a Provencal proverb: *avec le temps et la paille, les figues mûrissent*, which means "with time and straw the figs ripen," making an allusion, it would seem, to the need for time to elapse in order for things such as one's understanding of architecture to mature.[13] A similar expression exists in Italian: *col tempo e con la paglia maturano le nespole*: with time and some straw, the medlar fruit will ripen; in other words, be patient, all things come to him who acts at the right moment. This particular fruit, the medlar, was the first of the year to ripen in this part of the world. An equivalent expression exists in Spanish and was used by Cervantes in the text of *Don Quixote*: "Well,—but, as you know, days go and come, and time and straw makes medlars ripe."[14] The ripening to which this refers is a simple process: hard skinned fruits are set out on a wooden tray covered with straw. The same was true for figs. The point of the proverb was the same for both: they can be opened and enjoyed in time, having rested for a while on a bed of straw. A *timely opening* with Gray's house as our example: how could such an element be characterized?

Thus far we have described such an element as one capable of achieving a conjunction between the building and some occurrence or event in the wider milieu, the passing of the sun overhead, seasonal winds, or morning traffic. Accordingly, a timely opening would be one capable of taking advantage of conditions favorable to desired forms of occupation. It would not *wait* on events, nor would it mark *beginnings*. Its *timeliness* is the key. A non-architectural analog may be helpful. In ancient Greek rhetoric, the word *kairós* indicated a unique opportunity arising from the particular disposition of an audience, the exact moment when persuasion was possible. Professors giving lectures have seen these opportunities come and go; in pedagogical literature, they are called "teaching moments." The time to which *kairós* referred was one that called for a proper response, in order to gain advantage or success. It was a matter of making appropriate or fitting use of opportunities as they arose. The English word "opportunity" comes from the Latin *opportunitas*; its stem was the word *port*, which signified an opening, as in portal. But certain times can also be openings; hence the description of decisive moves in a game of chess, openings for checkmate.

Earlier, pre-classical meanings of the word *kairós* are even more interesting and helpful. For Hesiod, the word was less temporal than situational; it referred not just to the target at which one aims but more specifically to a penetrable opening or an aperture. An example from Homer would be the passage through the iron handle of an axe or rather of the twelve axes set at regular intervals in a straight line, as in Odysseus' famous "trial of the bow": shooting an arrow through the handle sockets of the aligned axes. *Openings* in this sense were places where one aimed to achieve success, but also moments to be "seized"; the whole tale of Odysseus' return to his house, his former life, hinged on this "trial." In more recent usage, we might say he acted just in the nick of time (nick as a notch cut out of un-eventful or prosaic time), exactly that instant when an opening appeared as an opportunity for success, one that required the right combination of force, purpose, and preparation.

The passage I've cited above and used as an epigraph gives us Gray's sense of architecture operating *in the nick of time*. To conclude this chapter, I'll repeat the observation one more time: "The fleeting patterns of sun and shadow play freely about, and the breeze flows in from the far horizon. It is a preferred location where one can, according to the hour and the mood of the weather, either hide from or stretch out in the full sun." Natural patterns and flows come and go, mostly according to past schedules, sometimes not. Their stay is invariably short; the time Gray describes is fleeting. But each of the propitious moments wakens architecture from its slumber, that immobile duration—permanence—that has been so often praised in criticism and sought in design and construction. Gray suggests that the durability granted to architecture does not occur despite but because of change. Locations, her building shows, are always only intermittently advantageous. Now and then, their settings and provisions occasion just the right time for "hiding or stretching out," which is to say behaving as one would like, according to a schedule the sun and wind couldn't care less about. Architectural design is essentially a kind of pre-timing or preparation for concurrency, a material and spatial groundwork for those times when natural rhythms and cultural habits can be precisely synchronized, though never for very long.

2.3

Tempered Terrain: Sverre Fehn's Villa Busk

Everything Time ever brings out of earth into light,
Time also buries, however splendid it is,
And takes it back into the shade.
LEON BATTISTA ALBERTI, *ON THE ART OF BUILDING*, 10:12;
AFTER HORACE, *EPODES*, 1:6

Sverre Fehn once replied to a question about the juxtaposition of old and new building parts with a statement of principle: "A dialogue with the past can [only] be achieved with a precise expression of the present moment."[1] To elaborate his point, he offered a comparison: "An architect must move into the past as he must move into nature … [aware that] the traces of your footsteps will lead the next man to the same route. The footsteps are a kind of architecture … like a letter addressed to the next walker." This principle—it can be called the *principle of concurrency*—implies that neither the past nor the future can be disassociated from the present moment; the first is a former present and the second a present yet to come. Applied to architecture, this principle means that productive works always alter but never erase pre-existing conditions, no matter whether they modify untouched nature or an urban location.

Representative examples from Fehn's work in both types of context would include the Archbishopric Museum, built in an open, though hardly untouched, landscape near the town of Hamar in Norway—the work that provoked his comment about "the present moment"—and the National Museum of Architecture in Oslo, Fehn's very last building, another instance of juxtaposing old and new.

Figure 2.3.1 Sverre Fehn, *Archbishopric Museum*, Hamar, Norway. Photograph David Leatherbarrow.

Vestiges as Clues

In the arguments that follow, I will be less concerned with the kinds of sites that join elements of the past and present together than the kind of architecture made by "footprints in the sand."² I shall ask how a building or any of its parts can offer experience of both imprints left behind and messages sent ahead, how architecture can record and anticipate patterns of occupation, how places that were constructed sequentially can present themselves *concurrently*. To pursue this question, I will describe and interpret just one of Fehn's buildings, the Villa Busk, built between 1987 and 1990 near the town of Bamble in Norway's Telemark region. Here, as with his sense of "traces of footsteps," the central topic will be the interplay between environmental conditions and human affairs, more exactly, the kinds of marks that attest to that interplay, which can be called unwritten or silent testimony.

While material evidence of this kind offers proof of many things, my initial concern is with a rather basic sort of report, the simple fact that time has passed, that the force that left its mark is no longer present, precisely because only the vestige remains. This observation varies a premise that Aristotle put forward in his treatise on memory: all memory is of the past.³ While this may seem an obvious truism, it is, I think, one that still merits thought. Of course, it makes no sense to speak of memories of things that are present, for they can be perceived, nor of things to come, which can only be anticipated. The difficulty is that while they are indeed retrospective, the types of vestiges that qualify architectural works also indicate events and behaviors that are likely to occur again, for the "letters" Fehn described as well as the "kind of architecture" they represented were addressed to "the walker" yet to come, rather like a prompt one can say or more politely an invitation, at the same time a cue and a clue. Hunters who wait for prey in the woods typically position themselves within sight and range of well-worn tracks, expecting a return. Detectives also have an eye for signs of past behaviors; Sherlock Holmes deciphered traces and discovered criminals more skillfully than most. Perhaps the connections between this topic (the trace) and technique (detection) are not surprising when one reflects on the kinship of the key terms: vestige and investigate are cognate words, the first the theme and the second the method.⁴

Figure 2.3.2 Sverre Fehn, *National Museum of Architecture*, Oslo. Photograph David Leatherbarrow.

Past as Prologue

Describing the land on which—or *within* which—Villa Busk was sited, Fehn wrote that "the fields and stones pour out like waves in the ocean. In this landscape, moss finds its foundations on the moist surface of the stone and in the earth-filled crevices of the mountain

Figure 2.3.3 Sverre Fehn, *Villa Busk*, Bamble, Norway, entry walkway. Photograph David Leatherbarrow.

the pine finds breathing space for its roots."[5] For ambient forces to leave tell-tale marks, there had to be some impressionable and durable surface that was capable of registering their effect. In this location, it was a material that might initially seem unreceptive and unyielding: a type of mountain stone, gneiss, found throughout the Telemark region, that is light gray, striated (foliated), and harder than February ice is cold, although it was also, Fehn said, characterized by a "moist surface" and "earth-filled crevices."

The Busk family had purchased land near the Oslo Fjord, but not specified the plot on which their villa would be built. Fehn chose a rather dramatic spot: a lengthy, but uneven ridge to the south of which the escarpment fell into a green slope that in turn inclined toward a tributary that emptied into a cove alongside the fjord. Still today the outcropping is partially moss-covered, as it was when Fehn left his footprints there for the first time; lichen can be seen too, also underbrush on the villa's front side. Closer to the house, tall pines shade the roof and partly shelter it from winter snow. In his description of the building Fehn stressed something else; through the sheets of glass that lined the rear side of the living spaces, "gusts of wind" were visible "in the branches of the trees." One of his frequent, if surprising, references to Palladio occurred at this point in the narrative. He compared the gusts at Busk to the wind rushing through the Italian's "silk shirt." Locations have dramatically changed in this comparison, climates too; he bound them together by restating the familiar analogy between the body of a tree and a man.[6] I haven't come across references to Palladio's dressing habits in other sources; this is no doubt one of Fehn's dream images, but even if so, it is evocative nevertheless. Silk wasn't insignificant to Palladio; sixteenth-century Vicenza achieved much of its wealth in the mulberry and silkworm industry, which were the main investments of a number of his clients.

At any rate, there was more to the Norwegian wind for Fehn than a refreshing breeze: the air at Villa Busk was "filled with all kinds of seeds carried across the temperamental terrain."[7] Once again, he probably had another architect in mind when introducing this image, for Le Corbusier, whose atelier Fehn often visited during his stay in Paris, told anyone who would listen that the roof garden of his Porte Molitor Apartment had been seeded by the wind and birds.[8] While Le Corbusier stressed the resiliency of his little plot (also the connections between his art and nature's), Fehn's concern was with the intermixing of elements and conditions we tend to think of as distinct: land and air in the case of the wind-blown seeds, sea and stone in the case of the terrain: "the fields and stones pour out like waves in the ocean." The first coupling is actual, the second metaphorical. From his sayings and sketches, it appears Fehn often thought in images of this kind. He may also have known, but to my knowledge never cited, Thomas Mann's mythical tale about a "holy sinner" (later Pope Gregory) who survived for seventeen years on an island of barren rock, chained in place under the roof of heaven with no more protection than a "hair shirt." What kept him alive? In the middle of the hard platform he discovered "a little trough in the stone, and a whitish cloudy wetness [that] filled it up to the margin, probably yesterday's rain, he thought, only quite strikingly cloudy and milky ... [a] drink [that] tasted sugary and sticky, a little like starch, a little pungent like fennel and also metallic like iron."[9] Fehn's moss, lichen, and well-nourished roots were comparable outgrowths, comparably site-specific, sustaining, and long-lasting.

For Fehn, the several landscape phenomena he observed at Villa Busk performed their roles hand-in-hand, wind plus seed, stone plus moisture and moss. The combined result, he said, was a "temperamental terrain," a landscape he also called an "inferno of nature." Before turning to the matter of the terrain's temperament, I want to stress his sense of the mutuality of the powers at play on the site, the notion that they performed in concert. The comparison between waves at sea and stones in soil was, I've said, metaphorical—boulders cresting the terrain—but the affinities to which the image refers suggest both common purpose and legible expression, with each player linked together in a performance so cooperative and reciprocal that all assumed responsibility for the continuance of the whole. All-of-a-piece, as if well orchestrated, the elements played their parts in a drama without beginning or end, only repetition, cycles that continued unceasingly, neither rushed nor finished, imperceptibly changing but not progressing.

The force and direction of the wind weren't all that could be seen outside the villa's large panes of glass; Fehn forecast that his clients would witness the "growth and decay" of all living things, alternately nurturing and defeating one another. Thus, the concert of environmental interplay shouldn't be called *harmonious* if that term means co-existing without conflict. Physical things like trees, stones, and waters didn't sustain the interplay and cycles as much as the powers or forces that animated beginnings and endings, even if "materials" were required as the media of these developments. It was the play of powers that allowed the metaphorical coupling we've seen: exposed stone and crested waves were similarly wind-swept and subject to subsurface movements. In the text I've been citing, Fehn didn't extend his comparison to the pictures and imagery of the great Norwegian painter Johan Christian Dahl, but the affinities he observed are vividly apparent in the latter's landscapes and seascapes.

The events inside the house played themselves out in an entirely different kind of time. Recurrings there, Fehn observed, narrated the "story of life." Life in a broadly theoretical sense is not what he had in mind; he was concerned with particular ways of living.[10] This family's domestic habits were the subject matter of the architectural "story." Chronology of this kind does not follow cycles but sequences: seasons repeat, but site labor advances in phases, and the incidents of home life precede and follow. To explain himself further, Fehn turned to the Palladio of his dreams or desires once again: "I suddenly think of Palladio's villas, the walls of the rooms tattooed with Veronese frescoes, the contents a manifesto of the events every room is designed for. These notes endure in time and action."[11] Even in Norway—a climate so different from Italy's—the geographically and historically specific villa culture of the Veneto could still be appreciated, not because moments of domestic life repeated themselves—he didn't address the issue of domestic habits—but because temporal distance invited comparison. The tricky part of this is Fehn's comment on "notes" enduring in time and action. Their staying power is not thanks to the returning tide of environmental cycles, but the durability of traces, a lastingness that depended to a large measure on the materials used for the building and the ways they were assembled and finished.

Construction materials for a house that Fehn could liken to Palladio's Villa Maser would not have been found on the site he was given; they had to be brought there. Perhaps the timber he used, so abundant in Norway, could be construed as local in some way—if one's sense of local is widely regional—but certainly not the glazing, nor the concrete, still less all the metal parts of the structure and the various furnishings and finishings. Just as the site pre-dated the project, so did its materials. Well before the project began, they were waiting in warehouses or yards, ready to be ordered and delivered to the site. Other parts were advertised and made available through trade catalogues, although Fehn was no fan nor frequent user of so-called professional literature.[12] Still other materials were familiar to him because they had been put into service in one or another of his earlier projects. Again, this pre-construction history of materials is entirely different from the past expressed by the elements of the environment, for the site did not have a *history* so much as a *cyclical pattern* of growth and decay.

The typical phases of building practice wrote the middle chapters of the building's story. Wet materials such as concrete had to be mixed and cast in place, while dry materials, such as timber, tile, and steel, had to be cut and resized, then joined or assembled, and finally finished, in preparation for use and inhabitation, which would in turn re-finish them. There is nothing special in this sequence; all I want to stress is that

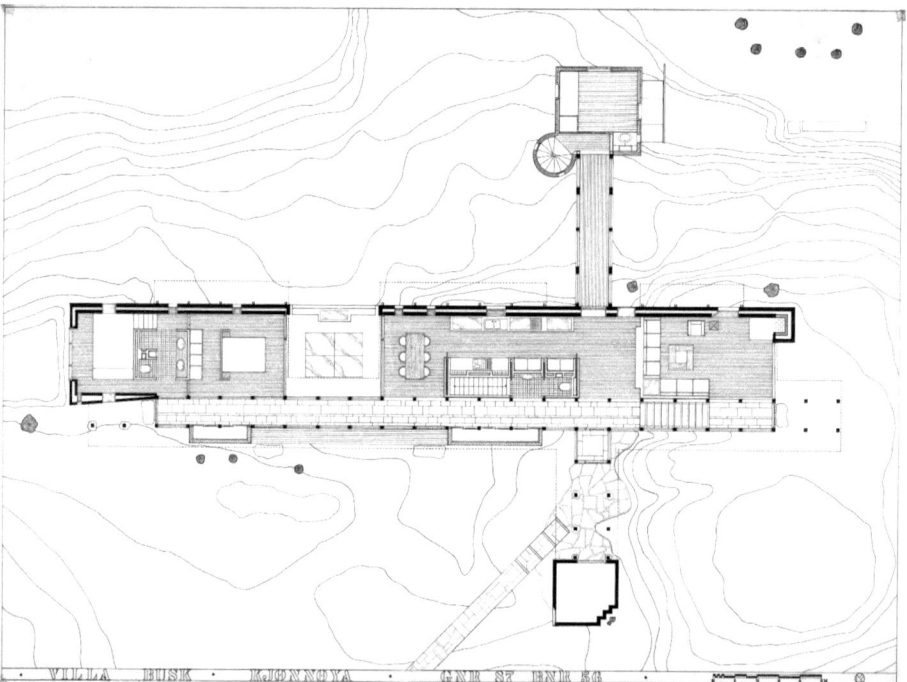

Figure 2.3.4 Sverre Fehn, *Villa Busk,* Bamble, Norway, ground plan. Courtesy of National Museum of Art, Architecture and Design.

it was *a sequence*, with a beginning in the warehouse or factory and an end on the site, sometime before the family moved in. Fehn's summary statement is as follows: "When the house was finished … I had the feeling of it being a dream about a journey I had not made … when we designed the house, I promised Sylvie, the youngest daughter, a secret room which only she and I knew about. When the house was complete, the secret room had vanished."[13] Such is the nature of the stories buildings and designers tell; they narrate events and have outcomes that sometimes surprise.

Fehn would not have objected, I think, to a comparison between an architectural plan and a dramatic plot, nor the notion that room sequences spatialize stories.[14] What he wrote about the plan of Villa Busk implies this association:

> Villa Busk has been given an architecture which seeks to provide depth to the topography of the terrain, from the marshy plain ending in the bay to the peaks of the mountains. The route from boat to hearth is mediated by a tower … other functions of the house such as entrance, kitchen, dining-room, living room, parental bedroom and bathroom, etc. are situated on the mountain ridge of the site.[15]

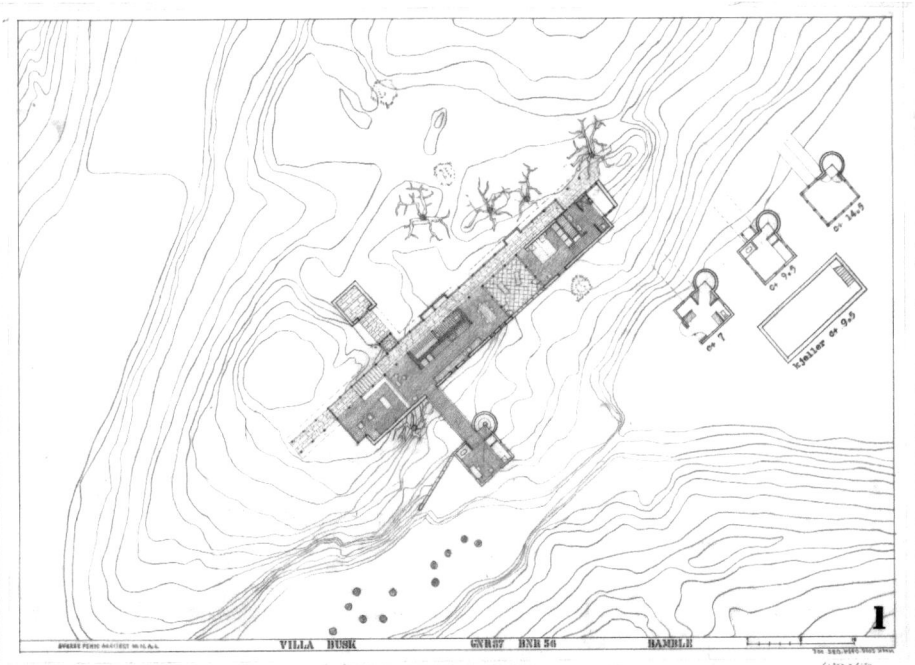

Figure 2.3.5 Sverre Fehn, *Villa Busk*, Bamble, Norway, location plan. Courtesy of National Museum of Art, Architecture and Design.

Figure 2.3.6 Sverre Fehn, *Villa Busk*, Bamble, Norway, bath. Photograph David Leatherbarrow.

Despite the inclusive character of this rather prosaic list, really only a couple elements gave the path and plan their primary order: the hearth at the end and a bath, not a boat, at the beginning.

Cresting the stone ridge before it tumbles into the green slope below are the arms of a long concrete wall that cups in its hands the house's two end points. Encircled at the east end is the large indoor bath/pool, just beyond the parent's bedroom. At the west end is a fireplace in the corner of the living room. These settings are in turn bounded by ancient stone outcroppings, the first seen glancingly from within the sunken bath—just above head height when the water is below your chin—and the second seen marginally to the right of the hearth. The views beyond also contrast; the ledge outside the bath is bounded by trees that close the prospect, making it hardly a view at all, while its counterpart opens widely to the cove that leads to the fjord, under the overhanging roof that extends the circulation spine.

As such, the long concrete wall binds together not only key elements of the house, but essentials of the terrain, water and fire attached to their respective boulders along a major cleft in lay of the land. The contrast between the endpoints is also sectional,

Figure 2.3.7 Sverre Fehn, *Villa Busk*, Bamble, Norway, outdoor terrace. Photograph David Leatherbarrow.

thanks to the eastwest rise in the terrain and the dip in between. The bath/pool is, I said, below the level of the boulder it adjoins, while the fireplace and living room sit at the same level of their nearby plateau, which has stepped up a full story above the rest of the house. Although they correspond in forming the limits of the enclosing wall, these settings sharply differ in a number of ways: in terms of use, the one is private, the other shared; as for topographical position, the first is sunken and the second raised; environmentally, the windows that border the bath open to the morning sun, while the one to the side of the fireplace watches it set; and lastly, one has a floor that is wet and the other a wall that burns. Unsurprisingly, the temporal indices of these settings are also dissimilar. Time doesn't pass slowly for the bather in the bath; it doesn't pass at all. The rock it hollowed obviously does not have water within it, but a body beneath the watery surface is more completely enveloped there than if he or she were all of a piece with the stone, and no less timelessly. Michel Tournier, in his re-telling of the Robinson Crusoe story, narrated an incident that provides a useful comparison:

> The next day the same thing happened. Time passed ... [But then, in his wanderings] he found ... the mouth of a narrow vertical chimney. [In order to slide down the tight opening] he stripped, and after rubbing his body with the remains of his milk [lubricating it], went headfirst into the bottleneck ... [and] landed on his outstretched arms in a sort of narrow crypt ... But what attracted Robinson more than anything else was a cavity or recess about five feet deep ... like the inside of a mold constructed for ... his own body ... which enabled him to fit so exactly ... that he forgot the limitations of his body ... He was suspended in a happy eternity ... Perhaps he slept. He could not have said ... When he racked his brains trying to determine how much time had passed since his entry into the cave, the picture of the stopped water clock confronted him with monotonous persistency.[16]

Fehn's encaved bath was not quite so close fitting, but I have a hunch that the time of the bath has similar latitude.

The chronology represented at the house's other end is the polar opposite of earthbound constancy, a time of incessant change or fugitive moments quickened by flickering flames. Below I will say more about this situation in consideration of its several elements—the white stone panel with its blue glass inset square, the dark stone base, timber surround, and so on—all that needs to be indicated here is the unending character of the play of variations that was put on show every time timber from trees outside the window was used to warm the night air.

What I have described thus far suggests the house was designed to be—and express that it indeed was—earthbound. That's not wrong, but only half the story. Just as there are two chronologies at play, the cycles of the natural world and the history of the building's physical make up; there are two basic types of construction, earthwork and framework, together with their topographical pre-conditions, soil or stone and sky.

Fehn introduced the land's counterpart in approximately combative terms: "In this inferno of nature, the straight lines of poetry are found in the concrete mass' confrontation with the mountain and the regular rhythm of wooden pillars [which are] slipped down

Figure 2.3.8 Sverre Fehn, *Villa Busk*, Bamble, Norway, exterior columns. Photograph David Leatherbarrow.

into the earth like responses to the static slide-rule of the roof construction."[17] The "slipping down" of each wooden pillar terminates in metal base plate or shoe, which reduces the support's dimension and load to a single point, abbreviating as much as possible its encounter with the stone, which in turn seems as indifferent to this manner of connection as it is friendly to the moss and lichen. Such an attenuated connection is the reverse of the way the concrete wall meets the earth: pointed not planar, dry not wet (when made), and mechanical not plastic (when formed), and fixed instead of bonded.

Nevertheless, one cannot say the grid of columns lacks congeniality with the location. Just as the line of the rocky ridge set the stage for the appearance of the concrete wall, a pre-existing pine tree served as the starting point for the rhythm of columns, specifically, an old one that stands to the side of bath/pool boulder, on the house's front side. Its inaugural role can be seen clearly on the building's ground-floor plan. The opposite end of the line of supports is capped by the overhang on the platform outside the living room and its fireplace. Between the two endpoints is the "slide-rule" measure that Fehn said mediates the house's extreme limits.

Figure 2.3.9 Sverre Fehn, *Villa Busk*, Bamble, Norway, rear wall meeting terrain. Photograph David Leatherbarrow.

The intervals between these limits, the column spacings that run the building's entire length, would make a mathematician happy. They are perfectly regular in the plan's full length (1.5 meters from one column center to the next) and accordingly form the increments of a rule of sizing to which the dimensions of every enclosed space conform.[18] For this rule to govern the sizing of rooms, not only the lengths of lines, but also the rhythm had to extend from side to side. The width-crossing ceiling span (three bays wide) is supported in a fascinating way on the building's back side: half-height columns were bolted to the outer face of the concrete wall. The detail is no less mechanical than the ground level supports on the other side (the metal shoes at the base of each column) identically point-like and dry. The topographical analogue and prompt for all of this were, we've seen, the pine trees, not so much for the linearity of the colonnade arrangement, but the arboreal, shadow-casting character of the roofs it supports, between the stone or concrete and the sky.

Considering the pre-existing stone and the trees together, I believe one can say that the characters that Fehn thought played dominant roles in the environment provided him with clues for the project, thus the earthwork coupled with a framework, in alternately

Figure 2.3.10 Sverre Fehn, *Villa Busk*, Bamble, Norway, half-height column bracket. Photograph David Leatherbarrow.

congenial and conflictual connections. The cyclical chronology of their interplay also had its effects. The column intervals, for example, were repeated within fixed if contrasting limits: at one end water in the morning, at the other fire at night, with equally spaced hours or paces in between. But, again, the earthbound chronology was only half the story. In any reckoning of the spatial calendar Fehn designed, one must also acknowledge the role played by the building's construction and materials, their history. The past served as a prologue to the project in two ways: as a pattern of recurring movements with which the building synchronized itself and a sequence of constructive acts that inaugurated a way of living there, as well as its subsequent modifications.

Lasting Impressions

The history that was (unofficially) inaugurated in the warehouse, quarry, trade catalogue, or Fehn's earlier work, and then extended by builders on the site was developed still further, he said, by events of domestic life: the children at play in the tower, the father at work in his basement sound studio, and the mother with her plants on the deck. Their requirements were not fully anticipated by Fehn's provisions; long-term use of the settings required some modifications to what he had designed and installed. But changes of this kind were not the end of the building's history either, still more chapters followed. The ambient environment had its effects too, some anticipated some unforeseen.

One more analogy may be useful in explaining this phase of the history that the building chronicles: what the stone of the site was to its vegetation—a foothold in which the seeds of regrowth could take root—the concrete was for similarly air-borne deposits. What kind of *receptacle* was the building's physical body? Like the boulders that crested the land, the concrete Fehn used inside and out might seem to take an insouciant attitude toward everything around it. Would such a stance render it insignificant? Given its wide currency in this phase of modern architecture, one should not assume concrete was thought to be mute or non-expressive. *Beton brut* has been described by some historians as the main ingredient of a post-war *style*. That's a big claim. My concern is more modest, only with the kinds of appearances that result from concrete's physical makeup and obdurate attitude: the material itself (rather like mud) and the way it is used or formed in construction (often suggesting stone).

Like all *plastic* materials used in buildings, concrete exhibits traces of the ways it was formed. The appearance we've come to see as "natural" cannot be separated from its "artificial" formation. Two types of traces are typical in architectural concrete. The first is the set of surface patterns and color that reveal the material's inner makeup, the sand and stone that went into its "mix." The other types of marks are those that attest to the kind of formwork that gave the wall, slab, or column its shape and dimension.

At the Villa Busk, there isn't anything unusual about the physical makeup of the concrete, hardly any of the aggregate has come to the surface, just the familiar light gray color. The vestiges of the formwork, however, reveal the imprint of timber shuttering: rough-grade, uniformly sized vertical boards used in the manner of much of the architecture of the time, particularly that of Corbusian lineage. Although the widths of the boards are similar in dimension to those used for timber cladding on its both inner and outer faces, the boards used for formwork were not reused as cladding materials.[19]

Nevertheless, the concrete surfaces one can see on both the inside and outside of the house provide evidence of the materials and techniques of the building's construction, pages in that chapter of its history, I've said, that were written before the family moved in, the story's middle chapters.

Much of the surface marking that was to follow as a result of environmental forces could have been expected. The natural cycles Fehn described allowed him to anticipate seasonal and diurnal changes, as well as the consequences they would have for the building: the baking sun on the south side, the wind-driven snow through the months of the very long winter, or the rainwater runoff down the slope where the concrete met the stone. Also expected would have been the deposit of dirt along the lines created by the edges of the formwork timber. After a number of years had passed, this accumulation created a rhythm of shadow lines in the skin of the rear façade.

At the base of that wall, however, dirt accumulated across the entire surface, regardless of the board-work geometry. Sediment carried by wind and rain didn't cause this coloration, instead absorption. One suspects that Fehn had ground water and ice on his mind when he designed the structural elements on the building's front side. Blocks of stone were placed under the column shoes which would have otherwise come to rest on soil. Over time, the metal has blackened. Like the traces that resulted from construction techniques, these evidences of environmental effect could have been expected. Fehn's specifications were in this sense anticipatory.

To make their marks, we've observed, traces require some reasonably plastic material into which their stamp can be pressed: the stone of a stairway tread, the timber of a tabletop, or the white plaster of a wall. Because such a formation requires some *external* force (an upward climb, seasonal rain, or an unknowing elbow), the mark is always somewhat strange to the material that receives it, alien one might say, sometimes

Figure 2.3.11 Sverre Fehn, *Villa Busk*, Bamble, Norway, concrete stain. Photograph David Leatherbarrow.

Figure 2.3.12 Sverre Fehn, *Villa Busk*, Bamble, Norway, column base. Photograph David Leatherbarrow.

surprising, like an unforeseen event. In any case, traces are not natural to things, even if their author or cause is well known. And their non-congeniality is a key to the temporal distance they measure and record. Impressions occur at the end of some exercise of power, an end that indicates a force's makeup, strength, and profile. The changes to a building's surfaces that result from unforeseen *impressions* testify to its capacity to allow and resist the forces at play in its milieu.

Consideration of another term I have been using, type (*tupos*), may clarify the forcefulness and externality of a trace's imprint. As a verb, the term *tupos* originally meant to strike. Not surprisingly, the noun signified mallet or hammer, and by extension any instrument capable of striking with considerable force. Something similar was signified by the word "character." Still today, the noun signifies the track or the trace that results from furrowing or stamping. When the stamping is very strong or the furrowing especially deep, the mark that results is often taken to be indelible, which is called a character trait.[20] The imprint of a signet ring also required pressure, pressure that preserved the signature once the hot wax that also sealed the letter had cooled. Likewise, with the production of a coin, a stamping or printing process, which is recalled when new terms are "coined." In all of these cases there is an active, extrinsic force and a passive, yielding surface. The trace is the impression that appears once the force comes to rest; or, put differently, it is the rest of the movement, its remainder, or remnant.[21] In perceptual experience, a remainder is often a reminder. Legible architecture offers experience remnants of this kind. But, again, when the stamp appears, the movement is over. It is primarily to this fact that the trace testifies. The partial and inadequate nature of the remnant—inadequate to the full reality of the force—also indicates the ambiguous nature of the image that results (an absent presence), whatever its place, as well as the interpretive task it invites.

Consider again the reshaping of profiles through frequency of use, the "cupping" or "dishing" of stairway treads that I discussed in the Introduction to this book. In buildings that are centuries old, this re-finishing radically alters original surfaces. Yet, insofar as these changes result from preferred movements, they could be said to improve or enrich the original solution. They certainly confer orientation by guiding movement along contours others have established, like Fehn's letter to a future walker, unintentionally and anonymously.

Fehn's anticipation of this type of alteration—at least of the changed profiles that would result from the paths most would prefer—can be seen both in and outside the Villa Busk, in his specification of white marble treads for the stairway that leads from the entry hall to the living room, and of the raised but still rough-cut stones that mark the house's corresponding thresholds (one into the garage and wood storage pavilion, and the other into the entry hall), both centered on the cross axis that also passes through the center of the tower. To date, neither shows much dishing, but both indicate his expectation that they will. In the terms introduced above: the harder stone has the capacity to resist the likely impress of a long history of steps.

Are these yielding surfaces, the white marble and raised stone, *inactive*? Because durability is one of architecture's chief virtues, we tend to think that buildings are both unchanging and passive. With these thresholds in mind one is inclined to ask if this is a defensible assumption. Although no wage is paid other than the cost of maintenance, building materials work for a living. In addition to "taking a stand" or "holding their ground," their job is to variously admit or resist ambient forces: recurring steps, in this case, but also, elsewhere in the house, wind, rain, sunshine and glare, temperature change, humidity, and so on. All the surfaces we touch and see testify to successes and failures in this kind of *work*, this kind of activity.[22] When external forces are allowed to show their effect, the result is accretion; when they are resisted, erosion occurs. Both stances, however, require what can be called *active passivity*, which is to say resistance, an internal force or capacity in a material's make-up that grants or refuses registration. On Villa Busk's north side, for example, the timber has become darker in color; on the sun side, the hue has lightened, saturated, and bleached surfaces. Neither stone nor steel would change so much. The timber of Fehn's tower has grayed so completely that a glancing view can mistake it for concrete. There is no need to decide if changes of this kind detract from the building's quality or enrich it; what must be granted, however, is the observation that they show its receptiveness to movements and elements that define the place, both environmental and practical.

Some of the marks that qualify Villa Busk today were probably unexpected. I have in mind the several instances of staining.[23] Here is the question: are the deposits of soot that mark a building evidences of its congeniality with its location, or do they detract from its intended qualities by recoloring its materials and redesigning its basic geometries? The same question can be asked of air-borne deposits that have variously qualified a façade's concrete, replacing the lines of formwork with spread of streaks. If the superimposed pattern gives voice to ambient conditions, does it thereby silence what the architect intended? Regardless of one's answer to this question, the fact remains that unintended marks also testify to the passing of time, not the time that follows natural or

Figure 2.3.13 Sverre Fehn, *Villa Busk*, Bamble, Norway, stair treads. Photograph David Leatherbarrow.

normal schedules (cycles), but moments or phases that divide time into periods unlike one another, breaking the "flow" commonly assumed to be continuous.

The concrete on the shade side of the garage and wood storage building is now marked by streaks of red. Similarly, the concrete base of the long, diagonal entry walk is darkened by patches of black. If one has design or expressive intentions in mind, these alterations would seem to be different from the bleached timber on the tower and the heightened formwork lines on the rear façade concrete. Why? Because they seem unintended and deforming. Yet, if one views the natural environment as an equally authoritative agency of surface qualification, which is how Fehn viewed the growth of moss and lichen on the stone, then all that should be said about a face thus saddened by tears is that it also bears witness to being in the world and the passing of time. After all, the red color results from the growth of algae, another gift of the same winds that crest the waves, expose the subsurface stone, and spread the seeds. Its significance is not a matter of attractive or ugly appearances, but an opportunity for the conjunction of two kinds of time: the seasons of the stain's (algae's) growth and decay and the history of its appearance and removal, also its likely return.

Figure 2.3.14 Sverre Fehn, *Villa Busk*, Bamble, Norway, threshold. Photograph David Leatherbarrow.

Pre-Recordings and Recordings

Two prominent surfaces inside Villa Busk can be used to summarize the points I have made about the ways for architecture to tell the time of the world, a world that includes environmental cycles and stories of particular ways of living. I have in mind the plaster walls that enclose rooms on their short sides (in the middle of the house) and the concrete walls and wooden ceiling above the fireplace (between the large sheets of glass that view the distant woods and cove). While both settings present qualified surfaces, they express different chronologies: the first, a *pre-recording* of likely marks (abrasions, partial cleanings, stains, and so on) and the second a *recording* of uses that have often been repeated, may have been anticipated, but could not be predicted in either intensity or regularity (smoke staining).

Let's first consider the plaster walls. Rather like the stairway treads that were protected and highlighted by sheets of white marble, the plaster walls that enclose the entry hall anticipate likely outcomes of practical use. Perhaps a useful (if pedestrian)

Figure 2.3.15 Sverre Fehn, *Villa Busk*, Bamble, Norway, plaster finishing. Photograph David Leatherbarrow.

Figure 2.3.16 Sverre Fehn, *Villa Busk*, Bamble, Norway, fireplace. Photograph David Leatherbarrow.

comparison is with "pre-washed denim," which is recommended because it can be worn comfortably and won't shrink. As for expression, it is designed to confer a sense of already-having-been-worn, of preparation for easy conformity to typical use. *Good fit* in this case is not only dimensional—the right size—but conformity to movement. These two senses of "fit" have a long history in architecture, codified in Vitruvius' text, but elaborated earlier in Greek philosophical writings, texts by Plato and Xenophon, for example. The Greek terms are "symmetry" and "eurhythmy", which have been translated as "norm-definition" (ideal or standard size) and "norm-realization" (the size that suits a particular body or situation).[24] A fitting material or surface treatment in this "eurhythmic" sense would be one that has been prepared for movements (activities, events, practices) that are likely to occur in a particular place. My concern is less with particular behaviors than with the kind of thinking that anticipates their effects by initiating their registration, a kind of pre-registration. The time of the Villa Busk plaster could be described as a *future anterior*, which is to say a statement about something that can be thought of as completed before it actually occurs. One imagines Fehn saying to himself: not long after the family moves in, walls in these places *will have been marked*. The pre-markings or pre-recordings ease occupation into a setting that has been prepared to accept the exigencies and accidents that inevitably attend to inhabitation, not just winding its clock, but making appointments on its calendar. Thanks to these walls, every "present moment" in the life of the house is also a retrospective future, one interval among others. These walls possess a strange kind of significance, seemingly accidental, yet nearly as composed as a landscape painting—especially an East-Asian watercolor (light brush strokes, a high degree of abstraction and compressed depth, so called vertical-distance). Even if there is nothing to see there is much to wonder about.

The smoke stains above the fireplace wall are similarly indefinite but offer a different chronology. Before the first fire was ignited, the concrete was uniformly gray and the timber evenly light brown. Each had its geometry, parallel lines resulting from board widths of formwork or cladding. And the differences don't end there: to the left of the flames is the white marble square with its corner cut out of blue glass and below is the slab of black slate, similarly square, but no less contrasting in color and texture. One gets the impression that Fehn intended the disintegration or fragmentation of the volume—the traditional enclosure of the Scandinavian fireplace—into independent and rather abstract planes. One outcome of a sequence of fires is that each of these planes will share some of the smoke residue. What is more, as the blackness increases the separation of planes will recede and the three dimensionality of the setting become apparent, surficial and soiled though it will be. Re-constitution of the setting through these means won't happen all at once. Several nights will be required, a comparable duration for acceptance of the stain. Even if the pace of recording turns out to be slow, the setting cannot be said to be static. Also, while silent, the stains will be read as signs of what has occurred there, the events of Busk family life. Maybe also and more widely, the life of the seasons would explain why Fehn installed an image of the sky, together with a view of the landscape, in and through the white and blue squares to the left of the fire. Time such as this will not have been added to these things, nor is it accidental to them; it would be better to say that stories and seasons are grasped in and through them, for without them they wouldn't be known.

2.4
World Rhythms: Álvaro Siza's Swimming Pools at Leça da Palmeira

Rhythm in the ancient sense is, at the moral and aesthetic level, the bridle which is placed on passion.

FRIEDRICH NIETZSCHE, *BRIEFE*

The forces at play in and around Álvaro Siza's Swimming Pools on the Leça da Palmeira waterfront were beautifully described in the first lines of an explanatory text the architect wrote a decade and a half after the first phase of the project was finished:

> Every year, with the spring tides, the sea takes away what is not essential. In that place, a rocky massif cuts through the three parallel lines: where the sea meets the sky, where the beach meets the sea, the long retaining wall of the street.[1]

Although the account is both personal and lyrical, I'd like to take what Siza wrote seriously. I believe these short lines articulate very directly and concisely the defining characteristics of the place and the basic subject matter of the design, as they can be seen today, more than half a century after the first phase of the project was completed.

Siza's first point concerns the time of the place: *Every year with the spring tides*. Three periods are implied—years, days, and months—each cyclical. The annual cycle is of course the longest. An equivalent formulation could be year-by-year, which is to say twelve-month phases repeating themselves without end, into the future from the past.

Figure 2.4.1 Álvaro Siza, *Leça da Palmeira Pools,* Porto, shore. Photograph David Leatherbarrow.

Seasons aren't noted, only implied. Next comes a much quicker phasing. Thanks to the moon's steady pull, high tides break upon the shore twice daily. Unlike the tides of public opinion or opportunity, which fluctuate without any discernable pattern, the rise and fall of the ocean's waters are reliably periodic.[2] Obviously there are low tides too, but they don't have the effects that concerned Siza. Lastly, there are the spring tides. Siza's term shouldn't be taken to imply a season (the one between winter and summer), for these tides occur throughout the year. Indicated instead is their ability to *spring* or jump forward, with increased amplitude, greater volume, and more violent force than others, as if suddenly released from Neptune's grip, the way a sprinter lunges forward at the start of a race. Violence is no less likely than force; memories of shipwrecks, ancient and modern, were probably not too distant.

Heavenly bodies set the schedule.[3] Twice a month, spring tides batter the shore, thanks to the combined pull of the sun and moon when teamed up in perfect alignment. Not so much cosmology, rather celestial mechanics provides the commonly accepted account. Newton's law of universal gravitation explained tidal force and timing, though Kepler suggested the influence of the moon decades earlier. A little more than a century later, Laplace took account of both friction and resonance when developing a mathematical model of tidal dynamism. Siza, for his part, didn't mention but no doubt observed the more frequent arrival of ordinary waves, every few minutes, by which the sea rhythmically re-presented itself, knocking at the city's big doorway—each wave just once—before slipping back, face down.

Paul Ricoeur once wrote that time becomes human when recounted.[4] I feel rather confident Siza's three waterfront calendars wouldn't have attracted his interest if they hadn't also presented themselves as episodes in a story—if the tides and waves had fallen onto the shore "just for the sound of it," as Francis Ponge beautifully observed.[5] For Siza, the spring tides had a decisive effect on the shore and city edge, epoch-making one could say: they removed what was *inessential*. One suspects Siza took this as a criterion of project development—waves of self-criticism. Spring cleaning also set the stage for project making, providing him with props, which is to say materials that were native or suitable to the place, with and against which he could work.

What might have been the shoreline *inessentials*? In reverse: what remained after the spring tides had their effect? A clue to the former was provided in the last paragraph of Siza's text: "In the first spring tides the sea took away a piece of the wall [an architect had built there], correcting what was not right." Obviously, this rectification occurred after construction, a later chapter in the site's history, to which I will turn shortly. What did remain after the gratuitous gesture had been taken away? What *was* right in such a place? Only those things that had the capacity to withstand the force of the tides. It was a talent or gift for endurance that determined their correctness.[6]

Let's imagine for a moment Siza hadn't built anything there. Before undertaking the project, he had "studied the outer limits, to the north and south." Looking from side to side, there's not much to see apart from spray and foam, only sand and stone and sky. Basic as they are, the elements under one's feet mostly hold their ground. Wind and water have their effect, erosion, thanks to which stone, the great symbol of lastingness, is also a site of unending change, slow though it has been and will be. What Siza designed, to which I'll turn shortly, thus stands between elements and times that couldn't be more contrasting, hydrodynamic and geological materials, impatiently fluid and implacably resilient. Degradation doesn't prevent the land from opposing the waves, first breaking then leveling them.

The operation is rather covert, however, unfolding well beneath the windblown crests. And its consequences increase as the angle between the surface and sea bottom tends toward 0 degrees. Friction between the ocean floor and the moving water drags and slows the wave's lower part, which in turn deprives its upper half of support, hence the terminal drop, precipitous if the wind blows from the shore out to sea, and is for that same reason loud: "The tide's countless wagons seem to unload their useless cargo just for the sound of it."[7]

Incapable of undercutting the waves, because they rise above them, the rocks also hold their ground. Siza says they do more: *a rocky massif cuts through three parallel lines*. He names lines but describes planar geometry, composed of levels or horizons: the water-level or sky-horizon, then the shore-level or land-horizon, and thirdly the street-level or city-horizon. The stone knifes into these domains, slicing through the levels they've established. Although cuts such as these might be suspected to result in a disintegration of the levels, the stone breakthroughs have the opposite effect: a single landscape is discovered among different horizons, similarly sliced, and sharing the same base. The procedure isn't surgical because the blade is blunt, but the edges are sufficiently sharp to expose the sea, shore, and street as sections of a single support.

The final part of the story's first chapter narrates the beginning of the project's beginning: *someone sought to protect a depression in that mass of solid rock*. The *someone* indicated here is not Siza himself, but the person whose initial observation led to the commission. Anyone could have come up with this idea, for the comparison—a pool is a big puddle—doesn't require penetrating insight. Less evident, perhaps, is the third virtue of the stone massif, hinted at with Siza's comment about solidity. We've seen, first, that stone has the ability to withstand the corrosive effects of the sea, though eventually the sea gets its way. Second, we noted stone's readiness to break the steady rhythm of waves. Its third strength is an unmatched capacity for supporting, holding, and retaining, a willingness to accommodate visitors arriving from anywhere, waters in this case, from who knows where, that want to remain there for a while, rather than slip back into the sea seconds after they arrive to the shore. Pools, like puddles and ponds, even the sea itself, make use of depressions in stone on the assumption that its hardnesses and softnesses meet two criteria: unbroken continuity of surface and a profile that anticipates water's easy compliance with gravity's pull.

Why would such a depression need to be *protected*? And from what? The answer becomes clear when the second part of Siza's observation is recalled: *someone thought to protect a depression in that mass of solid rock and use it as a tidal pool*. Tides come and go, repeatedly and incessantly. Rhythm may be apparent in forms that repeat, but once they appear, they don't last long. An entirely different duration was intended for the tidal pool. Once the depression was observed—one among many potentials contained within the massif—it was to be used and to remain as a pool, retaining or restraining the water's coming and going. This meant the tides would have to be both welcomed and resisted. Their contribution would be not only happily accepted as the supply of a fresh refill, but also refused now and then when they offered more than was needed. Despite

Figure 2.4.2 Álvaro Siza, *Leça da Palmeira Pools*, Porto, rock depressions. Photograph David Leatherbarrow.

the varying strength and volume of each arriving swell, the pool would have to be kept at the right level, meaning it would have to resist, more or less, the gravitational pull of the sun and moon. Odd as it may seem, the depression-as-tidal-pool had to protect itself against itself if it was to fulfill its purpose, which was the idea someone had and the beginning of Siza's project.

The Vocation of Construction Materials

Waiting is generally felt to be an imposition.[8] The bother is that one would like to get on with things that have been planned, and do so straight away, without delay, as expected. Of course, we sometimes choose to wait, but the time that follows such a decision no longer feels like an imposition, as it does when the delay is obligatory, at a traffic light, for test results, or a reply to one's invitation. With buildings, waiting is entirely different, just the opposite of an unwanted burden or bother; it is their chief purpose, one might even say their desire. The swimming pool waits for swimmers, as does a café for diners, and a ticket booth for theater goers, each setting being content in its inactivity because its fundamental charge is to remain available. Status quo expectations aren't required; settings can be prepared for a-typical as well as typical performances. All that's really necessary for a work to behave as it should is a willingness to let time pass. The kinds of preparations that define an architectural work are many. The measures that Siza pointed out were the work's physical or material arrangements, more specifically, their selection, sizing, and finishing—concrete not stone, for example, thick enough to support the load of the roof, and relatively smooth to the touch.

Before Siza made any decisions about materials, an initial indication about the right sort of preparations was given by the rocky massif. We've seen that a pool-like depression was ready to receive and retain tidal waters. Those preparations also made it just right for swimming. In this pre-architectural phase of the project, waiting had material and formal expressions: the stone waited for tidal waters to arrive and be refreshed twice a day, and the depression waited to be recognized as a possible pool. Although the massif never moved—how could it—a certain kind of activity was required for the appearance of a possible pool; the stone had to hold in reserve its potential to retain what the sea offered and the swimmers desired. Odd though the oxymoron may sound, this type of work required *active passivity*.

An analogous effort in human experience may be helpful in grasping this type of behavior: waiting can be tiring, inaction exhausting. In each case, doing nothing takes some effort, especially if alertness is also required. Thankfully, floors, walls, and windows don't seem to tire easily or quickly. Instead, they have a life-long passion for what comes their way without stable form or is never more than a tendency toward form—water's horizontality, for example, which is a result of its inability to stand on its own. Walls, for their part, seem to have an intuitive grasp of the rhythms that will come into play nearby. They have force, but they don't force themselves on what's around. Their service (work) is to wait and welcome what they've been designed to receive.

The patience of building materials is recognized in the second section of Siza's text: *concrete walls sustain the pine and copper roof and support the access paths to the pool ... here and there small interventions consolidate the natural platforms. Not much has changed.* In part, this observation repeats what has been said about the depression in the stone massif: a pre-existing condition served as a model for architectural development; small interventions consolidated the potential of natural platforms, changing what was already there just a little, only concentrating what pre-dated construction. The new thought in this part of Siza's text is indicated by his use of the term *sustain*: the concrete walls sustain the roof and paths. Support is obviously indicated. If the roof constitutes a dead load or downward force, the walls must act as a counterforce. Balance or the

Figure 2.4.3 Álvaro Siza, *Leça da Palmeira Pools*, Porto, rear walk and stair. Photograph David Leatherbarrow.

equilibrium of forces is the result. A second sense of sustaining is no less important. The walls give the work its standing through time, the times Siza's text implied at the beginning, the years, months, and days of tides and waves, as well as the rhythms of occupation, which include individuals or groups arriving in street clothes, leaving the changing rooms in swim wear, then retracing those same steps when they are ready to leave. *Sustained* in this sense means prolonged round the clock, continued without end or interruption, unbroken tempo. When construction materials are the topic of consideration, durability indicates both capacity and continuance. The key question concerns their mutuality, how materials or buildings keep themselves ready to act, for then their potential—their unexercised power—gives the work and its place specific character. Explaining this will take a few steps.

First, there is the matter of the building's patience and passivity, the two dimensions of sustaining that Siza mentioned. Consider again the unbuilt site. As soon as one wave breaks on the shore, the stone massif patiently waits for the arrival of another. The next may be stronger, higher, or faster, but the rock is prepared to hold its ground. It couldn't do otherwise, obviously. Siza intended the walls of the pools and changing rooms to be similarly patient, which is to say, keep themselves ready for wind and rain, violent or moderate as they might be, also for individuals and groups, who would be variously familiar with the building and its functions. The transition from the bright light of the access walk to the deep shadows of the changing rooms, for example, is disorienting on one's first visit. The word "patient" is cognate with a number of terms that indicate enduring or suffering (pathos, passion, pathetic, etc.). Each of them assumes inactivity. Patience and passivity are comparable postures and labors, efforts that are strenuous but stop short of action. Patience can run out, just as passivity can give way to action. But before that happens, there remains an untapped reserve, a state or condition of available ability, or prolonged capacity. Building materials exist in precisely this state, and in this state, Siza suggested, they sustain works of architecture.

Potentialities[9]

Since the arguments of Aristotle, in *Physics* and *De Anima* especially, activity and passivity have been coupled. Living things can act and can suffer the actions of others. Is the same true for so-called inanimate objects, bricks and boards, for example? Leaving aside the long history of writers in and outside architecture who discussed the life of stones (Theophrastus, della Porta, Alberti, etc.), it seems fair to say in a general way that buildings are inactive when compared to the movements of organisms—plants, animals, and people. Earlier, and following Aristotle, I made the distinction between two sorts of change: of state and position. The obvious truism concerning architecture's inactivity (positional fixity) should not be taken to mean buildings or their materials don't change or lack energy and force. Perhaps the kind of energy that stones possess can be grasped most directly by considering the non-use of human faculties: when one's eyes are closed, one does not lose the ability to see, for they remain available even when kept on standby. The power exists even when not put to use; it remains available or ready to be called upon. A capacity is a potential to act, no matter whether that power exists in a person or thing.

In physical things, particularly construction materials, potential arises out of the formative processes that unfold in the natural world or a factory, the means and phases of timber's or stone's constitution, leading to its disposition. Readiness not only precedes the exercise of effort but is preceded by the history of preparation. Resistance, for example, draws upon strengths that have been historically constituted, no matter whether that formation occurred by art or nature. Enactments, then, actualize and extend the clock of material disposition. I have in mind the concrete walls and slabs of Siza's pools and the timber of the changing rooms—their readiness to act as elements of the project: blocking the sun, resisting the lateral thrust of the soil or water, giving the feet a stable deck, and so on.

Again, an example from bodily experience should be helpful in clarifying this sense of capacity or potential. The *Discobolus*, or *Discus Thrower*, c. 460–450 BC, normally attributed to Myron of Eleutherae, but surviving only in a number of Roman copies, is not only one of the most famous works of classical antiquity, but one of the most vivid indications of the ancient understanding of rhythm (*rhythmos*). Several historians have shown that *rhythmos* did not signify movement or flow, as does rhythm today—the rhythm of houses on a street, columns in a building, or waves headed toward the shore—but *shape* or *form*. Werner Jaeger, for example, explained that rhythm, for the ancient Greeks, imposed bonds on movement and interrupted the flux of things. The idea was not flow but pause, the limitation of movement.[10] The epigraph from Nietzsche cited above makes the same point. The sort of action that is commonly adduced is dance, the movements of which flow between particularly expressive positions. Each pose doesn't so much interrupt movement as it summarizes one then initiates another of its sequential phases. Stops of this kind mark distinct intervals, one position then the next, with the measured flow of intermediate steps between. The character of the entire sequence—pose-flow-pose-flow and so on—is largely defined by the momentary positions, for they epitomize the movements that have preceded and will follow. Myron's *Discus Thrower* is obviously not dancing but holds a pose just the same. In this case, too, sequences are structured: the preparation for the throw has concluded and the process that will lead to the release is about to begin. The position and potential of his arm's backward swing have been usefully compared to the extreme limit of a pendulum's movement, the point and moment when it has gathered up its ability to move in the opposite direction, just before doing so, poised as if—for a split second—at rest.[11] In both ancient and modern sculpture (Myron, Michelangelo, and Rodin, for example), antithetical movements in single figures assumed and exhibited *contrapposto*, the axial disequilibrium that allowed the simultaneous appearance of front and back, as well as reach in opposite directions.

The interplay of elements and forces that alternately balance and un-balance one another on the site and within the building unfolds in both the history of the work and the experiences of the people who use it. Siza's brief text touches on the human body's encounter with the site's physicalities in just a few lines. In the middle part of his text, he observes that the *paths were there (on the hard ground, one knows where to put their feet)*. This knowing in one's feet is the counterpart to the disorientation that follows entry into the changing room darkness. The same re-grounding moment occurs when the swimmer's feet touch the pool bottom. His concern for feet at rest is apparent in his return to the moment four times in his text, as well as the anchoring metaphor used to describe the building's attachment to the retaining wall.

Siza's third level or horizon also plays a part in the building's work with and against the location. The retaining wall stops both the shore and the city. In spring tides, waves break against the wall no less than the stone massif rising out of the sand. Likewise, for the buildup of paths and intermediate spaces above the shore: the lawn, the sidewalk, and the road, which is bordered on its opposite side by another pedestrian walk, and still farther, the successive layers of the town, which gradually step upward, along an angle (in section) that parallels the descent of the shore into the sea (on the opposite side of the retaining wall). The wall's *pose* or *stop* establishes an equilibrium between the corresponding slopes and movements, in terms of both civil engineering (lateral forces canceling one another) and cultural history (ships and sailors arriving to the shore for centuries, also the growth of the town in "waves" of urbanization). With respect to the latter, the several phases of Siza's work on the site attest to the rhythms of Porto's urban development (1959–60, 1961–4, 1965–7, 1973, and then a master plan between 2002 and 2007).[12] In each case, movements came to rest against the sea wall, which also served as the threshold for the project's enclosed spaces.

Figure 2.4.4 Myron of Eleutherae, *Discus Thrower*. Creative Commons, Public Domain (CC-SA 4.0).

Figure 2.4.5 Álvaro Siza, *Leça da Palmeira Pools*, Porto, sink and mirror. Photograph David Leatherbarrow.

Figure 2.4.6 Álvaro Siza, *Leça da Palmeira Pools*, Porto, entry ramp. Photograph David Leatherbarrow.

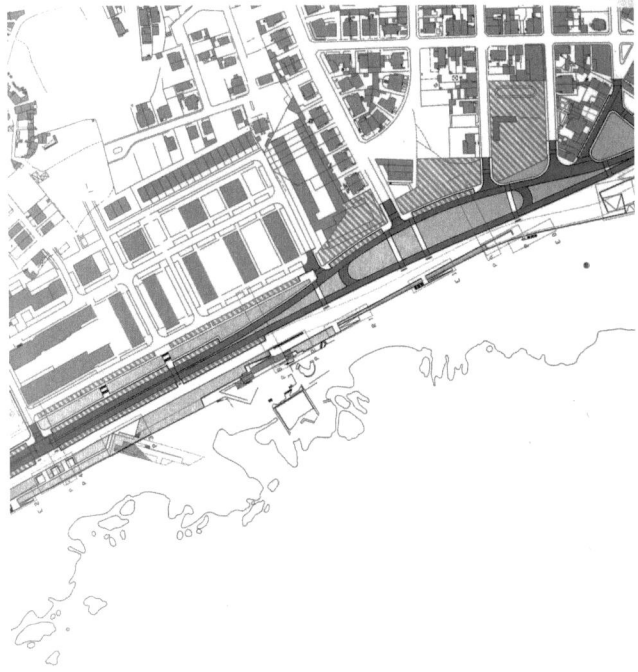

Figure 2.4.7 Álvaro Siza, *Leça da Palmeira Pools*, Porto, area plan. Courtesy of Álvaro Siza.

Waves repeatedly arrive and depart, as do cars on the road, the first moving perpendicular, the second parallel to the retaining wall and the interiors that thicken it. The same can be said for the swimmers, passing through the dark spaces of the changing rooms on one side of the retaining wall and then across the shifting surfaces of the sand and pools on the other. These kinds of movement are not as periodic as those of the sun and moon—they're more like gusts of wind—but are sufficiently regular to allow one to say they're *steady*. As such, they program future movements. What had arrived will return, even if the intervals between successive thens and nows will never be precisely the same, nor the speed and force of the arrivals and departures.

Variations are measured against what neither arrives nor departs, the retaining wall. Its primary function—from both civil engineering and cultural points of view—is to hold its ground against the play of ambient forces, managing the confrontation, steadying the rhythms. Just as it is correct to say the wall stops the forces, thanks to its capacities for resistance, it is also true to observe that the line between the shore and city marks the exact place in which the movements show themselves most vividly. After they change their clothes, swimmers move toward the pools. After that, once they've dressed, they move toward the town. The sun's movements are likewise seen in the slide

Figure 2.4.8 Álvaro Siza, *Leça da Palmeira Pools*, Porto, front lawn and roofs. Photograph David Leatherbarrow.

of shadows across the concrete. Similarly, the noise of the traffic ends when you pass behind the entry wall. Vectors of movement arrive and depart from a single line.

The times of the site, or more broadly the rhythms of the world, are known by virtue the work's capacity to stay as it has been, to keep itself at rest. One last analogy with the human body should help clarify this principle. Consider the rhythms of life: heartbeat or breathing, for example. Normally a few seconds pass between inhaling and exhaling, a pause or rest that seems to stop respiration, though life comes to an end if the stop lasts too long. Above, a comparably still moment was seen in the pendulum's swing, when movement to the left reversed itself toward the right. Siza's thickened retaining wall is precisely that moment of rest, that pause or pose, whose constancy brings the time of the world into relief, rendering it vividly legible, rather like the darkness in a theater that enables on-stage performances.

Part Three

The Time of the Body

3.1

Taking Steps: Nicolaes Maes' *The Eavesdropper*

It might very well be thought that… architecture works for the eye alone, but it ought primarily… to work for the sense of movement in the human body. When, in dancing, we move according to certain rules, we feel a pleasant sensation, and we ought to be able to arouse similar sensations in a person whom we lead blindfold through a well-built house.

GOETHE, "PALLADIO ARCHITECTURE" 1795

The center-stage episode of Nicolaes Maes' *The Eavesdropper* is polarized between two others: first, on the upper floor, in the deep middle distance is a dinner scene, performed by a small group awaiting a refill of wine glasses; second, on the lower floor, not quite so far away, a little closer to the foreground, is a tender scene of a different sort, the embrace of two lovers, of shared intimacy but unequal devotion.[1] While he is wholly dedicated to affection, she seems unmoved, though probably not unconcerned, because probably pregnant. Perhaps she is thinking of the work she should be doing or maybe she's heard someone on the landing, the person who occupies the center of the several scenes and the foreground. Although incidental to the events unfolding in depth, this third or middle position is beautifully integrative: the fact of the girl's descent—glass in hand—ties her to the dining scene above, but her gesture of silence indicates her orientation toward the embrace below. Yet, her eyes and smile are directed toward us, as if we are the ones to whom she is gesturing, like an actor on stage. But only we see what's behind and round the corner; she merely listens. Is she about to take the next step, then turn, and surprise the lovers? Or has she paused? The lower folds of her outer

Figure 3.1.1 Nicolaes Maes, *The Eavesdropper*. Courtesy of Dordrechts Museum, loan of the Cultural Heritage Agency 1953.

skirt ripple behind, tracing her steps, but the right foot—clearly off the step because of the shadow—only extends toward the floor, held back.

Pause is also indicated by the raised finger. To what end? Does it urge our silence, ask us to take note, direct our view vertically, or signal admonition? Probably all four. Maes tested possible indications of this gesture in several pages of sketches. The distance between her lips and finger was key. With too great a distance, simply pointing upward, she would limit the gesture to asking a question (I'll turn to what's above shortly); were it closer, maybe touching her lips, she would only be requesting silence. In other studies, she uses the finger instructively, as would a lawyer when offering evidence that speaks for itself—silent testimony. In this picture's alternative, the finger neither points directly upward, nor covers her lips expressing silence, but drops below and aside a wry smile that shows the lower-landing girl's guilt to be at once self-evident and amusing. The listener's pause allows the events above and below to unfold at their own pace, but thanks to her hesitation they've become part of a single narrative, despite their incongruity.

One Moment among Many

What about the margins of this three-episode drama? In the foreground right hangs a world map; below it, draped over a chair, are a gentleman's street clothes and sword. Another coat hangs from the door on the left; below it is the sort of lamp one would use outdoors. Paired and foregrounded, emblems of the street frame the central three scenes. Obviously, they were placed there some time before the events we see, the lamp probably a while ago, the coat and sword recently. One plane deeper in the space—not even half a meter farther back—a double archway framing the stair and hall serves the same enclosing and bi-focal purpose, leaving the street behind. Splitting the double is a significant vertical, an oddly thin pilaster that not only divides the arches but supports a bust labeled Juno, believed at the time to preside over home and marriage, as she does this arrangement of events. In this carving, the goddess turns away, rather ambivalently I think, her eyes might be closed.

Back to the foreground, the hat, scarf, coat, and sword are obviously male, hastily set down (who knows how they're standing), intrusive (hence the map), and quite probably sexual (undressed and phallic). Equally sexual, one supposes, seen through the doorway just past the coat, one plane deeper, on eye level with the lovers, is a cat on the kitchen counter stealing a bird that was no doubt prepared for the upstairs meal. Caught in his embrace, the girl has neglected her duty, serving the next course. The cat's paw has its prize, likewise the man.

Thanks to its architecture, the painting presents six separate episodes as one ensemble: a room through the door to the far left, the central staircase and corridor, the first-floor dining room, the kitchen to the far right, the lower passage with the lovers, and the garden and distant house outdoors. Listed this way, they stand as unrelated incidents, *episodes* in Aristotle's terms.[2] But that's like saying a good loaf of bread is nothing more than flour plus yeast, salt, and water. The staircase, landing, and pilaster, in front of which the listener pauses and begins her turn, make the mixture of moments something all-of-a-piece, a single story. The architecture of the interior—its levels, distances, apertures, and materials—integrates all the events into a chronicle that narrates a moment of crisis. What we see is a house divided[3] with decorum above and desire below, the conflicts of which cluster around a defining element and moment, jointly attesting to the breakdown of social order.

Each of the scenes has key architectural elements: the table that gathers the meal, the double arch that couples the middle-distance events, the lower threshold at which the lovers stand, and the step on which the eavesdropper hesitates. Maes signed the painting on the riser of this dramatic step. In the plan of a dramatic plot, each situation is given with elements that define it, as well as its right place within the encompassing topography (the levels and distances) and the unfolding of events (the sequences, surprises, and reversals). Absent these locations, the sequences wouldn't make sense. In reverse: if un-sequenced, the spaces wouldn't tell a story. Consider the stratification of the platforms: formal dining is elevated above the seduction scene happening at the same time, which is at the level of and concurrent with the hungry cat, the garden lower still, previously or yet to be entered.

The externalities that break in on the domestic scene polarize the setting from foreground to background and then to now and then again: the street (and map) from which the visitor has entered extends all the way back to the garden, which appears through a large window, not a door, though access beyond is implied in the stair rail to the right. In the very far distance, just in front of the house, another couple can be seen under a sky whose clouds foreshadow rain. Passage from front to back is accelerated by the axis and one-point perspective. In fact, there are four arches that frame this perspective, each quickening the pace. The upward movement to the left begins with the circular mat on the floor, in front of the first riser, and ends in the circular frame on the dining room wall, which is something of a dead end, for neither neighboring buildings nor sky makes an appearance, only soft light. Still, the paired circles limit the passage. The grid of tiny glass panes behind the table group reinforces the theme of containment, maybe confinement. And just as there are distinct settings, alternately discordant and concordant, preceding and following the listener's gesture, there are distinct characters, by my count eleven: the four around the table, the two lovers, and the eavesdropper, plus the two in the garden, the crazy cat, and above it all Juno.

Serving the same function as the paired circles are the recently arrived visitor's coat and the coming storm, terminal points of a spatial and temporal axis running through the archways on the right, expressing movements outside the compass and schedule of the domestic routine, the well-managed protocols of which shuttle between the circles on the left. At this moment, the seasons of natural time and the schedules of urban time are unsynchronized with the internal routines of domestic life, though they could have been, which means each plays its own part in the story. The listener and the landing bind together situations and settings that would otherwise be discordant. Plots and plans are reciprocal and equivalent forms of narration, timed for movements that bring the house not only to life but also into crisis.

Together with the distances shown in this image are times: passages, pauses, and advances, also progressions and retreats. Far from incidental to these movements, the spaces allow, invite, and recall them, for the mind certainly, hence the moral tale Maes has told, but also, and in concert with it, the body, eyes, feet, and hands. If we concentrate initially on the two distances that polarize the drama, up one set of steps to the family gathering and the down another (we don't see) that leads to the lovers' embrace, Maes has arranged rather distended sequences, relatively slow spaces, that take more than a minute or two to grasp. First, and obviously, they would transit across some steps, which would take a little while, then more distance and time inside the dining room or kitchen—who knows how long—because both are only cornered by the axes of approach.[4] People terminate each of these sequences, not places, at least not in their full extent and duration. Considering the upper room, neither its sides, nor floor nor ceiling is shown, only the cloudy, faceted glazing, plus two wall-hangings. I don't think Maes wanted to indicate a particular time of day. Nor have we been shown much of the kitchen's lateral spread, only a short length of the countertop, a window, and bits of the floor and ceiling. The partial presentation requires—but thanks to Maes' skill also invites—a step-by-step or moment-by-moment sort of apprehension in two phases: up or down the steps, and then into the spaces that turn inward.

Different dimensions of time are indicated by the more distant players, I mean the house and garden in the far distance and the unseen street on our side of the foreground landing, evidences of which, as we've seen, are the outer garments, sword, and map. The times of these spaces prolong the moment of the listener's gesture not only back to the time when the lovers first arrived but ahead to the time when the storm will break. The house's history is also extended, for the no-longer-there of the street and the not-yet-there of the garden are experiences and opportunities for everyone we see, not only these groups, at the time of this event, but others in the house too, before and after this moment passes. Interestingly, one's sense of what is behind and ahead (street and garden) is rather immediate, even though what appears is even more partial than the terminal points of the distances that require prolonged, two-phased perception.

Despite these four distances (dining, kitchen, garden, and street) and the times of sense they suggest, the gesture and the landing suggest they all have bearing of what is occurring at this particular moment, that they play their parts *now*. Regardless of their degrees of remoteness, or maybe thanks to their apartness, they are concurrent with this amusing but critical development, serving as the historical context of its unfolding and the chronological basis of our understanding. The simultaneity of these sequences is what I want to stress, alternately quick and slow, no longer and not yet, but all at once.

Again and Again

The times of these spaces are amplified by the pacing and spacing of several architectural elements. Throughout the painting, motifs are repeated and varied, alternately renewing and developing the moments each of them structures in sequences. As before, the insistent and obvious figure to begin with is the set of steps, not only the run of treads and risers, but the landings.

There is nothing special or unique about the steps of the stairways; seen and assumed, each step is more or less the same as the others—risers, treads, and nosings—so that a person's paces, one way or another, won't require thought, except the kind that resides in one's muscles, because the steps to come will be just like those before, ticking off approach and departure like intervals on the face of a clock. Repetitive sameness is not the principle that governs the landings, however; they vary or dilate in order to establish connections between the spaces at their edges, making them equally available upon arrival. In this sense, a landing is an upper-level equivalent to an entry hall. While the risers that step up from or down to the landings are of the same height as those of the steps, the widths of each landing vary. The two that extend to the sides of the hallways at the end of the run that leads to the dining room differ from the stairway treads in depth only.[5] The central landing, by contrast, is more than double the hallway width. It has also been shaped to meet the two doors on either side and presumably the foreground entry door through which the visitor recently passed. The greater depth and wider spread of landings invite pauses, of course, like the listener's, but also viewing and a fairly speedy sense of the surroundings, thanks to the concurrency of prospects mentioned above. All of this is to say two kinds of time unfold in or on the steps of the stairway: a serial, sequential, or step-by-step time of identical treads and risers, and a discontinuous but simultaneous time of the landings.

Another architectural element used repeatedly in this internal landscape is the arch. Despite the use of quasi-classical elements—pilasters, capital details, and bases—one doesn't feel that Maes was a serious student of Vignola, that a well-informed sense of proportions governed the formation of these arches, all five of them. Still, it seems the intention was to make them all the same, even if the frontal pair are coupled by the Jove-supporting pilaster and enriched with emblems of abundance, rather like trophies on ceremonial arches. Because they repeat, each serves the same spatial purpose, limiting a segment of the route through the house, ending and beginning the phases of that passage, making connections by repeating sequences.

Lastly, the least architectural, almost graphic instance of repetition and variation is Maes' use of the circle. The initial and most prominent figure is the landing mat, between the listener's downward step and Maes' signature, with the street lamp to the far left, at the foot of the coat-bearing pier. Then comes the prominent, though distant, circle on the dining room wall. One can't say if it is a mirror or wall-mounted candle, but it functions as a terminus of upward movement just the same. There are also the circles on the foreground map, the lower, smaller, and a complete one, probably a wind rose. Lastly, least conspicuously but most centrally is the rim of the empty glass. Surely that circled emptiness summarizes the story most simply. But the form repeats, as do the essential elements of the architecture—the thresholds, archways, and treads—each inviting and recalling spatial passage between the moments of rest they accommodate and represent.

3.2

Pacing and Spacing: Bo and Wohlert's *Louisiana Museum of Modern Art*

> *Veritas filia temporis.*
> Truth is the daughter of time.
> ANON

The history of the familiar epigraph cited above sets the stage for the inquiry into the temporal dimension of buildings and landscapes I intend. Briefly noted, a few of the key moments are as follows. In the seventeenth century, Francis Bacon argued for the progressive unveiling of truth. Learning would advance as time passed, if inquiry abandoned the "idols" he described. Bacon was not, however, the first to see truth descend from time. Leonardo da Vinci, more than a century earlier, understood time as the cradle of invention, as did Aristotle in antiquity. In *Laws*, Plato asserted that the truth of any piece of legislation is arrived at through long processes of correction and improvement. And in the fifth and fourth centuries BC, Hippocratic writers described the discovery of medicine as the outcome of extended periods of research. Earlier usage can be assumed, but the origin remains unknown. As time passes—not hours and days but years, decades, and centuries—the order of existence becomes apparent, the reality of current conditions.

The time intended in these observations can be characterized as historical. Some interpreters have suggested it also chronicles scientific progress. The acceptability of that reading hinges on one's conception of science. Yet, there seems little doubt that through the centuries, the maxim assumed different kinds of time and truth. The

Figure 3.2.1 Bo and Wohlert, *Louisiana Museum*, Copenhagen, view toward the Sound. Photograph David Leatherbarrow.

former, for example, was personified in sharply different figures: *Chronos* and *Aion* in ancient Greek myth, the first typically depicted as an old man, the second a young boy; or, centuries later in Renaissance culture, Father Time with wings or Saturn with an hourglass and scythe; and so on.[1] Might the same conclusion about *temporis* and *veritas* be drawn if we consider this parent and child in rather more concrete terms, not as represented but directly experienced? I have in mind the time of bodily movement, of *passage* through buildings and landscapes. If the extension can be granted and the hypothesis allowed, then truth, or more modestly the sense of reality that results from architectural experience, would also be the daughter of time—not time with a "tooth," eating away at things, but "time the revealer," a mirror or lamp. Let me pursue this idea a little further before introducing the specific case to be studied in detail.

In architecture, some types of settings offer their contents all at once, others successively. Instances of the first type await one's arrival or return, fully prepared with all their parts in place to be used in the typical activities of everyday life, without demanding much attention. They quietly convey a combined sense of suitability, stability, and settled repose, *still* as they were. Examples of the second, successive type, through which we move at varying speeds, are known in *passing*. Often, they are laid out to join the still-spaces together. Not only do they link places together, they join times: when one is moving along a passage or walk, behind means no longer and ahead indicates not yet. Passing movements are less segmental than transitional. Passages aren't used in quite the same way as still-spaces, nor are they as amply provisioned. In passing-space, one rarely has a sense of fullness. Incompleteness may be conveyed because some other place was left behind, but there is also a positive sense of the yet-to be-discovered, maybe the fulfillment of a desire that hadn't be met previously. The distinction is not watertight, of course. Passages often run through still-spaces, and moments of rest can begin or end transitional ones, landings or terraces, for example.

Despite their occasional overlaps, still- and passing-spaces indicate in a preliminary way two distinct temporalities in architecture: the time of present circumstances, when current conditions are grasped in full, and the time of incremental unfolding, when the discovery of what this or another place has to offer is phased or unfolds successively. Obviously there are other kinds of architectural time, but none are quite so recognizably different as these two. When coordinated through design, as they are in most buildings and landscapes, they join together periods of approach and arrival, followed by times of rest or work, and then departure. Although the term is contradictory, I'd like to describe the two together as configurations that are *still passing*. My aim is to show that still-passing experiences typically unfold in settings for movement and repose, without which—here's the difficult point—time itself would lack the structures through which it is known. Passage and rest do not *take*, they *make* time. There is no pre-existing fund from which spatial currency can be borrowed; rooms and gardens generate their own temporal resources, the pulse and rhythms by which they are experienced and known.

Considering the first type a little more fully, one can say that each time we return to a given space we expect it to be just as it was, still the same. I suspect that August Schmarsow, the early twentieth-century architectural theorist and historian I cited in the Introduction, had this reliable and restful sense of settings in mind when he described architecture's provision of lasting places in times of forceful change.[2] A person's self-awareness provides a useful analogue. To be still is first of all to be motionless. When inactivity is coupled with quiet, the result is tranquility. That both stillness and tranquility assume staying put in a single place is hardly surprising when the etymological root of still, *stall*, is remembered, for its range of meanings all point toward place stability or positional fixity. At the bottom of the word "stall" is *sta*, cognate with the Greek *stello*, parent to a very large family of place terms. But the temporal implications of still are my concern just now.

Still means persisting in self-sameness or remaining as before: after all these years, Richard is still a close friend; though my daughter recently married I am still her father. Likewise in settings: when he returned in the early morning, the workman's bench was still as he left it; in the late afternoon, the librarian's desk is still piled with books; despite Saturday night expectations, the restaurant still has a table late in the evening. Albeit awkwardly phrased, the dictionary definition is beautifully precise: still means then or now or for the future as before. The key is *as before*. An associated and usefully compact definition is as follows: even to this or that past or present or future time.[3] In each instance, some time now offers itself as if it were the same as some time before or after, still the same, promising to remain so.[4]

The second temporal type contrasts sharply with this settled sufficiency. One's grasp of passing places is phased or additive, one moment then the next, each giving only part of itself, while recalling those that came before and pointing toward others that will follow, without overcoming their distance and difference. Even though times that are no longer and not yet are obviously distinct, they can be connected, as indicated by the term *now then*, which indicates summary understanding at the same time that it inaugurates advance. Like the instant a decision is made, its resolve is buttressed by a conclusion and a beginning; its self-definition *now* includes another period *then* without ceasing to be itself.[5]

When the topography one moves through is densely structured, as in most urban areas, partiality is the norm: the boulevard extends past the street corner, the gardens in the interior of the block continue behind the building I'm facing, and the hills of the cemetery hide the river that forms its edge. The same sense of *still-more-to-be seen* can be said for many landscape gardens, particularly those in the so-called informal traditions, as developed in England of course, but also, though differently in China, thanks to various techniques of distancing, concealing, and borrowing topics of interest.[6]

Art in these instances elaborates prosaic experience. In everyday perception, views catch no more than the visible sides of things: these bays of an apartment building, that length of shops on the street, the tops of several taller trees, not the garden at their base. Even when the "projective cast" is wide, from a roof deck or garden clearing, some aspects of elements and places keep themselves hidden. Although practical vision not appreciative looking typifies perception in passing space, marginal awareness remains alert to fringe phenomena.[7] The *still-to-come* of a setting's unfolding results from its depth, for no vantage takes hold of more content than figures are willing to give or show at a given moment; and depending on the distance, even this may be hard to take hold of properly. The three-part structure of prospects—nearby, neighboring, and distant—distinguishes distances in terms of grasp and reach: beyond this vicinity, for example, the trees, windows, and doors I see are too far away to be recognized clearly, let alone entered.

Because most buildings, landscapes, and cities are generous with their holdings, one tends to believe that whatever is out of reach at this moment can be taken in more fully in a while. Immediacy is all that's lacking. Jacques Derrida repeatedly discussed the ways that figures differ from yet defer to one another.[8] What is behind an object has deferred the time when it will make an appearance. This sense of occasion means that the perception of spatial depth requires the acceptance of delays. Arrivals occur for many reasons: sharpened focus because the right viewing distance has been reached, increased interest overcoming boredom, a new orientation thanks to turning, relaxing, etc., or a change in the landscape itself, resulting from all manner of environmental comings and goings. Architecture can prompt re-orientations such as these and give them pace and rhythm. Like the arrivals and departures at a taxi stand, phenomena emerge into and recede from visibility in unbroken, if sometimes unplanned, continuity.

The intention of the study that follows is to examine how movement through and residing within spatial ensembles enact these two temporal types, how anticipations and arrivals pace passage between rooms, through buildings, and across landscapes. Perceptual orientation will be one of the key topics, likewise viewing distance and viewing angle, in and outside buildings. Each of these themes bears upon the more general problem of movement toward, within, and around settings, as well as the kinds of time in which that movement unfolds, times that are still and passing I've said, but also quick or slow, cyclical or sequential, and known through anticipations, discoveries, and recollections. Although issues as basic as these could be taken up in any number of works, I'll concentrate on those that have found their place at a single site, the architecture, gardens, and park of the Louisiana Museum of Modern Art in Denmark.[9] In this Museum, like any other, the layout gives more space to passage than rest and intends experiences that are more optical than practical, but the range of settings it contains should be sufficient to exemplify the times of space I want to describe.

A Museum without Walls[10]

In 1965, the Sculpture Park at the Louisiana Museum was opened 20 miles north of Copenhagen, in a village called Humlebaek.[11] Before there was a Museum on the site, there were the house, barns, gardener's lodge, fishing hut, and gazebo of a pre-existing

Figure 3.2.2 Bo and Wohlert, *Louisiana Museum*, Copenhagen, entry. Photograph David Leatherbarrow.

but deserted villa. It was called Louisiana because the estate's founder had been rather remarkably remarried three times to women with the same name, Louise. The villa's varied topography included gardens, terraces, an orchard, stream, lake, and the shoreline of the Sound, with a view of Sweden in the distance. The villa had been abandoned and the grounds neglected when it was obtained for the Museum in 1955. The architects used the word "jungle" to describe the landscape. Nevertheless, these pre-conditions played significant roles in the makeup of the new building and landscape, though they themselves were transformed in order to meet the Museum's requirements.

From the very start of the project, Knud Jensen, the owner, and his two architects, Jørgen Bo and Vilhelm Wohlert, wanted to avoid the introverted, treasury type of museum they thought common at the time. Jensen referred to the National Gallery of Denmark (*Statens Museum for Kunst*, 1896) as "a true horror cabinet, very much the nineteenth-century bourgeoisie's exaggerated view of its own importance."[12] His reaction was rather like Paul Valéry's polemical comments four decades earlier: "However vast the palace, however suitable and well-arranged, we always feel a little lost, a little desolate in its galleries, all alone against so much art … We cannot stand up to it. So what do we do? We grow superficial. Or else we grow erudite. And erudition, in art, is a kind of dead end."[13]

Pacing and Spacing: Bo and Wohlert's Louisiana Museum of Modern Art

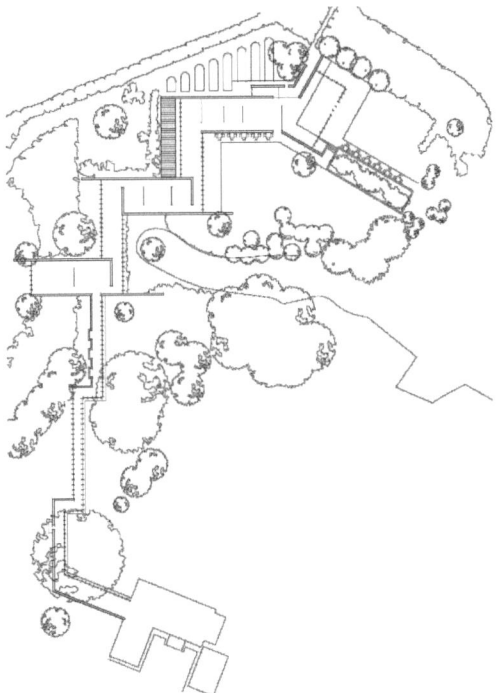

Figure 3.2.3 Bo and Wohlert, *Louisiana Museum*, Copenhagen, general plan. Drawing David Leatherbarrow.

The Louisiana alternative involved opening the walls of the institution to the opportunities of its milieu, literally through the use of window walls, and conceptually in the transformation of what typically would have been a single-block-of-a-building into a number of pavilions connected by gallery corridors that linked together not only the enclosed exhibition rooms but the house and the site's several prospects, across terraces and gardens, toward the old orchard and forest on one side, the lake on another, and the open sea on the third. A simple pattern of walkways allowed for the clear differentiation of rooms, inside and out, each with its own character or atmosphere, thanks to their individual dimensions and geometries, but also the site's varied topographical conditions (of enclosure or expanse, shade or bright light, and views), which they variously absorbed and amplified. For example, a depression near the lake became part of a wonderful two-story gallery for a group of works by Giacometti; the expanse of the upper terrace extended the prospect and illuminated a pair of walkways; a shallow pool under ancient trees served as the site for alternately compact and vertical sculptural works.

Variations in the exhibition spaces did not prevent the ensemble from expressing coherence; however, for simple techniques of wall and roof construction were repeated

Figure 3.2.4 Ole and Edith Nørgård, *Louisiana Museum*, Copenhagen, garden rooms, view.

throughout, as were the types of display panels and a few types of materials: tile, painted brick, and clear-varnished timber. The zig-zag plan also formed the sides of a number of outdoor rooms, again with varying character, though built, like the buildings, with a limited palette of materials (horizontal boards covered with ivy in the "garden rooms," for example), sometimes locating sculptural works, other times providing good spots for sunbathing, picnics, or evening concerts. While these uses transcend what we typically assume to be museum functions, they do allow the institution to ease its way into everyday life, restoring the links between its representational and participatory dimensions.

Landscape Configuration

Immediately after the architects accepted the commission (1956), the client invited them to stay for several days in the house, to survey and study its grounds. He had obtained the villa one year earlier but took a while to select his architects. While there, Bo and Wohlert walked and wandered the site, discovering what they took to be its potentials and deciding what changes would need to be made, what clearings, cuts, terracing, and planting would accommodate both the works that Jensen already owned and those he intended to obtain. To get a better sense of possible settings for display within the pre-existing conditions, they hung some of the paintings on large trees—seemingly improbable though the notion was, and risky for the paintings—in order to assess lighting, angles of approach, distances, and sequences.

There isn't evidence that sculpture was similarly tested; Jensen's initial collection seems to have consisted largely of pictures plus some small carvings, both ancient and modern. Yet, he did arrange outdoor exhibitions of sculpture, with works borrowed from other collections. In 1964, for instance, he mounted a show called *Middelheim Visits Louisiana*, with works on loan from the Middelheim Museum in Belgium. This experience seems to have taught him the importance of careful placement, for years later he wrote that "in the open-air sculptures swim," not something he recommended.[14] Surveying was also required for the second campaign of design and construction, undertaken by the landscape architects Ole and Edith Nørgård, in the early 1960s. Their work resulted in another set of walkways and rooms, "garden rooms" they've been called, as varied and individually characterized as those inside, thus scaled better to some works than others, linked together by steps, but unroofed. Sadly, these rooms no longer survive, except as remnants alongside newer buildings that took their place.

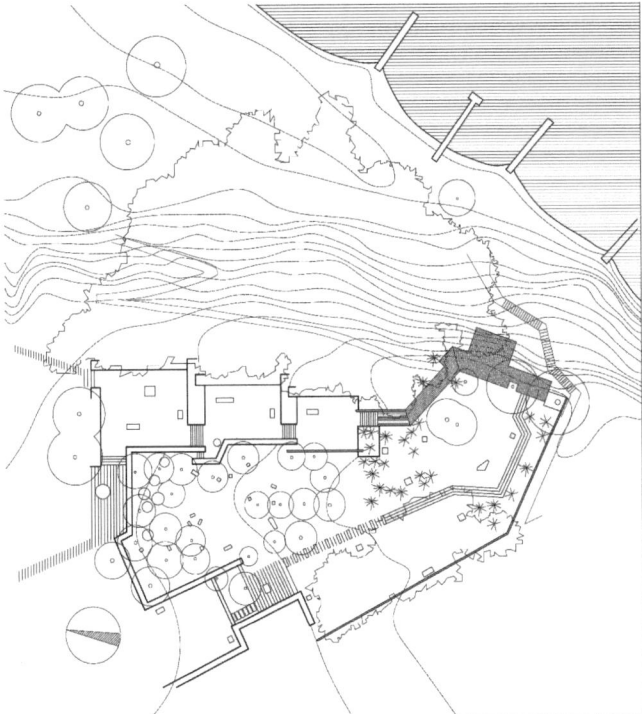

Figure 3.2.5 Ole and Edith Nørgård, *Louisiana Museum*, Copenhagen, garden rooms, plan. Drawing David Leatherbarrow.

Figure 3.2.6 Bo and Wohlert, *Louisiana Museum*, Copenhagen, gallery corridor elevation. Photograph David Leatherbarrow.

Landscape Movement

Nothing was more important to the client, the architects, and landscape architects than avoiding the boxed-in sense of enclosure that had become typical of late nineteenth- and early twentieth-century museums, temples of art, in which pure aesthetic experience was unleavened by practical affairs or external engagements. At the Louisiana Museum, by contrast, interior passages and enclosed rooms always open to points or places in the landscape.[15] Thin load-bearing columns lying behind window frames plus window walls made this openness possible, though contrast and focus were aided by the careful placement of bulky planes of white-washed brickwork. Nor was the route closed in on itself as a single aesthetic experience. Although a work by Henry Moore (*Reclining Figure*, 1969) now greets the arriving visitor, entry to the Museum properly begins in domestic space, at the door to the pre-existing house, with its modest scale and traces of residential life. The end of the route has all the opposite qualities: the shore-side bluff's open expanse, the Sound's wide horizon, a very big sky, and another country in the distance. Mediating these contrasting conditions, the route through the several galleries—some corridor-like, others ampler spatially—offered a series of spatial or sculptural events, analogous to a journey Jensen said, but not goal-oriented, because the destination could be decided at any moment, in any one of the passages, walks, indoor or outdoor rooms. The paths and places were meant to be continually stimulating and inviting, without dominating one's attention.

The arrangement of spaces through which movement passed was governed by the principle of variation. They were to be alternately high or low, narrow or wide, bright or dark, and everything in-between. Variation did not mean insistent individuation, however, for no less important than difference was a sense of rhythm. Recurring intervals of building structure, wall cladding, and glazing set a regular tempo for movement between the works/events Jensen called "birds on a wire." Also modulating passage were repetitive alignments—first one gallery corridor, ending where the passage turns, and then another corridor beginning after the corresponding turn, so, again, station points. But rigidity was not the result. Rather like the recalibration of skills and habits that is required when a craftsman is faced with unique requirements and materials, the repeatedly used elements were slightly adjusted or adapted to local opportunities, giving passage not only measure and cadence but grace. Attunements were typically prompted by variations in the pre-existing terrain, its different enclosures, openings, elements, and prospects, as well as the physical qualities of the lawns and groves, plus the pools, pond, and sea. Yet the terrain wasn't always amplified; sometimes variety was achieved by working against the grain: leveling a terrace, for example, where the land had previously fallen to the shore. Nor was the range of spatial types only topographical. Movement from one spot to another meant encountering settings—still-spaces—that were alternately aesthetic, natural, and practical, the latter including places for concerts, picnics, swimming, and children's play. Concentration thus gave way to distraction and possible involvement, with areas for musing in-between.

Viewing Distance and Angle

Perhaps the first task of design when locating a work of sculpture in either a museum interior or a landscape setting is the determination of *viewing distance*. When the distance is right, the work gives itself to perception without reserve, completely and all at once. When not, when the separation is too great or slight, perception and understanding are blurred or blunted, through deficiency or excess of content. Another step or two, forward or back is all that's required. Time passes when this occurs, prolonging the approach. Putting the matter mathematically, optimal viewing distance is inversely proportional to indeterminacy.[16] Remote works have slipped out of one's grasp. This doesn't mean they are nowhere to be seen, only that they are not fully present at this particular moment. If, by contrast, their locations allow them to advance too far forward, when placed tangent to a curve in a path for example, pressing in on us too closely, or we on them, they disintegrate into bits of material and color, fragmenting, at least for the moment, the whole intended by the artist.

When turning into one of the Louisiana Museum's gallery corridors, works at the far end of the passage are sometimes too distant to be appreciated, like the face of a person you know but can't quite recognize on a train platform. David Summers introduced the term "defect of distance" to describe this situation.[17] But passing-space is not only deficient, it is also germinal. Once a few steps reduce the separation, after the summons for a closer look has been accepted, the profiles spring into relief, shadows and highlights giving shape to legible form, and the work offers its qualities unhesitatingly and without end. A *still point* such as this could be reached near the end of an approach, thereby defining it as such, or just as a corner is turned and the view opens onto a new prospect, the sense of which, once again, depends on the right distance. At these times, what places and prospects have to give is offered unstintingly.[18] In works of art, the offering is often excessive, which is why we stay a while, and sometimes return. Targeted views needn't be interior; at the Louisiana Museum, they often look outward. In one striking case, the interval between the vantage point and the work is measured by equally spaced paving stones. When works simultaneously attract focus and reward concentration, one sometimes has the feeling of submitting to the work's expectations or requirements, of accepting one's part in the drama the work has scripted and the architecture staged.

Viewing distance is not, however, a matter of so many meters, precisely determined; instead, a range is intended, rather like a perceptual norm, within or around which meanings crystalize, neither too far nor too near, as I've said, but at the extent of reach that allows one to grasp the work fully. Below I'll consider the crystallization or germination of still-space more fully, but the point I'd like to secure now concerns perceptual freedom or choice within a designed configuration: the fact that control over viewing distance is never perfect or absolute—the length of the gallery/passage or the interval between a corner doorway and the end of a line of paving stones—does not mean that the conditions under which meaning may be maximized should not be attempted. Admitting defeat so quickly would deprive design of one of its main responsibilities.

Approach is not only a matter of distance, the angle of the view also matters, and there may not be a single slant that seems best, but several together. Determining lines of sight is a second essential task in siting sculpture, indoors and out. Some of the works at the Louisiana Museum were positioned so that they would be approached and viewed frontally, squared off, face-to-face. A pertinent case is the upper level of the first large gallery room designed by Bo and Wohlert, the Lake Gallery, where Astrid Noack's *Kneeling Figure: Young Man Planting a Tree* (1942) was originally installed, but now stands a group of Giacometti figures.

The approach to both the room and the group is orthogonal, along the lines of the gallery corridor that leads there, but also, and more importantly, those of the ceiling and roof structure, two parallel timber beams. Between them, a circular roof-light has been cut through the ceiling, under which the sculpture rests on its two-part base, bathed in light. Even if the moment that's been captured is only one chapter in a longer story, a sense of calm tranquility is expressed by both the work and its setting. With the cycle of approach and arrival concluded, passing-space has ended. The backdrop plays an important role in the limpid stillness; floor-to-ceiling whitewashed brickwork does its very best to escape attention, playing the part of barely taking part. The backdrop, lighting, beam structure, and line of approach all contribute to the presentation format, concentrating the focus and allowing for a "meeting of the eyes."[19] Oblique views are always possible and no doubt taken—Jensen wanted this kind of release—but the configuration privileges the axial line, to which one eventually returns, because the 90

Figure 3.2.7 Bo and Wohlert, *Louisiana Museum,* Copenhagen, gallery mezzanine. Photograph David Leatherbarrow.

degree angle answers the expectations of the work itself: eyes looking forward, shoulders square, face to face. The gallery walls, together with the room's ceiling, anticipated this stance; the white backdrop concluded it. The before and after of spatial passage have condensed themselves into an extended moment's full immediacy.

Similarly paced and axial is the walk across the shallow pool of water that aligns with a wide corridor gallery (Astrid Noack's *Standing Woman*, 1937, terminated this walk in the early years, in its place now is a work by Jean Dubuffet). Above I alluded to the measured distance between the gallery door and the work. Both the initial view and the approach demarcated the axis, inviting one to step outside and approach the work. The line of stones bridged the pool and inscribed the route into the terrain, suppressing its differences (wet then dry) beneath the march of steps, the insistence of which slightly recalls the performance of some archaic rite. All the views that followed the first (from the corridor or doorway) reinforced those that came before (in preceding corridors and doorways), making the cycle reiterative and the sense cumulative, stopping the clock of the visitor's stroll when the right viewing distance and angle, the still point, was reached. A turn off axis would have meant turning toward another work or some other prospect, rewinding movement's clock and beginning the journey anew.

Figure 3.2.8 Bo and Wohlert, *Louisiana Museum*, Copenhagen, stepping-stone walk. Photograph David Leatherbarrow.

Still-space offers its contents immediately because it has gathered itself together into a single situation, at once inhabitable and legible. At the end of the route through the Museum, a setting of this kind coordinates interior and exterior elements, in support of uses that are no longer essentially aesthetic, though they are beautifully composed. Benches, chairs, and tables orbit around the fireplace, the social pleasures of which are illuminated by a window wall that has been shaded by a cantilevered roof orienting one's view to the wide expanse of the dining and Calder Terraces, as well as the Sound beyond. So unified is the setting that it can be read as an epitome of the entire landscape, in and outside the building, across the wider landscape, with its performance spaces, picnic areas, and swimming beach, facing Sweden. One sees the distant figures partially, but their remoteness does not suggest deficiency, rather the right degree of involvement. It's the setting's quiet sufficiency that is so striking. What has been given is all one would want and expect, at least for a while. The room's other sides have entirely opposite qualities but are similarly *still*. Adjacent walls are much shallower in depth (there's no glass) but are equipped with compartments and shelves. If the window wall view encapsulates the wider landscape, this archival one summarizes what has been put on show.

Other works at the Louisiana Museum invite many angles of approach and view, giving themselves to experience in distinctly different phases or moments, not *still-* but

Figure 3.2.9 Bo and Wohlert, *Louisiana Museum*, Copenhagen, fireplace and dining room. Photograph David Leatherbarrow.

Figure 3.2.10 Bo and Wohlert, *Louisiana Museum*, Copenhagen, dining room catalogue wall. Photograph David Leatherbarrow.

passing-space. Because no single vantage is preferred, movement in these instances is not frontal but orbital; one circles around the work, inspecting or discovering sides that had been unseen from a preceding angle, sides that perforce conceal still others yet to come. Sense such as this follows a completely different temporal register, distinct moments or phases that are neither repetitive nor complete, incidents that diverge from one another as much as they precede and follow. At the Louisiana Museum, this kind of approach reveals the qualities of works by Henry Moore, Joan Miró, and Max Bill, works that show themselves in-the-round, above the soil, and beneath the sky, but never all at once, nor from any preferred vantage.

The staged type of disclosure can occur inside buildings too, at a larger scale, but no less successively. In fact, at the Louisiana Museum, this type of space and the temporality it embodies are more or less the norm, accommodating the "journey" Jensen had in mind. Consider one of the sliding-door entries in the gallery corridors, for example. The sidewalk approach that cuts a diagonal through the lawn has neither the rhythm nor the orthogonality of the glass-enclosed walk to its side. It arrives to its destination, nevertheless, just after it has passed by a large-size sculptural

Figure 3.2.11 Henry Moore, *Three Piece Reclining Figure-Draped*, *Louisiana Museum*, Copenhagen. Photograph David Leatherbarrow.

work (different sculptures have held this position through the past decades). The corner entry splits one's view. The prospect to the left, compressed by the white brick wall, accelerates very quickly along an oblique line, first toward a painting in the immediate foreground and then the wider landscape in the distance. Each figure is grasped incompletely because of the extreme angle and rapid pace of the view. The other, more frontal prospect, hurries less, as it rejoins the orthogonal linearity and steady pace of the gallery layout; but it, too, keeps its objects remote, in some cases largely hidden. The hollows or dark spots on the left side set the tempo as much as what can be seen. Three recessed bays in the middle ground promise contents we can't yet see, while the passage ends in a white wall that first serves as backdrop to a sculptural group and then implies others (to the left), in part of the room we will get to shortly. Finally, the adjoining landscape outside the passage extends the verdant deck indefinitely, recalling the openness sensed at the beginning of the diagonal path. Three views and three sequences, each suggesting more than they show, extending rather than concentrating topography, at different speeds, but equally intent on prolonging the route.

Figure 3.2.12 Joan Miró, *Personage, Louisiana Museum*, Copenhagen. Photograph David Leatherbarrow.

Comparable instances of passing space can be seen in the many gallery rooms that exhibit works on partition walls. As with the partitions one finds in the free and open plans of early modern architecture (by Le Corbusier, Theo van Doesburg, Mies van der Rohe, and countless others who followed), the basic presumption is lateral continuity and phased unfolding through spaces that are "free" or "open" for the more pleasurable work of defining and qualifying discreet settings. Once four-sided containment is abandoned, partitions are put into service for structuring and timing passage. In the Louisiana Museum's galleries, spatial definition often moves from the margins to more central elements: ceiling supports and skylights, artificial lighting, floor levels and surfaces, and light-weight panels and screens.

In one gallery, the central partition folds in on itself under the half-story volume of the skylight. Because works appear on its outer sides, one naturally assumes others have been sheltered within. There's nothing new in this; similar suggestions have led to similar spaces elsewhere in the Museum. Successive space is a style of configuration whose elements and tempo repeat characteristic movements. A comparable sense of more-to-come is conveyed by the end wall, which promises continuation of the side panels, while offering a glimpse of the exterior landscape as a sort of interlude. Space such as this both fragments and dilates; each of its aspects presents itself in succession. Nothing definite can be said about the duration of each view; all one can know for sure is that more will follow, just as others have come before.

Every setting or prospect that presents itself partially has other dimensions that keep themselves remote, dark and light interims succeeding then reversing one another, offering or withholding their contents. Settings seem to seize any opportunity to put their attractive sides on show, delaying the appearance of their other parts. At the same time, those yet to come (the contents of the three bays, the larger gallery whose threshold the sculpture group occupies, and so on) will be experienced in due course.

Each moment in passing-space indicates its own individuality and a set of implications, vectors of movement that cumulatively generate temporal sense. One side of the two-story Giacometti gallery faces the nearby lake and wooded landscape beyond. It is a remarkably beautiful view, with the impressive depth of the prospect complemented by a well-proportioned foreground (work to window). The exceptionally vertical statue, *The Man Who Walks*, is backed up by floor-to-ceiling glazing that has been sub-divided into similarly tall and thin sheets of glass. The view

Figure 3.2.13 Bo and Wohlert, *Louisiana Museum*, Copenhagen, gallery. Photograph David Leatherbarrow.

presents its contents without reserve, sufficient-in-itself, still. The other side of the room also includes a deep prospect, but one that invites movement beyond the room, *passing*. Although framed at the sides and centered by Giacometti's carvings and castings, the asymmetrical middle ground (wood screen, open-riser stair, and white wall) invites passage to the next gallery, the depth of which is apparent behind the top of the stairway wall, as is the arrangement of beams and skylight that opens toward the sky. Still farther in depth, but no more complete, are indications of passages that will extend the route through the Museum into additional corridor galleries toward their exhibits and the surrounding landscapes. While the majority of these are hinted at above the Giacometti room, some can be glimpsed at its level. All of this is only intimated—partly recalling the kinds of settings through which one has already walked, partly anticipating others—for passing-space, with its phased structure, always requires further inspection and the time that it takes.

Occlusion and displacement are not the only techniques of spatial articulation; corner entries, diagonal movements, and divided pathways serve the same function. Permeable edges extend one's orientation outward and endlessly. A number of the

Figure 3.2.14 Bo and Wohlert, *Louisiana Museum*, Copenhagen, Giacometti room. Photograph David Leatherbarrow.

Figure 3.2.15 Bo and Wohlert, *Louisiana Museum*, Copenhagen, Giacometti room. Photograph David Leatherbarrow.

prospects include views of the distant coastline, as if it were a permanent point of orientation, as well as the source of many of the garden's motifs. Prolongations from within building into the garden are apparent in the striking instances of change in the ground level. Perhaps the most poignant example is the descent from the Giacometti room to the pond outside its great window. Here, the sense of the earth's fecundity is impressively strong, to say nothing of the relief from the building's enclosures—varied though they are. At the room's edge, unforeseen content is both made apparent and kept out of reach, which is to say, awareness is excited and appreciation postponed.

Spatial order of this showing/concealing kind is contingent on temporal structures. The premise, I've said, is that the past is a former present and the present a recent future. At any given moment, places and times have linkages to lapsed conditions that are *present as hidden*, which is to say recalled and anticipated, seen partially and implied. The key point is that the building's or landscape's recessive aspects allow it to *give more than it shows*, to yield content that exceeds what is seen at any moment as well as what might be expected or remembered. I have differentiated two temporalities—still and passing—and associated them with the great categories of continuity: the same, the different, and, when coupled, the similar. Assuming that these categories have descriptive and analytic value, it is also true that they are indivisible in our unreflective involvement with a particular location. Insofar as architecture is a way of knowing our place in the world, the times of nature, history, and memory confer orientation no less clearly than spatiality's several distances. The ages of the earth, cultures, and habits give to experience a vivid sense of where it has been and where it might yet go. Time embodied in architecture is thus an evidence of the conditions of our lives and our freedom.

3.3

Wandering Sites: Wang Shu's Hangzhou Guest House

On the river, anxious mind, a thousand layered mountains,
Patches of green float in space like clouds and mist;
Are they mountains? Are they clouds? Too far to tell;
When mist parts and clouds scatter, the mountains are just as always;
…
A fishing boat like a leaf where the river swallows the sky.
SU SHI, *INSCRIBING "MISTY RIVER, LAYERED PEAKS"* c. 1090

Wang Shu once observed that Xiangshan Hill, which rises above the roofs of the China Academy of Art in Hangzhou, was "heavier than anything [he] would design."[1] It was not only weighty, he added, but speechless and ancient. Before he took up his pencil and paper to labor in its shadow, the hill looked down on his site alongside the stream, as it always had and would, long before and after his buildings were finished. But the hill's steady silence wasn't all that impressed and intrigued him. Like many mountains represented in traditional Chinese landscape paintings, poetry, and gardens, this one sheltered spaces for a range of activities: having a drink or light meal beneath the canopy of some small grove, conversing with friends at the riverbank, or wandering on one's own, re-enacting in one way or another experience at the core of traditional culture, as understood by Wang Shu, who can still reconstruct its world by association, despite all that happened socially, politically, and environmentally in the twentieth century. But the hill had even more to give: promptings for the tradition's possible renewal, not only through new paintings or poetry, but contemporary building.

Figure 3.3.1 Wang Shu, *China Academy of Art,* Hangzhou, mountain and river. Photograph David Leatherbarrow.

For these memories and possibilities to play a productive role in design, the hefty physical presence had to be seen and understood as an *image*.² Once it was, architectural design could renew its cultural task: reinterpreting the physical fact and its associations by providing an equivalent representation. If it were to be architectural, such a representation would be material and spatial, but also legible, which is to say, an expression that could give rise to thought. No less importantly, it would accommodate ways of living in the modern world. In the text from Wang Shu I've just cited, these aims took the form of an imperative: "Build a World to Resemble Nature."

Construction at the site started in 2001 and continues today. The buildings that have been finished in phases one and two successfully accommodate the activities of the Academy, in many instances beautifully. But functionality in the narrow sense—discrete settings serving specific purposes—was not what Wang Shu stressed when explaining the design, nor what I would like to address in this study. The matter of "resembling nature" was just as important as accommodation, probably more so. This is not to say the matter of likeness or similarity was either simple or straightforward, for his target was not only *that* hill and river, in their brute actuality, though their palpable qualities were important, but equally the images of mountains and rivers that could be rediscovered in traditional art, poetry, garden art, and landscape painting. Wang Shu is particularly fond of landscapes from the Song Dynasty (Northern Song 960–1127, Southern Song 1127–1279). Although sited at the foot of the hill and alongside the stream, the Campus buildings were designed to be seen, sensed, and enjoyed as full-size translations—resemblances—of typical elements, spaces, and environmental qualities in "mountain-river" or *shan-shui* paintings.

An important commonplace of these paintings is the absence of centralized perspective, together with its conventional apparatus of construction: coordinated axes and points of convergence, metric proportionalities governing size diminution, regular and congruent figures or enclosures resting on a continuously receding ground plane, and most importantly for what this chapter will address, unity of action, time, and place—a single event unfolding in a well-defined location.³ When depth and movement are unburdened by these conventions, distances and elements extend beyond the horizon and past the frame, which in handscroll paintings are of course also beyond the viewer's manual reach and immediate apprehension.⁴ Such a landscape's lateral spread allows its figures to stand apart from one another, to reduce the overlapping that would fix them in positions of more or less prominence (in the back-, middle-, or fore-ground). A third consequence of this kind of structuring is that the painting's open spaces are pervaded by an atmosphere of indefiniteness, rendered with smooth brush strokes as mist, low-lying clouds, or less-than-limpid light, sometimes all three together.[5]

Rarely if ever in these paintings is there a single point of concentration; instead, one's focus is allowed, in fact expected to move, wander, or drift around and through places that emerge into the fore- and then recede into background, as a result of that very movement. A traditional Chinese landscape painting is an invitation to a journey, the step-by-step choices of which are alternately rewarded and disappointed by unexpected discoveries: happening upon a beautiful prospect would be a great pleasure, stumbling onto a riverbank with no bridge in sight the reverse. One of Wang Shu's several published explanations of what can be seen, felt, and enjoyed in landscape paintings is as follows: "Chinese landscape paintings never depict the visual image statically, but rather convey a perception of the experience of travelling amidst real landscapes of natural beauty, accompanied by memories and imagination … a garden or a painting is just a temporary pause [in that unending movement]."[6]

In what follows, I will show that this exploratory or meandering sort of movement is key in both the paintings and the architecture he designed to resemble them. And with movement comes time, the time both of change and of permanence. Wang Shu's models—bodies of water and mountains—possessed both: water's fixed level at the horizon, together with the unending changes that result from its flow, plus the mountain's unmatched durability, despite the changing aspects that present themselves to any traveler who climbs or descends its heights.

In explanation of his Library for Wenzheng College of Suzhou University (2000), Wang Shu wrote:

> My purpose was to make people aware that they live between mountains and water, which is the garden style of Suzhou. Backed by a mountain full of bamboo in the north and facing a lake that used to be a disposed brickfield in the south, the sloped site descends southward with a difference of four meters in the level. According to the principles of gardening, buildings between mountains and water should not be prominent, so nearly half of the library is underground. The three-story building actually shows only two-stories to the entrance-side. The rectangular main body is floating over the water, facing south, the dominant direction of the winds in summer … The pavilion-like building in the water—the poetry and philosophy reading room of the library—is from the Chinese literati point of view, in a position where man and nature are balanced.[7]

Figure 3.3.2 Wang Shu, *Wenzheng College*, Suzhou, rear elevation. Photograph David Leatherbarrow.

The explanation is useful because one's first impression of the building suggests the opposite of congruity: white columns rising out of the water and white walls against a verdant background, level decks indifferent to the flow of water and slope of soil below, hard edges contrasting with soft contours, and over-sized cubic forms. But this initial view neglects the fact that the landscape was both a physical thing and a living environment. It was with the latter that Wang Shu sought agreement. His idea was that the building would breathe the site's air, modulate its light, and take part in its metabolism. To this end, movements of several kinds had to be accommodated and represented: breezes through permeable walls, passage between spaces, views between rooms, courts, and pavilions, and the "travels" of a reader's imagination when paging a favorite text.

Discordances of this kind were also established at the Xiangshan Campus of the China Academy of Art, Hangzhou, at several scales: building to building, room to room, and one construction material to the next. High differentiation is the result, also more than a little fragmentation; but also, as a result of repeated revealings and concealings, an open invitation to passage, choice, and sensations of change. In imitation of the nearby hill, the architecture was to initiate or prompt these choices and changes, but then

Figure 3.3.3 Wang Shu, *Wenzheng College*, Suzhou, entry. Photograph David Leatherbarrow.

Figure 3.3.4 Wang Shu, *Wenzheng College*, Suzhou, interior. Photograph David Leatherbarrow.

rely on forces it couldn't control (rain, wind, temperature change) for their continued unfolding, sometimes to the detriment of the project itself, as can be seen in the current state of the Wenzheng College Library today, as well as the buildings in the Xiangshan Campus' first phase.

Describing the initial design, reportedly completed in four hours—ten buildings enclosing 80,000 square meters, pencil drawn in aerial perspective on an A3 sheet of paper—Wang Shu stressed that all the façades of the Campus would be broken down into side views opening toward the hill. Why, when the hill is not all that unique? "Well," he said, "it is still more important than the buildings."[8] When climbing its slopes or descending into its recesses, one discovers an internal dynamism, the hill's capacity for change, not only of its own aspects but of constructions nearby, likewise for the mountains represented in traditional paintings. The *same* mountains always presented themselves as continually *different*. The thesis was for centuries a commonplace in writings on landscape painting. In the eleventh century Guo Xi, for example, famously wrote: "viewed at close range [mountain forms] have one appearance; viewed from a distance of several miles, another, and viewed from a

Figure 3.3.5 Wang Shu, *China Academy of Art,* Hangzhou, preliminary sketch. Courtesy of Wang Shu/Amateur Architecture Studio.

distance of scores of miles, still another. Every time one moves away, one gets a different view. This is why it is said that the mountain forms change with every step one takes."⁹ As such, the hill/mountain—a fact and an image—guided the resemblance the architect sought to fashion, but only partly, for the existing hill also resisted design's ambitions.

Both phases of the project developed land at the base of the hill, along the course of the area's two streams that edge its north and south sides and then merge on the eastern flank before they flow into the river. Some existing farmlands were preserved, also small gardens and fish ponds. Today, Academy staff and students grow grains, vegetables, and fruit in small-size plots. Pastoral though it may now seem, it was to this site that 7 million shards of building rubbish were re-located for reuse in building construction. Given the rate at which old villages are being destroyed for new buildings in contemporary China, there is ample demolition debris available to both architects and countless anonymous builders who see the merits of the reuse and recycling of building materials (long-term savings, thanks to embodied energy and cultural memory). Phase one of construction was completed in 2004. But what one sees today is not what the builders finished. Chapters of the site's prehistory can be read, but also the changes that have occurred since construction, the project's afterlife.

Already, in the two decades the early buildings have been standing, alterations that seem unintended are apparent. Different kinds of change can be distinguished: the re- or mis-use of spaces, unintended weathering, and two kinds of overgrowth—trees that are now too tall for the courtyards and vines on façades that obscure apertures. Unforeseen,

Figure 3.3.6 Wang Shu, *China Academy of Art*, Hangzhou, gardens. Photograph David Leatherbarrow.

but in hindsight understandable, these changes show the terrain's capacity to re-make itself, sometimes according to expectations, sometimes not. What Wang Shu designed and built is not gone, only exceeded by evidences of a metabolism beyond his control. What had been inserted into the site—with all the best intentions—has been absorbed by it, as if the sympathies construction once enjoyed were secretly accompanied by a corresponding measure of topographical indifference. The hill's disinterest was known from the start. Above all else, Wang Shu was impressed by the hill's brooding silence and implacable reserve—absconded, ponderous, and deep, always capable of giving more than it had previously shown. Site surveys, no matter how well intentioned and thorough, were unable to penetrate to the full depth of this capacity, nor to this reserve.[10]

The Time of Spatial Passage

Yet, another sense of change interests me in consideration of the buildings of the Xiangshan Campus, as it does their architect. The *time of spatial passage* is a topic that has been important to Wang Shu for a number of years. Explaining his "Picturesque House," for example, he wrote:

Figure 3.3.7 Wang Shu, *China Academy of Art, Hangzhou*, classroom building. Photograph David Leatherbarrow.

I looked at many traditional landscape paintings related to this region ... a painting from the seventeenth century depicted the lifestyle of rural scholars. A path twisted its way deep into a hollow space formed by the trees, which also implied the depth of thoughts. [A peasant's] line of vision was solely from left to right, uninterested in the splendid world outside. That hollow space impressed me ... I could see the strong lines in the vague woods, half natural and half artificial ... There is no hierarchical difference in this ever-deeper space.[11]

The absence of hierarchy did not signify a lack of structure, however, just a different kind of order, *temporal*. Like the movements of the body along the "twisted path," there were movements of perception, by virtue of the scholar's body and its several instruments of apprehending. Perhaps the movement of the eyes is the most obvious. In a text called "A House as Sleep," Wang Shu wrote: "You could stand under the eaves of one house and see the distant view through the shadow of another house."[12]

Broadly speaking, perceiving an object means grasping aspects that show themselves at a particular moment—the visible surface of the desktop, for example, as opposed to

Figure 3.3.8 Wang Shu, *China Academy of Art*, Hangzhou, courtyard and mountain. Photograph David Leatherbarrow.

its unseen underside. To see what is below, one must bend a little or take a step, *and then*, after the change of vantage or position, look at the desk from a different angle. While it is correct to say that each momentary glance opens onto a view of the world, it is no less true to observe that each prospect is both partial and passing. And just as each part suggests its counterpart, each moment invites another to follow, having succeeded the one that came before. One assumes that the parts correspond, perhaps as a matter of perceptual faith. Rarely does one doubt the wholeness of the object or setting—unless it is broken in some way or unusually beautiful—despite the fact that it is never grasped as such, all of its aspects all at once. Partial or oblique views pace the temporal structuring of spatial order. The only way to imagine and then build a spatial configuration that makes sense is by taking account of the ways it can reveal itself through time, coupling views that occurred previously with those at a given moment and still to come. Exploration never begins nowhere; it moves forward in a landscape that has already presented itself. Perceptual synthesis is perforce temporal synthesis.

Such, I believe, was the lesson of traditional paintings for Wang Shu, an art form often characterized as essentially temporal.[13] The same would be true of any equivalent art form, in his case architecture. Hence the observation cited above: "Chinese landscape paintings never depict the visual image statically, but rather convey a perception of the experience of travelling." Even more emphatic is the following account of traveling through the Xiangshan Campus: "This route [constructed through buildings and landscapes] is precisely controlled in the design: it creates different sceneries and allows different positions of viewing. [However,] when one sees the hill over and over again [along the paths], the experience then becomes coherent."[14] But coherence or synthesis in traditional paintings took many forms. The kinds that allowed architectural translations still need to be determined, for it is not only repetition that determines interconnectedness.

Here's the fundamental question: with respect to temporal structuring, did Wang Shu have in mind some kind of simultaneity, in which several scenes or spaces could be grasped at the same moment? Or was sequence, the progressive unfolding of discrete settings, the structuring principle of the landscapes he designed and built? Each of these alternatives raises an even more basic question about the unity of action, time, and place. Was each prospect or perceptual moment single and whole? Are sharply defined distinct events what one sees in the several scenes of traditional landscape paintings? Did a pavilion for rural retreat, for example, include all the furnishings, natural elements, lighting, and views that were appropriate to the act of enjoying tea? Or was each setting, painted or built, shown and meant to be seen partially: paths without beginnings or endings, for example, or other landscape and architectural elements whose incomplete showing allowed a sense of unending transition? If neither simultaneity nor transition characterized the time of appearances, were they perhaps incremental, or cyclical? There is also the matter of memory and recollection. Was the time of recollection structured through the repetition of figures, elements, or materials, or was recognition achieved by approximation and gradual change?

Non-synchronic Passage

Let me return to my earlier observations on the spatial ordering of traditional (especially Song Dynasty) landscape paintings. Above I noted the absence of centralized perspective, the lack of coordinated axes, metric proportionalities, and enclosures, and the question concerning temporal unity. Absence or lack here does not mean deficiency. The point is not that these paintings fail to communicate depth, only that three dimensionality is constructed in different ways. In this difference—which could be called *a-perspectival* space—they resemble European works painted both before and after the five centuries of the perspective tradition, those of Duccio, Giotto, or Martini, for example, and Cézanne, Klimt, and Matisse. Depth is visible in their paintings, despite the lack of "legitimate" perspective.[15]

One way that movement was expressed in the a-perspectival space of traditional Chinese landscape paintings was through the extension of the image's several distances beyond the scene's immediate horizon, which is to say beyond the picture's borders (along the further length of a hand-, or the height of a hanging-scroll). Above, I also noted that space for traveling or wandering was commonly constructed through the avoidance of close overlapping that would have fixed elements in locations before or behind one another. This type of composition was particularly conducive to spatial movement when the painting's middle ground was pervaded by an atmosphere of indefiniteness—low-lying clouds and rising mist, as I said.

Buildings, bridges, and city walls portrayed in painted landscapes also "break the box," for they, too, are governed by a principle of *divergence*. While most architectural elements are laid out parallel to the picture plane,[16] some advance toward and beyond the picture's edges at oblique angles. City walls commonly do this, also roads, canals, and covered walkways. This makes sense given their wide compass, external sources, and neighboring connections. Diagonal movements lead the eye out of the picture, or "over the horizon," as Wang Shu once said of a drawing he made of a project that recalled a mountainous landscape.

The depth one sees in these paintings has been carefully constructed; generally, the classical theorists explain, through one or another of the three kinds of distance or depth: level, deep, and high (though some writers argued for an additional three: broad, hidden, and obscure).[17] No less important in traditional composition is a lateral spread or sideways expansiveness that gives free play to the movements one can imagine—especially when landscape terrain is constructed as "level distance." I'll cite the key passage from Wang Shu a third time on this point: "Chinese landscape paintings never depict the visual image statically, but rather convey a perception of the experience of travelling amidst real landscapes of natural beauty, accompanied by memories and imagination … a garden or a painting is just a temporary pause."[18] Through the use of diagonal lines, obliques, or zig-zags, he approximated the same kinds of movement in his architecture. Shadowed spaces serve the separating or joining function of low-lying clouds or mist. Sometimes he uses clusters or bands of bamboo for this purpose. Yet, the absence of hierarchy among elements thus separated did not mean lack of structure, just a different kind of order, *temporal*.

Although moments of rest occur in landscapes, no less than in buildings, gardens, villages, and cities, Wang Shu's work shows that there is no reason to think that changes

Figure 3.3.9 Wang Shu, *China Academy of Art*, Guest House, Hangzhou, interior stair and court. Photograph David Leatherbarrow.

of location or position are any less important. I mean spatial passage in the obvious and everyday sense of the term: from here to there, and then to another place, possibly still farther, or maybe back again. Each of these relocations unfolds in time, but not clock or calendar time—intervals of regular length—instead, a time of varying speeds, prompted by desires, guided by anticipations, and recalled by recollections. Every present moment is *mid-way* between where one has been (but still recalls) and is going (already anticipates). *Here* is of course positional—where one stands—but also where one is *currently*, which is to say, no longer where one has just been, and not yet where one is going.

Advances and retreats rarely pace themselves out regularly; contractions and dilations are more typical. Some spatial configurations compress time, accelerating the arrival of what's been anticipated, while others extend it, delaying the appearance of what one had expected to come into view. When you go to a building designed by Frank Lloyd Wright and pass through its entry spaces, it seems as if the architect had sought to prolong the approach, in order to orient you to the wider vicinity while advancing you toward your principal destination. Not only is the space slow, it is typically tight and low. The consequences are striking. Having been confined for longer than one might like during the approach, arrival is not only welcome but often stunning: the ceiling is twice the height of the corridor and the wide interior opens in ways one would not have imagined. And once you reach the main hall, you then see that other passages head toward other spaces, each with its own delays or accelerations, arrivals, and departures. All of this is to say that one important way of thinking about temporality in architecture is through the spatiality of movement.

The same is true for the temporality of painted landscapes. First, there is the time of viewing a handscroll, in phases freely determined by whatever length is unrolled. If the seated reader's elbows are used to hold the scroll open, there is a postural or embodied determination of view extent and duration (even if that length will vary reader-by-reader and, probably, also reading-by-reading). Next, there is the time of viewing the several scenes, also freely determined, as a result of shifting focus. An intriguing scene might invite lingering inspection, while another might fail to hold one's attention because what it shows is a little too familiar. The premise here is that the pictorial scroll is poly-scenic,[19] the moments of which have their own unity. This is no less true for scenes that link up along a path, a shoreline, or in a valley, than for those that are clearly not meant to be seen consecutively. As the eye moves through the spaces, hesitating for a while in one or breezing by another, there is always still more to be seen, insofar as each evokes others. Passage thus unfolds as a series of anticipations, buttressed by recollections.

Sequence is possible because of the high differentiation of settings, sometimes overlapped in layers, other times set out along implied diagonals.[20] Each place has its own qualities that are legibly distinct because intervening clouds, mists, or waters serve the double purpose of separating and joining—a single atmosphere pervades the terrain, but in so doing isolates its several elements. Despite the differences between the many and varied places (the valleys, plateaus, caves or hills, plus the streams, rivers, and lakes, as well as groves and forests), the landscapes are visibly coherent, thanks to carefully constructed arrangements of depth, the three "distances" I briefly mentioned earlier: level, deep, and high.[21]

Distances and Depth

Spatial depth both assumes and expresses a three-part structure of perception: a figure, its background, and the perceiving subject. Distance in these paintings can be understood similarly, but only if assumptions about metric regularity are suspended. A house or hill that is ostensibly far, as a matter of measurable distance, may appear to be near, depending on how depth is structured. Prior to reflection, in everyday experience (and outside traditions that have naturalized concepts of metric space), near and far mean proximate and remote, which is to say within or out of reach, for the sake of whatever one might happen to be doing or want.[22] Embodied sense plays its part here, as do habits, skills, and desires. For the unskilled swimmer struggling toward *terra firma*, the shore is a lot farther away than for someone with more ability or training. Liquid or fluid metaphors often invoke temporal sense ("no man ever steps in the same river twice," Heraclitus; "an hour is a sea between a few and me," Emily Dickinson). The pictorial depth that contained "hidden distances" was typically rendered in watery landscapes, at the foot of mountains, where remoteness was expressed by foggy or misty atmospheres that concealed or obscured the destination, hence the phrase cited above in the epigraph: "patches of green float in space like clouds and mist."

Level distance ranges laterally. Figures sweep or drift sideways, in a fairly shallow space that is often, though not always, panoramic. Chinese painting theorists ascribed to this bleak type of terrain a psychological sense of being forlorn or vacant. An elegiac mood prevails, perhaps due in part to the blending of bright and dim spaces, rendered in a faintly misty air. But all is not soft: there is typically a rugged shore, a burdened traveler, and barren trees. It would seem natural that this kind of depth would be presented in horizontal format, handscrolls that unroll from side-to-side, but there are also instances of level distance in vertical or hanging scrolls, particularly when they are part of a composition structured according to the principle of deep distance.

Deep distance—which on the face of it seems a redundant term—is sometimes said to result from the combination of the other two configurations (level and high). By contrast with the panoramic landscape, however, this type is structured through multiple overlappings, resulting in pictorial space that has great density, even congestion: "hundreds of waterfalls and cascades," for example, or rocks lost and seen again, presented in all sorts of disposition or posture. The "hollow spaces" to which Wang Shu often referred are common in the folds of deep distance, with destinations of paths hidden behind hills, river bends turning into concealed lakes, or travelers beckoning to unseen friends.

Spaces thereby secluded give ample room for imagination, alternating between a sense of yearning or desire and remembrance triggered by repetition. Each of these expressions prompts continued movement, the advances of which are sustained by recent accomplishments. The travelers' next steps drag in their wake reminders of those that came before. Thus, climbing *continues*. A clearing in the distance, though edged by a river, is like the one that came before, but without the small pavilion. The foot of the bridge can be seen, but not its full length, still less the opposite bank. No passage proceeds without pauses, each of which resumes what has been achieved so far. Looking ahead is indivisibly prospective, but at the same time necessarily retrospective, because the direction it follows was preceded by what is apparent at the present moment. In a certain sense, one has no choice but to remember; forgetfulness is never absolute; a clean break or fresh start is no more possible than a complete return.

Lastly, there is the so-called high distance. Mountains typically set the stage for these types of scenes, giving rise to lofty views, in the face of imposing figures. Densely packed foreground horizontals fill the bottom parts of these images, separated from the towering height by mist rising from an unseen river or lake. Small-size figures seen up-close add to the sense of extreme verticality, by contrast. Here, too, movement is suggested, but a more rugged sort. On the far side of the fog, travelers might be seen climbing, reaching, and coming up short, though sometimes a mountain-top retreat is shown, as a place for rest and relaxation after the long journey. Contrasting with the slow effort of the climb is the accelerated drop of the waterfall, whose velocity doesn't seem to require a destination that can be identified. Power or energy is often expressed in these landscapes, as well as authority and grandeur, thanks to the remoteness they express so vividly.

Depth and Duration

Depth, then, is known most concretely in movement. It offers itself to reflection in rest. The eleventh-century painter and theorist Guo Xi listed different kinds of movement in Song Dynasty paintings: "There are landscapes in which one can travel, landscapes which can be gazed upon [requiring, one would think, a pause of some duration], landscapes in which one may ramble, and landscapes in which one may dwell."[23] The four were not equal in his mind; best were those in which one could dwell, or imagine dwelling. Residing, or being at rest "under the eaves" in Wang Shu's terms, would seem to bring the patterns of passage (traveling or rambling) to an end. Not exactly. Guo Xi also noted that when the body is at rest, the eyes still move. Thus, traveling, rambling, and surveying are distinct from dwelling, even though all four "take time."

Vantage points take many forms in these paintings: a balcony under the eaves, a window in an otherwise shuttered-up house, the side of a boat, or from the apex of a bridge. Outside architecture, views are occasioned by several landscape situations: a turn or a path that reaches some elevation, for example, a level plateau that breaks the climb up a mountain, or at the threshold of a wide clearing. Given the accent on change in all of the accounts of spatial movement, it is not surprising that the writers (consciously or not) associate *kinds of time* with these *types of depth*: a deferred, gradual or slow unfolding of content commonly characterizes the experience of level distance, recursive or reiterative disclosures as one moves through deep distances, and an abruptly sudden appearance of lofty figures in landscapes that are arranged with high distance.

The external walkways on a number of the buildings in the Xiangshan Campus are good examples of a way that spatial content can reveal itself *gradually*, deferring sense until a passage has been followed for a while. To distinguish these kinds of circulation from quicker and more immediate instruments of passage, Wang Shu alluded to the unhurried style of rural thinkers. He called his long, marginal types of circulation "philosophical" paths. On first thought, it would seem there is little content along these routes—that they are truly vacant—for paces along the paths continually repeat similar intervals, step after step, climbing or descending slightly, on route toward or away from a minor bend, hardly changing direction, noticing little that's new, always more to come. Content seems bypassed not discovered. Yet, if one is in no hurry, progress gradually yields some subject matter, on both sides of the route, within the interiors of the buildings they align, as well as the outer surfaces of those nearby, sometimes even the mountain that served (in silence) as their model. As with "level distance" in the Song Dynasty paintings, the mood along the philosophical path is often pensive and the progress leisurely, if also alert to what is unfolding at the margins—the hill, as I said, or a canal that regulates part of the river, a ground-level walkway that's no less delaying, or a distant grove of trees. Not one of these figures presents itself fully; the walk continues and propels movement that seems to have no end.

A sharply contrasting pace is apparent on the other side of the walls that support the "philosophical" walks, I mean the interiors they bypass or encircle. In a number of his study drawings for the project, Wang Shu drew interior elevations that tested the ways the external walks could be viewed in the context of spaces that had their own, speedier forms of interconnection. The drawings typically couple volumes of different height, one or two stories, whose corners overlap and thus introduce an implied diagonal movement that requires linkage through stairways of various sizes, normally single runs. When the apertures are large, one or another of the external ramps can be seen passing by, but always glimpsed partially, with no beginning or end in sight, because of its interminable length. This is to say, the interior elements that serve to connect discrete settings accomplish their task at a different pace than the ramps, without delay, because residing in the room, for however long one might like, is more important than traveling there.

Figure 3.3.10 Wang Shu, *China Academy of Art*, Hangzhou, external walkways. Photograph David Leatherbarrow.

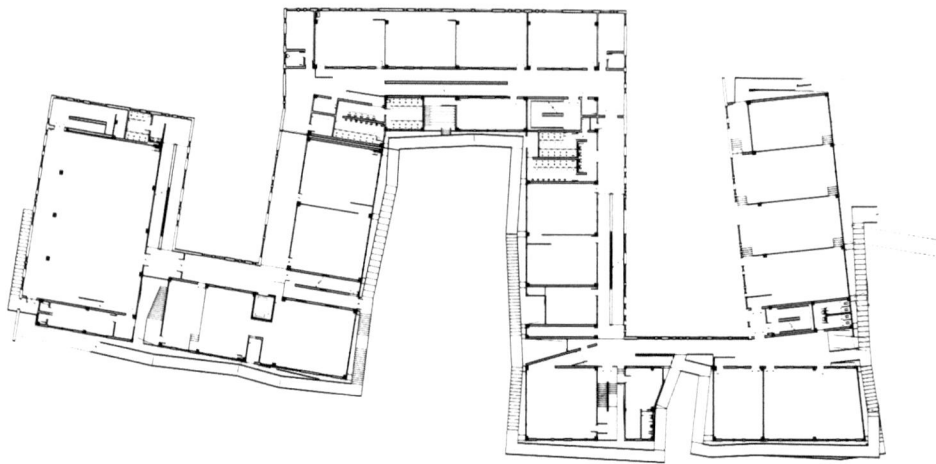

Figure 3.3.11 Wang Shu, *China Academy of Art*, Hangzhou, classroom building plan. Courtesy of Wang Shu/Amateur Architecture Studio.

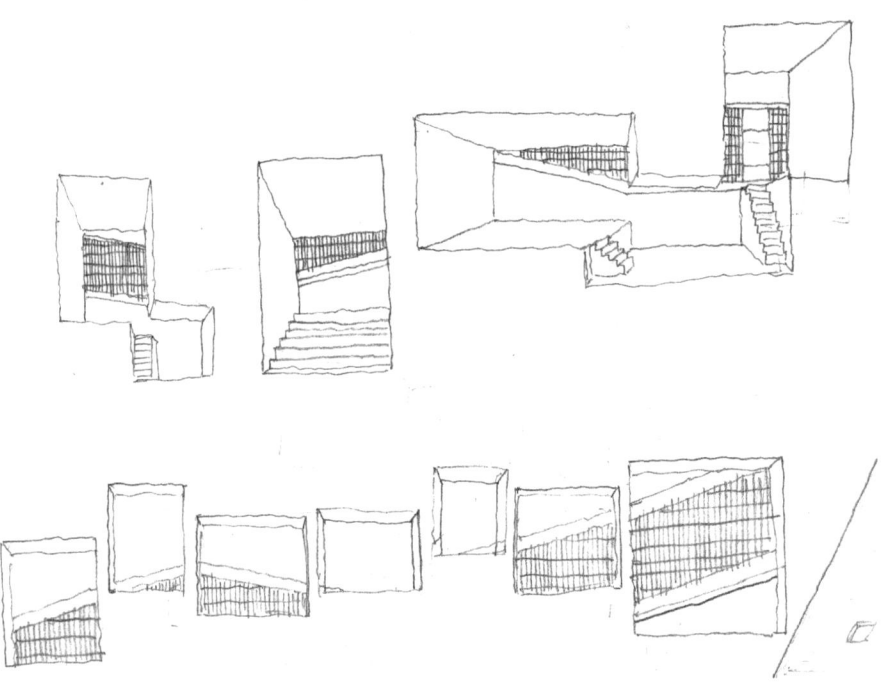

Figure 3.3.12 Wang Shu, *China Academy of Art,* Hangzhou, sketch. Courtesy of Wang Shu/Amateur Architecture Studio.

Differences in pace are plainly evident when the types come together. This normally happens at the second level, in the open spaces between buildings where the ramps meet landings, which in turn give access to interiors, by means of short single-run stairways. At these points, the slow time of "level distance" is mixed with the quicker time of "deep distance." We saw in the paintings that multiple overlappings resulted in pictorial space that had great density or congestion, and that it occasioned a combined sense of yearning and remembrance, triggered by repetition. In the buildings, too, one gets a sense of now-plus-then at these moments, of having been in a similar place before, one that led to a place of arrival, though different in kind from where one had just been. What's more, the change that is soon to occur seems immanent in the route itself, as if moments that recall also prefigure, more or less simultaneously. This is, in short, the function of transitional spaces.

In the Xiangshan Campus generally, but the more recently finished Guest House especially, elements used in the composition and construction of interior settings repeat themselves. The recurrence is inexact, but the likeness is close enough to cause one to think that one of the ways the ensemble holds itself together is through a family resemblance of parts. We saw this, too, in the paintings Wang Shu studies: similar mountains within a range, familiar waterfalls or hollows in their flanking sides and below, and comparable bridges, boats, pavilions, and travelers who populate their

Figure 3.3.13 Wang Shu, China Academy of Art, *Guest House*, Hangzhou, pool and bridge. Photograph David Leatherbarrow.

shores. Again, one never detects exact sameness, only likeness, sibling forms and kinship among descendants.

Historically, this characteristic of the paintings is one outcome of literati culture, where works resembled one another as much as specific places. Poetry was often the intermediary. The principle of *ut pictura poesis* (as in painting so in poetry, from Horace) was no less forceful in Chinese literati culture than in classical and neo-classical European art and art theory. Hence the blunt summary of Su Shi: "If anyone discusses painting in terms of formal likeness, his understanding is nearly that of a child."[24] In the case of Wang Shu's architecture, family resemblance is apparent not only among projects, but also between designs and their precedents, paintings we've seen (as a matter of structure and configuration, rather than specific elements) but also models in old villages, the parts of the landscape that are fast disappearing under the heavy weight of contemporary urbanization.

Nevertheless, the depth of "deep distance" is structured through the arrangement and variation of similar forms or elements. In the Guest House, these include the internal ramps, the nearly parallel rammed earth walls, the open galleries and balconies, courtyards and terraces, and sections of the massive and all-inclusive roof structure. As sibling forms repeat, the phases of passage recall one another. Again, precedents can be found in the paintings: the visitor's forward steps drag in their wake reminders of those that came before. Sometimes the resemblance of one place to another is so close that the resulting sense of topography approximates disorientation. I have a hunch that this observation wouldn't displease the architect, for he has written several times that estrangement or de-familiarization can help him accomplish one of architecture's most significant tasks: to encourage people to see the world anew—even if it is the world of a single building in an art or architecture academy.

The time of "high distance" I suggested earlier is neither delayed nor reiterative, but sudden or abrupt. Given the fact that the majority of the buildings at the China Academy of Art are two, three, or four stories (though a few are taller), the project as a whole might seem an unlikely place to find an architectural equivalent to this way of timing spatial depth. Yet, in the Guest House, there are a number of places that are surprising in their verticality, so much so that the slow passage along a ramp, or the familiar turn of a walk, is stopped in its tracks by a scene that presents itself all-at-once, in full immediacy, despite the absence of anticipations and without any indication of likely successors. The dramatic change in scale renders these figures largely not just towering but remote. Moreover, the reduction in the number of elements makes those that do appear seem larger than life.

The most obvious and insistent example of a lofty and over-powering figure in the Guest House is its massive roof. As built, it is a single folded plate, or plane, supported by oversized and insistently prominent trusses. Apparently, this idea for a single roof developed late in the project. Originally, six pavilion-like buildings with individual roofs were meant to shelter the guests—much like the buildings in the Campus' second phase, though the Guest House pavilions would have been smaller. But after reflecting upon the near uniformity of roofs in Wannan villages, Wang Shu decided on a single roof for all of the spaces included in the Guest House. Each time a section of the roof appears, no matter whether one is in- or outside the building, it dominates the prospect, over-powering the paths that meander at its feet, making out of several spaces a single project, always under the same covering. The high distances that appear in the paintings rose to levels that few travelers could reach. When translated into a single building, however, this roof was made accessible. The prospect one gains is certainly magnificent, even lofty, as the art theorists said of landscapes with deep distance. But insofar as the Guest House roof also serves as the substrate for a "philosophical" walkway, it also opens into a wider horizon that unfolds more slowly, in level distance.

Wang Shu structured the plan of the Guest House to allow occasional views of his old friend the nearby mountain, as he did the other buildings of the Xiangshan Campus. Each prospect is partial. Intermediate elements always block some of this hill's aspects, its top, base, or sides. In a sense, its changing aspects are made more apparent by the ways

Figure 3.3.14 Wang Shu, *China Academy of Art, Guest House*, Hangzhou, roof landscape. Photograph David Leatherbarrow.

it is framed by the building, as if its character were made more apparent by the forms that took it as their model. Yet, the mountain is unmistakably all-of-a-piece: heavy, long-standing, and inaudible, as I said earlier. The changing aspects revealed by the building do not, however, present themselves in any particular order. Nor is the building's arrangement of places and times the basis for anything like a legible narrative. Still less is the sequence of views cyclical, despite Wang Shu's repetitive use of forms and elements.

Viewed as a whole, the time of the project would thus seem to be rather more aleatoric. Were one to suggest that the configuration as a whole possesses a plot, one would have to say that it seems to be the kind of composition that Aristotle criticized as episodic, with events following or preceding one another without an intelligible order or sequence. Wang Shu tends to emphasize choice when describing the decisive moments in the plan: passage is allowed to determine its prospects, paths, and speeds. But I believe it is incorrect to say that the configuration is for that reason without order, that the depth is unstructured, or that the movements have not been arranged.

The varying prompts, together with the successive beginnings and endings, certainly allow movement its freedom, but always within the limits of a schedule that remains attuned to the patterns of day-to-day life in a hotel and academy, the rhythms of eating and sleeping as well as going to class or the vegetable gardens, for example, but also, and more minutely, passing from public to private spaces, and then within each, increasingly more social or intimate settings. The narrative that can be read in the times of this building's spaces is less aesthetic than practical. Wang Shu's aim was to coordinate two ways of living: the spontaneous and seasonal changes in mountain-river environment with the freedoms and schedules of everyday life in the campus buildings and grounds. Architectural intelligence is apparent in the places where the two temporalities appear to be one.

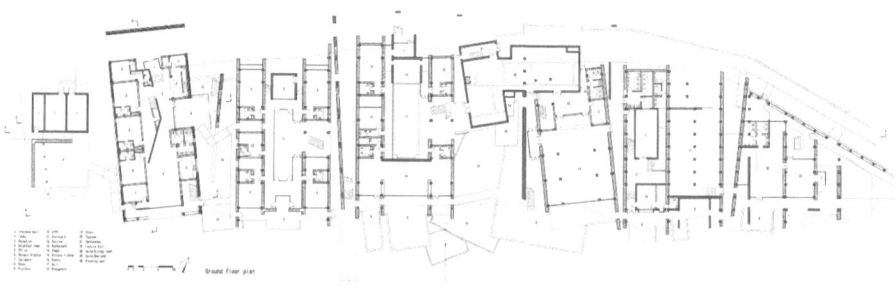

Figure 3.3.15 Wang Shu, *China Academy of Art, Guest House*, Hangzhou, ground plan. Courtesy of Wang Shu/Amateur Architecture Studio.

Figure 3.3.16 Wang Shu, *China Academy of Art*, *Guest House*, Hangzhou, terraces. Courtesy of Wang Shu/Amateur Architecture Studio.

Figure 3.3.17 Wang Shu, *China Academy of Art, Guest House*, Hangzhou, interior. Photograph David Leatherbarrow.

3.4
Pedestrian Rhythms: Álvaro Siza's Swimming Pools at Leça da Palmeira

This ceaseless rush of shadows and shades, that, like the fantastic rush of clouds cast darkly upon the waters on a windy day, fly past us to fall headlong before an implacable horizon.

JOSEPH CONRAD, *MIRROR OF THE SEA*

Topographies are structured in two ways, spatially and temporally. I imagine no explanation will be required for the first half of this observation, for the *here and there* of a street or shore are obvious to anyone in those and other locations, obvious not only in their appearance and character, but in their respective distances and configuration, approximate though that knowledge may be. From *here* at the apartment, or the café on the street directly below, the ocean is ten blocks away and getting *there* means passing by the school and the park. Measure and shape define all spatial situations: this alley is narrower than most; that perimeter block is big enough to have gardens and workshops in its interior.

The *now and then* of topography, by contrast, seem less clear. I don't mean topographical time is unrecognizable when one thinks about it, but that it is generally implicit in one's experience of the café, street, school, park, or shore. To say the walk to the shore will take twenty-five minutes locates time's passing on the face of a clock or watch, not the street.

Figure 3.4.1 Álvaro Siza, *Leça da Palmeira*, Porto, showers and rear walk. Photograph David Leatherbarrow.

Nevertheless, no one will deny that walking or driving a car between places has both spatial and temporal dimensions. Passage takes place *in* time, just as it does *in* space. Yet, when time is formulated this way—container-like, *in which* walking or driving occurs—it exists apart from you and me, in itself, which is to say objectively, indifferent to our movements, even if it provides them with a certain kind of context. According to this conception, time passes impassively, as an unbroken and unbreakable flow of moments, each atomic or dot-like, and therefore short-lived, erasing and erased by one another in turn.

Like many commonplaces, however, this one about time conceals questionable assumptions, not least of which is the container-content premise, together with the objective-subjective distinction it invokes. Let us begin our study of movement in Siza's shoreline architecture by adopting the stance taken by St. Augustine when he famously asked himself about time: "What, then, is time? If nobody asks me, I know; if I must explain it to those who question me I do not know."[1] The basic premise of what I will argue is as follows: when we rephrase the question and ask not about movement *in* but *as* time, we bring into focus the several temporalities that topography offers experience and knowledge, its speeds, configurations, and pleasures.

On the way to the swimming pools at Leça da Palmeira, the neighborhoods left behind, together with the sea yet to come, are clearly not present in the way that any place along the route is, but neither are they entirely absent. While on route, the neighborhood trails behind and the shore approaches from ahead, thanks to both recollection and anticipation, as they are sustained and provoked by the patterns of the urban landscape. At any given moment, it is very hard to say where the neighborhood ends and the ocean landscape begins, both mentally and physically. Memories and expectations can fill one's thoughts, but they can also play their parts more concretely, in one's eyes and feet, as they range across the sidewalks or shops. The walls and pavement that make up the route at any particular moment extend what's been traveled so far and lead toward what's still to come. Like the walk's beginnings, *now* and *then* are rarely, if ever, categorically distinct from one another. Helpful in grasping this coupling is the compound term *now then*, which simultaneously summarizes and starts temporal change.[2] Every step along the route vibrates or modulates a single temporal wave, whose force and speed provide passage with orientation. Making progress along the way depends so largely on grasping where one has been and is going that any substantial lack of concurrency among *nows* and *thens* means one is lost.

Concurrency in urban and architectural experience is neither necessarily nor insistently cognitive. It is equally corporeal. This thesis is implicit in Siza's repeated stress on the ways feet *know* whether the ground they travel is solid or shaky, safe or scary: "The architect merely chose where to put his feet and where not to go, fearful of the dangers and of the sea rocks."[3] Admittedly, pace and tempo weren't Siza's primary concern in this passage, but the spatial knowledge to which he refers has an echo in temporal understanding: the body can know duration in the same way it can grasp durability.

In order to pose this chapter's opening question, let us assume we've made our way to Siza's site and have stopped for a minute at the top of the entry ramp, where, before descending, we can look across the roofs of the changing rooms, past the sand and pools, into the sea. The water that rushes toward the shore approaches in waves whose number and sequence, tumble and fall make the horizon both intelligible and expressive. The force of the wind, for example, is apparent in the height of the waves, their speed, and their sound. Intelligibility is also granted from behind where we stand, by the parallel streets, open lawns, and diagonal paths that lead up to the building. They contribute to the durable character of the neighborhood, as well as its dimensions and configuration, as I said.

Just before entering, then, one occupies a stretch of time that couples the phases of approach, arrival, entry, and occupation. Behind means before, ahead after. How, then, is the coupling, concurrency, or interlapsing of these apparently discreet times of phases to be understood? How can the knowledge possessed by the moving body be rendered in terms that make it amenable to thought, and then to both description and design? What are the configurations, dimensions, or structures of movement that give the project's settings temporal sense and amplitude?

In what follows, I shall reply to these questions by working my way through the settings Siza designed, through what could be called the waves of passage from city to sea, in order to observe the correlation between the work's spatial and temporal structures, as they present themselves in movement.

Pacing

By the time one steps onto the descending ramp that begins entry into Siza's buildings and pools, one has passed along the several parallels that define the northwestern edge of Porto's urban fabric, between the Matosinhos and Leça da Palmeira neighborhoods. The primary virtue of city texture is its permanence, Aldo Rossi insisted, regardless of whether its rock-hard staying power is "pathological" or "propelling."[4] The configuration stays as it was while one moves through it, no matter whether that movement is quick or slow, by car or foot. Although they may be equally sized, some of the blocks, the dull ones, drag along slowly, others, more interesting, pass by in no time at all. Porto's center and near suburbs have been left behind, while the shore and sea lie ahead (including the Boa Nova Tea House, Siza had previously designed and built). His early site sketches singled out a few of the pre-existing parallels for particular emphasis: the coastal road (Avenida da Liberdade), its sidewalk, adjoining lawn (shaded in this view) and parking, as well as the seawall, a perpendicular avenue, and the cluster of lines that would after construction enclose or extend the building's several settings, including the pools. The clustering of lines, densest at the project's margins, indicates a slower, more measured pace of passage, suggesting structured simultaneities that concentrate ambient patterns.

Among the lines of walls, roofs, and walks, some prolonged the urban geometry, while others initiated new directions. In the pattern of parallels, bends were also required, to re-start and then extend the route, often at the same pace that defined the approach. Most of the turns are so short that they never develop their own stride. Nor do they suggest or reward any kind of pause. Following a comment by Siza himself, a number of critics have observed a zig-zag, or switchback pattern of movement, as if the

Pedestrian Rhythms: Álvaro Siza's Swimming Pools at Leça da Palmeira 153

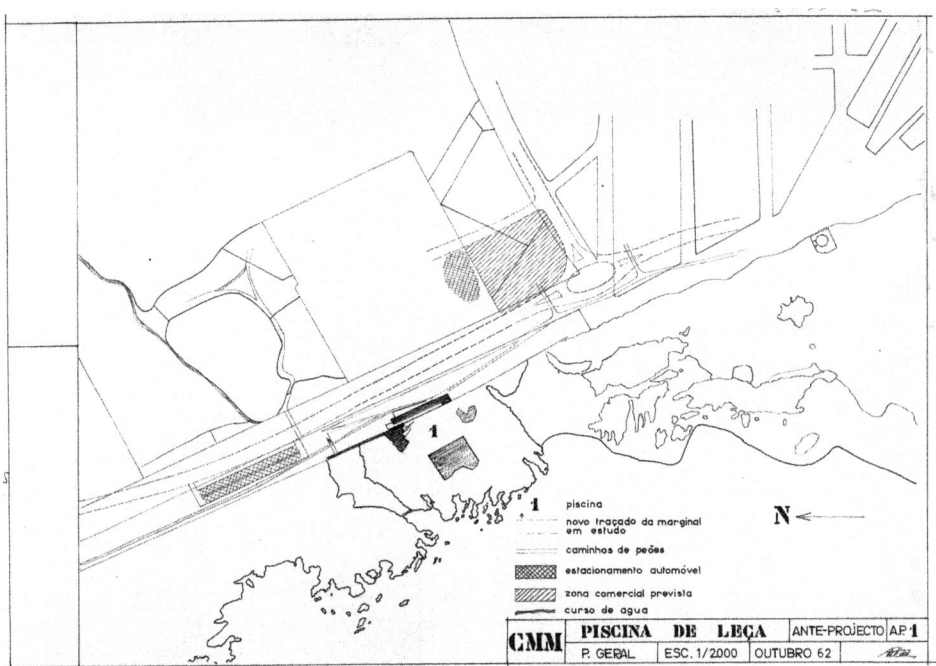

Figure 3.4.2 Álvaro Siza, *Leça da Palmeira Pools,* Porto, preliminary site plan. Courtesy of Álvaro Siza.

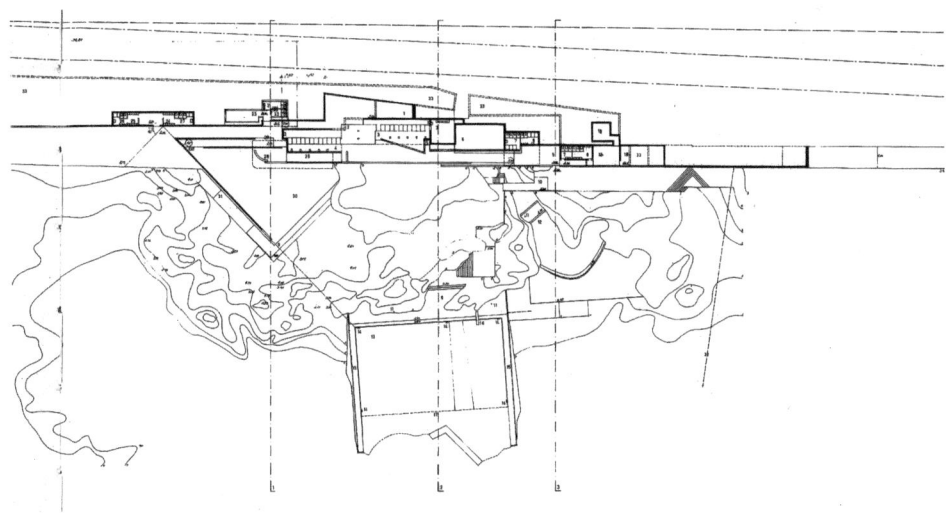

Figure 3.4.3 Álvaro Siza, *Leça da Palmeira Pools,* Porto, preliminary plan. Courtesy of Álvaro Siza.

descent from the entry resembled the rather more dramatic passage down a hillside or mountain. Given the parallelism of the walls and walks, a better comparison might be the tight meander of lines at an airport security or immigration checkpoint, though that geometry is as unbearably tedious as this layout is enjoyably varied, partly because of the latter's occasional diagonals. Moreover, the widths of the sequential lengths alternately dilate and contract. But here, too, no appreciable change in speed results, only an increase in the social sense of the wider walks, and the lingering they encourage.

Despite their short length, some of the 90 degree turns have decisive effects on the rhythms of movement, for they break the steady tempo into momentary pauses.[5] *Landings* typically do this in stairways that turn back on themselves, so-called dog-leg stairways, ending one sequence of treads and beginning another. In Siza's project, rhythmic turns often shift one's orientation from the horizontal plane upward or downward, thanks to an opening to the sky or a descent of steps. In the darkness of the changing rooms building, for example, the bright light admitted by a ceiling aperture is exceptionally theatrical, dramatically staging one's appearance in a full-moon disk mirror, above a white receptacle that catches both light and water. Sometimes the break is less dramatic: a patch of blue might appear above a wall that limits one's view of the near horizon. But the turns can also introduce completely contrasting spaces: dark to bright, upon

Figure 3.4.4 Álvaro Siza, *Leça da Palmeira Pools*, Porto, roofs and distant shore. Photograph David Leatherbarrow.

leaving the changing rooms and showers, for example (thus transforming personal into social space), or bright to dark, when it is time to get back into street clothes. So, while the parallels would seem to suggest a steady tempo, the passages actually structure sequences of steps, bracketed by moments that conclude one progression and restart another.

Entry to the building descends step-by-step down a ramp encased within the newly discovered thickness of the seawall, the site's and project's primary parallel. We've seen that the site plan's diagonals prolong, then terminate lines of approach that diverge from the coastal road. The seawall is primary among the parallels for two reasons: it defines the entire territory and initiates the arrival sequence. As for the speed of this initial descent, it is unhurried and effortless. The acceleration that would typically result from aligned walls (that appear to converge) is slowed by the reverse perspective of Siza's non-parallels. The lateral spread also makes the lower landing wide enough for the business of checking in. Before getting there though, the downward slope makes one's body feel a bit too heavy, rather like the posture of the waves that tumble toward the shore across the slightly sloped sea-bottom.

Despite its measured pace, the downward slide or glide is unclear about what's to follow, however, given the implacably blank terminal wall. At this point, one is under

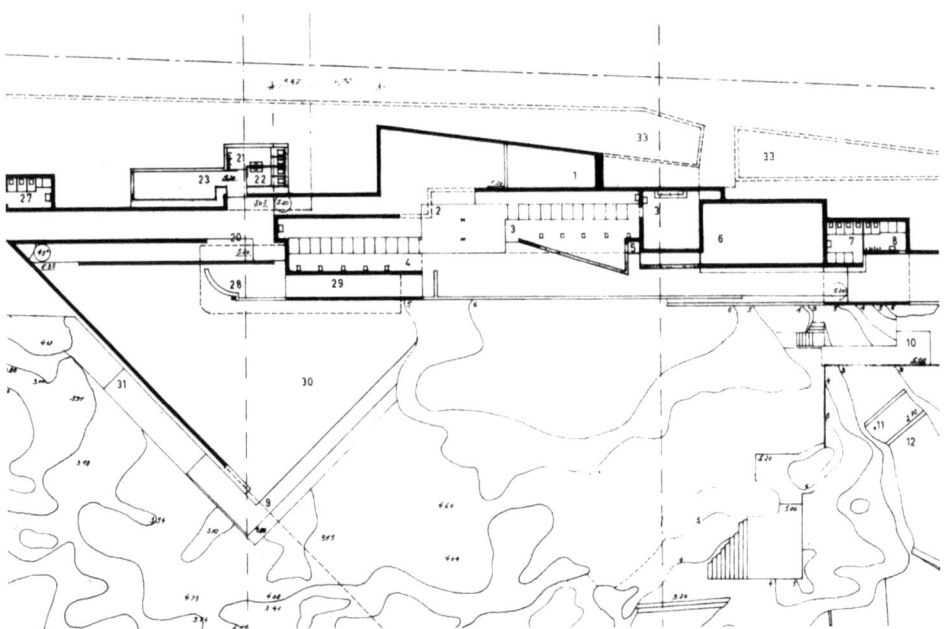

Figure 3.4.5 Álvaro Siza, *Leça da Palmeira Pools, Porto,* partial plan. Courtesy of Álvaro Siza.

Figure 3.4.6 Álvaro Siza, *Leça da Palmeira Pools*, Porto, entry ramp. Photograph David Leatherbarrow.

ground level, but the sky above hasn't changed. Arriving in the building's interiors means leaving the city's behind—though not completely. The eye-level urban horizon increasingly disappears with each successive step, but in due course opens again, laterally, above the showers. From that restart, the measured paces begin again, not across but under an extended horizon that substitutes the sky.

Ramps are not the only instruments of design that pace passage. Beyond the enclosed spaces, but before the pools are reached, a couple of short-run stairways change levels between the buildings and swimming areas. Some of these steps are direct in their descent or climb; others are widely expansive. Along the indices of topographical time, the first are the un-delayed type, speedy in their climb, while the second are un-hurried in their rise or fall, as if there were no particular urgency about changing from a higher to lower level. There is a corresponding change in tread depth: the shallow treads quicken the steps, while the deeper ones slow the pace. At the edge of the pool, examples of the latter type approximate benches for seating. In point of fact, these slower sequences invite rest as much as movement. The speedy steps that scale between levels—often between paved and sandy surfaces—seem by contrast single-mindedly dedicated to regularity and continuity of passage, as if considerations of scale were not only instances of analogy and dimensional correspondence between buildings and bodies but measured pace and repetition.

Opportune Beginnings

Moments of disorientation often signal experiences of arrival and departure. One way to structure opportune experiences of losing one's way is to modulate ambient light, which is to say to cast shadow. Siza's shadows are constructed for both practical and expressive purposes. At one point along the route, he marks an important transition by carefully arranging three elements, no one of which is physical: a shadow projected from a high, side wall; another from a cantilevered roof; and a patch of exterior brightness projected onto the floor and wall, which has the effect of guiding movement toward the absolute darkness ahead (no less blank than the entry ramp's terminal wall, but black). The lines will move as the sun does, but their relationships to one another will remain, as will their compounded effect. Likewise, the sense of occasion arises when the constituent elements are in the right balance or mixture.[6] As I've noted already, spatial dimensions have temporal correlates: the shadows that are partly behind one's present position (the diagonals on the floor and side wall) made their presence felt some time before we reached this spot, and the ones that are partly ahead conceal most of what will be seen after we take a few more steps. Disorientation is the name we give to the momentary pause between approach and arrival, a brief hesitation that ends one sequence of steps in order to inaugurate another, halting steps perhaps, probably short and slow, but also aware and expectant.

The building's secondary elements, its door frames, handles, furnishings, have been blanketed by the dark cloud ahead. Although one can't be sure, it would seem likely they will be ready for use once they are located. This willingness to wait is true of all the "equipment" that makes settings inhabitable.[7] Even if they can be moved from one spot to another, furnishings keep themselves prepared for the time—the opportune moment—when they will be called upon to greet an exploratory hand, foot, or eye. Considering the shadowed spaces along the route through Siza's buildings, one shouldn't say the destinations and means of access are wholly unclear, but the radical contrast with steady passage through well-lit spaces is obvious and inescapable, thanks to three kinds of uncertainty: of depth, direction, and distance. These types of setting are more profound than fog, and no less disorienting. All that's really stable is the ground surface, as Siza stressed "where you put your feet."

Movement comes to a full stop in the changing rooms and showers, also where one's feet are washed. Unlike the fog entry that initiates this sequence of spaces, these tight enclosures offer their contents openly and all at once, with nothing in reserve. And they do so jointly, under the pattern of roof beams (already glimpsed at

Figure 3.4.7 Álvaro Siza, *Leça da Palmeira Pools,* Porto, cantilevered roofs. Photograph David Leatherbarrow.

the entry). Acting in concert, they modulate the interior by rhythmically darkening the darkness. The sense of envelopment they occasion is no less complete than the threshold shadow.

After one has changed clothes and turned on a shower, water envelops the body the way the threshold darkness had. Perhaps disorientation isn't the result, but there arises a comparable sense of restarting the entry, at least beginning its next phase. Although barely apparent, this second covering (washing) is more comprehensive than the first (blanketing), because of water's close adherence to everything it touches. But the liquid surround is unlike what will be granted by the pool, for it is always only a matter of surface wetness. Still, the setting can be described as inaugural, for once washed, one is ready for the pools. The clock of spatial passage restarts, and the paces toward the next, more profound immersion begin.

At the edge of the changing rooms and showers, along another one of the parallels, the low horizon of darkness through which the paces have progressed turns toward its opposite, a wall of bright light. This break is no less profoundly enveloping than the preceding two, the shadows and showers, but wholly different regarding verticality, stratified in three distinct levels. Beneath one's feet, irregular ground is discovered

Figure 3.4.8 Álvaro Siza, *Leça da Palmeira Pools*, Porto, showers. Photograph David Leatherbarrow.

below the platform that pacing had previously enjoyed. Siza's accomplishment is clearly apparent in the contrast between the two surfaces. The second level opens above eye height. It comes into view beyond the shadow cast by the outer edge of the cantilevered roof and releases an unlimited brightness that is unforgiving in its intensity and stunning. Between these two levels extends the third or middle horizon, where the sand, pools, and shore give way to the sea, which reaches its limit in the line that stops the sky. Such a line is what Le Corbusier had in mind when viewing this conjunction:

> The level is fixed where
> the waters stop flowing
> to the sea
> the sea daughter of droplets
> and mother of vapors. And
> the horizontal regulates the
> capacity of liquid.[8]

Figure 3.4.9 Álvaro Siza, *Leça da Palmeira Pools*, rear deck. Photograph David Leatherbarrow.

As with the shadows and showers, the newly apparent brightness is entirely enveloping. Maybe it's a little too bright. When the breeze exhausts itself, the air is also hotter than one would like. Another radical change is the modification in the route's social dimension. Shared space is on the horizon. It is not urban, in the sense of the nearby neighborhoods, but it recalls the sidewalk and street nevertheless, thanks to the little café, the music, conversations, and so on. Hence, a different phase of lateral movement: across the terrain, toward the pool, with steps less regular than those just completed, though still sequential, but now somewhat familiar, even recognizable, as if one had moved at a similar pace before.

The end of the route begins with another vertical change: a plunge into the pool (the children's or adult's pool). One could say that this beginning is also a resumption, but only if another kind of passage is allowed, one without a destination, somewhat like a ramble or wander but even less goal oriented, rather like the back and forth steps that animate dance, which is to say a kind of movement that never intends to go anywhere, despite all the effort, retreats that cancel advances, alternately short and long steps that follow their own pace, just for the pleasure of it, rhythms for their own sake, within the supporting medium, fluid though it is.

Figure 3.4.10 Álvaro Siza, *Leça da Palmeira Pools,* children's pool. Photograph David Leatherbarrow.

And again, like the surroundings provided by the shadows, showers, and sunlight, these watery circumstances are wholly enveloping, which is to say oceanic, even if the sea is outside the pool's proper limits. Unlike the sea, this context keeps its level, thanks to the perimeter walls and rock, in the absence of which it would disperse, into the play of waves and tides, or underground. When swimming stops, the feet once again know their place, even if that place is slippery.

Still There

Standing on the coastal road, facing Siza's project, one hardly knows it is there. The interior spaces are below grade and the pools, together with their sandy surrounds, lie at the level of the shore and sea, at the foot of the sea wall. Nothing could be more contrasting with the sky overhead, which is no less insistent than obvious, nor with the sea, seen in the far distance. From this initial vantage, three distinct horizons present themselves, each expansive but limited: the sky, the sea, and the soil. Siza carved his rooms and pools into the third, but also prepared them to face the second, under the overarching influence of the first.

The several times of passage organized by the project— the beginnings and endings, the fast or slow pacings, and the unscheduled or repetitive sequences—positioned those movements against the relative stability of the three horizons. Siza's project, like any design that's aware of its temporalities, coupled two great empires of time: the time of sequences and duration. I've noted that in antiquity two deities ruled these kingdoms: *Chronos* and *Aion*. Distinct though they seem to be, they were also understood to be reciprocal, hence, Plato's famous statement in *Timaeus*: time is "a moving image of eternity," which is to say *Chronos* is an icon of *Aion*.[9] To fully grasp the ways movement and time are structured in this project, we need to consider lastly the temporal dimensions of the project that didn't and don't change, the three horizons.

Little more than a series of surface modulations confront movement against the grain of traffic, waves, and tides. Despite their unobtrusiveness, each inflection serves as a limit to some sector of the expanse, marking one or another of its phases or sequences. First, there is the depth of the town, as it reaches its limit at the road's edge. Next, there is the line where the sidewalk meets the lawn. Lastly, the line divides the expanse of the lawn from the dense thickness of the sea wall, beyond which all one can see are the roofs over the enclosed spaces. It was into or alongside this wall that the parallels of Siza's building were cut and constructed.

While only the upper edges can be seen from a distance, some lines also have vertical depth. These "lines in the sand" also shelter (hide, protect, and contain) the spaces below.[10] Surface geometry thus signals changes in the project's horizons: first, from the level of the urban landscape to the sub-surface interiors, second, from the concrete decks and sand to the pools, and third, from all that Siza built to the sea. We've reviewed each of these already. A particularly striking manner of implied depth has been seen in the initial descent, for example. The landscape that was plainly structured gave way to a downward gradient that had an unclear end—the end wall is plainly apparent, but what will greet a turn to the left is unknown. Although the lines marking the upper edge of the wall that encloses the entry ramp are plain as day, only when the lower landing is reached does it become clear that the depth of the descent equals the ceiling height of the enclosed spaces—rooms are sheltered in those shadows.

From within the enclosed spaces of Siza's project all intermediate distances are blocked. There's no middle ground, only the surfaces within reach, which is to say the vertical and horizontal slabs, bound to atmospheric conditions that extend beyond one's reach. Are

Figure 3.4.11 Álvaro Siza, *Leça da Palmeira Pools*, entry roofs. Photograph David Leatherbarrow.

these two horizons (concrete plus clouds) or one? At any given moment, the walls suggest the pacing should continue, for the pools are still farther ahead. For its part, the sky stays as it was. The first is an image of change that takes for granted the second, which doesn't.

The boundary function of the horizon has been seen already in our initial vantage from the street: the upper edge of the wall is like the distant limit of the sea, the place or moment when the heavenly blue shows its overarching constancy. But the interior limit tops a vertical plane rather than edging one that's horizontal—thus the blockage. The unseen middle distance could be imagined, but that's pointless given the emphatic denial; it is simply a middle distance whose appearance has been delayed. Probably there is some proportionality between desire and delay: the stronger the first the more disagreeable the second. Nevertheless, the sky descends to something *there*, to be reached in a while, just as it does *here*, now, but how the two connect spatially is anyone's guess. Sounds also suggest unbroken continuity, but they, too, only intimate sense. The delay is unmeasured: the space in-between waits indefinitely for our arrival, just as we take a while—who knows how long—to get there. The slabs succeed one another as we advance while the sky remains.

Figure 3.4.12 Álvaro Siza, *Leça da Palmeira Pools,* rear wall. Photograph David Leatherbarrow.

Figure 3.4.13 Álvaro Siza, *Leça da Palmeira Pools*, horizontal openings. Photograph David Leatherbarrow.

The denial, delay, and promise of the spaces that movement seeks (to the pools) are even more emphatic from within the changing rooms or showers, for then the blockage is frontal and close. Not only *no longer* but *not yet* seems a long time from now. Yet, this particular interval lasts as long as one would like—long enough to comfortably change clothes, shower, or secure one's belongings. In fact, this is the kind of delay one could easily choose to extend—take a longer shower, take more care dressing, etc.—unlike the breaks in the horizon of movement caused by intermediate walls, prolongations of passage that are unnegotiable. When moving through the passages and then into a changing room, the level of one's view remains at the same, searching for distant prospects.

The last type of walls that build horizons are those that limit the flow of water, particularly in the pools. Their task is to interrupt water's downward tendency, to keep it at a desired level or depth, one that's right for swimming, which alternates aquatic movement with periods of rest or standing, for adults and children. If there is blockage in this type of walling, it is not of one's view but of water's escape. Thus, a horizon is formed that is contained and surrounds, like the outer edge of a huge disk, which is what the ancient Greeks meant by the word—a bounding or limiting circle. The edges of the pools are polymorphic: concrete walls, pre-existing rock, walks, etc., but not one of them rises very high above the water level. Thus, they resemble the walls one first encountered: top edges are visible, but the drop is hard to fathom, except by diving. And like those first limits, these stay put, otherwise there would be no pools in which movement can enjoy its exercise for unlimited periods of time.

Figure 3.4.14 Álvaro Siza, *Leça da Palmeira Pools*, adult pool. Photograph David Leatherbarrow.

Part Four

The Time of the Project

4.1
Past and Present Possibilities: Leonardo da Vinci's *Adoration of the Magi*

Coming events cast their shadows before.
JAMES JOYCE, WORKING NOTES FOR *ULYSSES*, c. 1915

In architecture, there is no time like the present. Rephrased, this truism could read: current conditions are wholly un-precedented, this moment is unlike any before. While these statements are perfectly intelligible, they also obscure the reality of the architectural project because they neglect the ways that built works exist *in* and *as* time, through the several phases of design, construction, and reconstruction, or the sequence of adaptations that define the work's real duration. Many of the claims made about *this moment* are anachronistic and indicative of a non-architectural conception of duration and the design project. In neither the built work nor the project does an isolated present exist. The term is not senseless—we use it commonly—the mistake is to confuse a familiar idea with the concrete phenomena it abstracts. Architectural reality is distorted by notions and terms that presuppose and partition time, while neglecting the inevitability of alteration, transformation, and innovation. In the introductory comments that follow, I want to show how the project's prospective and retrospective dimensions infiltrate and qualify its assumed currency, extending its clock, while conditioning its beginning and end.

The Time of Given Conditions

"No new architecture can arise without modifying what already exists."[1] Modification in this phrasing approximates adaptation but isn't quite the same; the first is a more abstract index of change that tends toward affirmation, and the second pursues a goal of increased suitability or better fit. A setting that has been *adapted* is more *apt*. The "what already exists" of this principle, the priorities that architects typically call given conditions, can refer to any of the basic topics of design: the site, the program, or construction materials. Consider a building's location. Any work that is to be built must be built somewhere, in some spot that exists prior to the project—the site a client has obtained—the conditions of which will make it variously suitable for the spaces and settings the project intends. Similarly, construction materials and elements also pre-date project development; they might be "found" near the site or more commonly today in a catalogue or warehouse, where they wait for selection, delivery to the site, and then assembly. The key point is that work on given sites and with existing materials always involves the alteration of subject matter that bears the stamp of the anterior, even if it is so recent a past that it seems contemporary.

What exists in the past, prior to the project, *persists* through the adaptations it proposes. Project development never erases all indications of what made a site or material suitable for shaping and sizing. Nor would such erasure be desirable, for then the place would be unrecognizable, and there would be no basis for measuring the project's success. Even if a site's slope is drastically changed, let's say cut into a set of stepping terraces, pre-existing conditions below the surface, such as geological pressures and hydrological movements, will still show themselves in time, through processes of settlement and erosion. Similarly, when pre-existing materials are cut, shaped, and polished, the properties that define them will still be seen and felt through the new finish. The sorts of change that result from construction are always significant but never absolute. Construction finishing often continues natural processes, making what shines, for example, shine even more. Once is never enough: refinishing repeats steps that had been taken on the site. Thus, finishing extends processes that preceded it and continues after construction ends. The same is true for the adaptation of a program of uses. New works can indeed offer new types of accommodation, but these patterns will only be sensible if they are sufficiently familiar to invite appropriation, if the café that now screens sports programs on big digital monitors still serves coffee. The continued force of pre-existing conditions is especially evident in urban architecture, for primary topics of design, such as orientation and frontality, are conferred upon the project as much as they result from it. A building's back is where it faces the pre-existing block interior, its front, the main street.

Even though these prosaic observations may seem to take the wind out of the sails of design innovation, the thesis of adaptation is neither a constraint on invention nor a restriction on divergence, still less a concession to the status quo; it requires difference and some measure of disorientation as the measure of the project's particularity. This means the project is something other than both the building and the design, although the three are closely related. What, then, is an architectural project? A process? An idea? Somehow both? One plausible definition is as follows: through the means specific to architecture, the project is "a critical dialogue with the present."[2] Critical? Perhaps. The present? Its autonomy is precisely what we must question. One thing can be said with confidence: project making is always interpretative and conditional, at least when design is seen as projection not production. But that distinction needs close attention, for today, when projects are so often "fast-tracked," we tend to equate the two.

Project vs. Product

Production assumes that much if not most of the work of design development has been completed. Like all progressive endeavors, productive work is oriented toward the future. It is unique insofar as it converts orientation toward what is ahead into full engagement with it, abbreviating approach in order to accomplish arrival. The prefix *pro* means before or in advance, in front or in favor of. Architectural projects, for example, advance *pro*-posals. Etymologically the word project means "to throw forward"; a *projectum* is something thrust ahead, a projectile. Earlier I referred to projection as design's prospective moment. Production, by contrast, *completes* the project's advance, achieves its goal, and along the way insulates design's procedures against future interferences. Single-mindedly dedicated to its ends, approximately locomotive, production marginalizes all possibilities but one in order to arrive at the work's concluding stage. This process draws the yet-to-come of the project back into the now, placing the future in the grasp of the present, as if project making were planning, which it is not. Through these means the product discards its preliminaries in order to achieve a form untainted by traces of its formation.

Production is the explicit goal of today's new instruments of "design development." Many software programs promise to close the gaps between the several phases of project development and implementation, overcoming the problems of "associativity" between packages, linking together in one seamless flow the work of documenting the context, sketching a possible solution, developing the design, refining its articulation, specifying materials and products, and controlling their assembly, perhaps robotically, at least in part. Possibly the most significant recent addition to the list of new instruments is "building information modeling" software. Whether or not the promises for speedier and more controlled process are kept, the change in thinking allowed by this and similar programs is significant. When the outcome is assured at the beginning, unforeseen possibilities have little or no role to play in project development.

Project Making Prospects

Projection, the real core of project making, is different. Like probability in scientific discourse, projection in architecture remains within the limits of the likely. The basic idea here is that architecture, designed and built, never offers more than *the conditions under which* something is likely to occur, more than a possibility but less than a promise. Although project making is indeed forward-looking, it is never more than a prefiguration of a final product, the foreshadowing of an outcome. Furthermore, its advances are always coupled with delays, even retreats. Before it can anticipate anything final, let alone achieve it, the proposal must define its relationship to what exists, partly tearing itself away from the present, because its provisions no longer suit current needs, and partly remaining there, for that is where changes must be made and where their effect will be seen. A complete break is refused, and adhesions are required. Adaptation as transformation requires this. In every project there are, I have said, prospective and retrospective dimensions. The difficulty for the conventional sense of design development is that despite its mechanisms it cannot completely separate these dimensions, which always overlap and intersect.

It could be said that projection has a kind of blind logic that unfolds *during* not *before* the project, detouring after advancing, then turning back, renewing beginnings by rethinking premises, and moving forward once again. Paul Klee once described drawing as letting a line go for a walk, moving freely without a goal, a walk for a walk's sake.[3] If allowed a goal, the ramble he had in mind illustrates the path of a project very well, forward-looking but open to the attractions of unforeseen encounters, as well as their distractions. Perhaps project making could be described as a mixture of chance and reason: chances must be taken because mechanical repetitions get us nowhere, yet reason must intervene because the problems with which we began have not been solved. The games people play would lack structure and never develop momentum if players did not know with reasonable certainty the outcomes of certain moves. At the same time, they would fail to excite if foresight could be extended indefinitely. Projects play with circumstances and are played by them. In his last text Le Corbusier said only one thing was key: to play the game.[4] The processes of project making are less a matter of foresight and calculation than of cunning, requiring wide-eyed alertness to possibilities as they emerge. Alison and Peter Smithson had a good term for this *mêtic* intelligence: wit + eye.[5]

Contemporary criticism favors a more emancipated sense of projection, neglecting the "rules" Le Corbusier thought essential. Design today is often viewed as an instrumental kind of transcendence, whereby the difficulties that surround us are overcome. My sense of the matter is rather different: through project making, existing conditions (in the present) are both surpassed and preserved. This double movement will never result from the kind of experimentation that closes the work in on itself, nor from methods untainted by extra-disciplinary involvements. Project development requires movement away from its own methods toward conditions that are not of its own making, an eccentric procedure dedicated to the unseen potentials of the world it seeks to remake. To grasp the temporal richness and ambiguities of project time through an image rather than argumentation, I'd like to turn to a painting from centuries ago that clearly articulates a comparable coupling of potentials and reversals of expectations.

Anachronisms

In 1481, Leonardo da Vinci started work on *The Adoration of the Magi*, for the church of San Donato a Scopeto, just outside the center of Florence. Although unfinished, Leonardo's ideas for the painting are clear, especially his representation of what happened during the moment of the Epiphany, the *adoration*: linear time was broken and distant times were joined together.[6] I'd like to use this as a key to what happens in the unfolding of a design project, no less a surprising turn of events when considering given circumstances.

Leonardo's composition poses a number of surprising anachronisms. Although one tends to focus on the central group of figures, given the crossing of compositional diagonals at the child's raised right hand, the margins introduce the painting's temporal propositions most directly. Figures that represent radically distinct ages are positioned at both the left and right, and the back- and foreground. The least complicated pair appears at the painting's two sides.

Figure 4.1.1 Leonardo da Vinci, *Adoration of the Magi*. Courtesy of Galleria degli Ufizzi.

An elderly man stands at the extreme left, his back edging the panel. Because he is cloaked in a way that recalls the appearance of an ancient sage, some scholars see a philosopher, others the prophet Isaiah, whose account of the Epiphany seems to have guided Leonardo's thinking. Philosopher or prophet, he is wholly absorbed in thought. Arms crossed over his massive bulk, a closed left hand supports his downward-turned chin. One can't really say for sure if his eyes are shut, though they seem so; if not, he is looking without seeing—not seeing but foreseeing—or more generally, expressing inward focus, no less encircled than Rodin's *Thinker*, who is similarly self-enclosing and concentric, though seated. Another sculptural comparison is Michelangelo's *Lorenzo de' Medici*, who also embodies contemplative life, with downcast eyes, knuckled chin, and sealed lips, closed in on himself, brooding and un-distracted. In Leonardo's version, the sage/saint's concentricity suggests isolation from the action at the center, as if the past he represents were a closed book. We'll see it wasn't.

On the painting's right side stands the elder's polar opposite: a youthful figure, entirely out-going and animated, also more limber, twisting on his vertical axis, in *contrapposto*, right and left arms turned toward the center and eyes in the opposite direction, who knows where, just not here, toward something just departed or not yet arrived. He could be greeting a latecomer to the event we see. Some critics have said this is a youthful self-portrait, but not explained why that would make sense, given the Epiphany theme. This figure's equivalent in the Medici Chapel would be *Giuliano de' Medici*, who is also poised to act, though not oriented quite so obliquely. Some scholars see refined dress in Leonardo's figure, at least according to fifteenth-century norms, also a figure who is well equipped. Whatever has caught his attention, its off-center location couples him to his senior on the other side because both ignore rather than adore the center.

What about the painting's vertical organization? On most accounts the panel divides in two parts when viewed from top to bottom or back- to foreground. The division is about one-third above and two-thirds below, slightly more background than was typical in Renaissance paintings. One assumes this is because Leonardo had much to say and show about the events that preceded the Epiphany. A commonplace of language is assumed in this type of compositional history: *behind* indicates some time *before*, which is to say, the foreground *now* emerges out of the background *no longer*; distant means some time ago and nearby this particular moment.

The background third is roughly divided into two sides by the tree rooted in the stones that serve as the seat of the foreground's central scene. On the left a double stair rises from an unpaved clearing to the parapet wall of a raised platform, with a three-bay arcade between the steps (below the parapet). Oddly, but prominently, a single pseudo-Corinthian (Egyptian?) column rises from the upper deck. Workmen move up and down the steps, also along the platform's edge. Parts of the building are in ruin. Two saplings rooted in the stone make this fate plain, but other parts of the fabric are being rebuilt—at least that's what the sketchy tangle of figures on the second stairway and parapet suggests.

To the right of the steps are horsed and unhorsed riders, who seem to be violently at odds with one another. A battle or some sort of skirmish is generally inferred. Also there, at risk of being trampled, are other animals, dogs at the center and cows and oxen to the right. In an earlier sketch for the painting, farm animals like those barely visible here rested outside a rendition of the nativity stable. In fact, a number of elements of that initial sketch were transferred to this panel. In addition to the farm animals, a single timber column of the stable can be seen, just to the right of the distant mountains.

On the opposite side, at the far left, are more horsemen, in front of the stairways and under the incomplete vault, in and around the piers, with unseated riders and unruly horses caught in-between. Horses also press in on the central scene; at the left and right, but like the elder and youth at the extreme margins, riders don't pay much attention to what's happening at the center, though the left hand of one and the eyes of another rider indicate some interest in the main event. Lastly, a landscape profile can be seen in the remote distance, bordered on the right, I've said, by traces of an earlier support for the stable, and visible on the left between the piers that once supported the broken vault. The ruin and fighting seem to indicate troubled conditions before the Epiphany: conflict, discord, and destruction, but also, I'll discuss below, rebuilding and restoration.

Lastly, one of the most remarkable groups in the background is the pair (is it a double pair?) of figures standing in front of the first stairway. Leonardo is still undecided here, though the aim for *contrapposto* is very clear, for profiles overlap and limbs extend widely, indicating competing interests or attractions. Rather like the twisting youth at the foreground right, these bodies show concern with what is happening beyond the landscape we see, what has just departed or is about to arrive.

As for the panel's bottom two-thirds, which fills out the foreground, we are shown not what was happening some time ago but what is occurring right now, the new dispensation. In brief, the momentous change takes the form of a double donation: the mother gives her child (relaxes her hold, allows his reach), while the magi offer their treasures. More precisely: this is the moment when the infant offers his blessing, without having accepted the gift which the magus has raised but not yet released. Geometrically, the lines of sight—the mother's, child's, and magus'—parallel the slightly lower axis of giving and receiving. The arm, wrist, and hand that offer the blessing run perpendicular to those parallels, but the index finger points upward. One assumes the sign of the cross will be traced in the air. Despite this matrix of connections—the sign of the cross, the giving or receiving, and the meeting of the eyes—the mother and child remain divided from the magi and all they represent (the gentiles), thanks to the strong vertical line that falls from the baby's left shoulder, behind his elbow, all the way to the ground. Some distance above the child, this line reaches upward, from the rock root into leaves of the central tree. But below, the line edges a purple robe, the bottom length of which folds across the ground.

The foreground's background is an upward tilting plane of rockwork, especially vivid—maybe too distinct—when compared to the un-rendered lightness of the deeper space. Compositionally speaking, within the compass of the stone outcropping is a set of concentric rings circling around the mother and child, notwithstanding the implied diagonals.

First among these circles is the ring of close onlookers, each of whom indicates un-distracted absorption, rigidly submissive in orientation. The central group includes the three magi and a fourth figure, probably Joseph, who is holding the lid of a gift already received. According to a legend popular in the fifteenth century, this first gift was gold. In due course, Mary and Joseph will donate the gold to local poor. No less current, but a little more recent—the actual moment Leonardo depicts—is the gift from the magus to the lower right, as we've seen. His orientation and submission are strung out along a single line that directs not only his glance but his entire body, from his left toes and heel, along his spine, through his eyes, toward the receiving hand and eyes of the child and mother. Behind her, Joseph's gesture reinforces this axis. If the first gift was gold, the second, received and blessed at this moment, was frankincense, traditionally associated with Christ's sacrifice, which would be a lifetime away in the future, though recalled and anticipated by the sign of the cross. The crucifixion would also have been remembered in countless performances of the mass this painting was to adorn, had it been finished and installed in San Donato.

A corresponding diagonal, 90 degrees to the first, links the intense focus of the elderly man to the right of the child (eyes shaded, *aposkopein*, against a bright light above we can't see but should imagine) to the blessing gesture at the center, as well as the bowing and kneeling gestures of the two magi to the lower left. The gift in the younger magus' right hand will be the third and last. Myrrh was an oil commonly used in preparations for burial.

The next ring consists of rather more marginal figures, alternately independent and engaged. They are diverse in age and involvement in the Epiphany, except for the two who share an interest in the central tree. One figure is clinging to its base, the other acknowledging its height. If it represents the Tree of Jesse, the root from which the child descended, still more events from earlier times would be allowed a place in current affairs, indicating again the break with the past that wasn't absolute. It is also possible the figure clinging to the root (an angel announcing the child's coming, or John the Baptist, who had performed the same service) is pointing not to the new branches, but the star, presently unseen, that had guided the magi to Jerusalem. This would also be the light to which the nearby figure gestures so expressively. But these are just a couple of the several intrusions of the past into the present. After all, the downward fall of the background ends in the paired indications of ancient and modern times at the far left and right.

Despite all the twists and turns of times and places around her, the mother sits rather calmly at the painting's center. The panel is nearly square. Diagonals from its corners cross near her chin. She, too, indicates divergent interests; she would seem lifeless if she didn't. Her lower half turns outward, along the line that extends from her right foot, while her upper inclination and focus parallel the line that coordinates the gift and blessing. At the same time that her inclination and tilt combine giving and caring, she also expresses calm stability, though it is hard to say if she is seated on a stone ledge or a seat of some sort. Prior to Leonardo's version of events, Mary was often shown seated on throne, as an indication of her majesty. That's not the role she is playing right now, instead, a *Madonna dell'umiltà*. She is at home in a landscape, under one tree (the rock-rooted one) and backed up by another, possibly a palm, an emblem of peace traditionally associated with the Virgin. Like the foreground tree, she is at rest on the rock, as are the figures ringing around her, though they seem less stable.

As a physical support, the rocky base plays a part in the story too, though tacitly. It supports the tree root, as we've seen, also the mother, her seat, and feet, and third, the outward fold of the child's robe. There's more: Joseph's elbow used an upper self of the stone for support, the foreground magi its lowest level. No less indicative than the robe's fold is the gesture of the King whose gift has been received: he not only bows but has lowered his head far enough to kiss the ground. Presumably, its sanctity is why shoes have been removed from all the feet we see.

What about the stone and soil behind and before the Epiphany, out of which this event emerged? In the middle distance, on the left-hand side of the painting, a female figure stands in front of the pier that buttresses the first stairway and supports the remains of the broken vault. Her back is turned toward us, so she can turn toward the riders beneath the vault, with an outstretched left arm, possibly brandishing a sword. More interesting is her stance. Her right foot rests on a rather large but unshaped stone block that has either broken off the building or not yet been prepared for the work of renovation: no longer part of the ancient building, not yet part of its restoration. Its irregularity is striking when compared to the regular form of the piers and the geometry of the deck. Nothing of the platform's regularity appears on their other side of the stairways; instead, an unmarked and presumably uneven stretch of terrain extends to the right.

But at the far right, another unshaped large block appears rather prominently, at the foot of the wooden support for the nativity stable. The uneven terrain between these stones—on which the enmity between the horsemen and animals plays itself out—also extends into the depth of the image, over gently rising hills and hidden valleys, to the foot of the mountains. The odd profile of the remote range has led some critics to infer that its contours were added after Leonardo abandoned the painting. Possibly, but topographically speaking, they are no more unusual than the outcropping of stone that encaves the foreground events.

Both back and front show unshaped land. The terrain in between, the unshaped plane plus the level platform, as they lie between the two unshaped stones, shows the task and outcome of design and construction—if we were to construe this turn of events as the subject matter of an architectural project. The stable on the right and classical building on the left tell the same story: how both primitive and sophisticated building technique make use of natural conditions, conditions that not only pre-date design and construction but provide them with the means of their renewal. Apart from the antecedents that preceded the present moment (the time of an event or of a project), any sequel would be deprived of the context in which its accomplishments could be measured. In both human affairs and project making, no such present can be said to exist.

4.2
Proposing Precedents: Rafael Moneo's *Museo Nacional de Arte Romano de Mérida*

The dialectic of repetition is easy, for that which is repeated has been—otherwise it could not be repeated—but the very fact that it has been makes repetition into something new.

SØREN KIERKEGAARD, *REPETITION*, 1843

My concern in this chapter is the reality of the architectural project, not the idea or ideas that we commonly think define it, nor the actual building that results. Advancing the inquiry will require addressing two symmetrical objections to the concept-fact alternative just introduced. The first objection is raised to the notion that it is *built works* not projects that give architecture its reality, its perceptible solidity and concreteness, by virtue of which it accomplishes its basic purposes, accommodating and representing the ways we live or would like to. The second, opposite contention I'll need to challenge is that *ideas* are what mostly matter in project making, that they alone are truly essential because they determine the work's singularity, despite any errors in construction or subsequent modifications. Because I think the choice between these two is false, I'll proceed along the lines suggested by Rafael Moneo, who observed that there is something "essential" in the "crude reality of built works," that prior to analytical reflection, in the living reality of the work, the ideal and actual are indivisible, no matter whether the ideas are dull or original and the realization is faulty or highly accomplished.[1]

Figure 4.2.1 Rafael Moneo, *National Museum of Roman Art,* Mérida, front court. Photograph David Leatherbarrow.

In that short passage, Moneo doesn't note but elsewhere observes that the project's temporality holds a key to its "reality."[2] Examining the correlation between the concrete and essential dimensions of an architectural project means grasping how they jointly unfold in time, how anticipations depend on recollections, advances on reversals, and, more specifically, how built realizations—for example, these parallel walls, that room's atmosphere—expose previously unnoticed pre-conditions as their preparation, as when a child's behavior shows something new about the parent you thought you knew.

Projects are obviously prospective; the word's prefix designates just that, as it does with propitious and productive, associated anticipations in design and construction. Each project holds potential because it is oriented toward what is yet-to-come. But here's the difficulty: *prospectivity* is no more than half the story. I'll try to show that a project's real possibilities for architectural sense and quality depend not only on the work's novelty but equally on its adherence to current norms and disclosure of preceding conditions, making it simultaneously prospective and retrospective. It is the *concurrency* of the no longer, now, and not yet in projects that I want to explain. I realize the sense of time we take to be obvious and sensible—linear time—doesn't allow the simultaneity I have in mind. Nevertheless, I'll explain that new dimensions of the past come into visibility by means of solutions to current problems that propose rearrangements for the future and do so time and again.

Because architects typically do not make buildings but representations of them, it seems natural to assume that the project's reality is what is rendered in two- or three-dimensional images: manual or digital cuts and views, or scale models, if the whole building is under consideration, full-size mock-ups if a discrete part needs assessment. Concepts are different from project drawings because they're very abstract, largely lacking tangibility, especially when kept in one's mind, slightly more concrete when discussed. Built works are no less contrasting with graphic representations because they are far more substantial than lines on paper, fully three-dimensional and full-size of course, palpably manifest, and therefore communicative. Moreover, they partner with extra-architectural factors, such as the work's environment, its builders, patterns of use, and so on. Project drawings, we tend to think, *mediate* these two, rather like a visa stamped in your passport, thanks to which border crossings between different worlds become straightforward.

When understood as a set of drawings, the project endows the idea with a helpful measure of tangibility. Not as concrete as a building's, I've said, for drawings are paper-thin, scaled, and show views no one will ever see. But they're substantial enough to govern construction practices, which in turn demonstrate the architect's foresight. I don't doubt that the notion of mediation can help us see some aspects of the project's reality, but only if one's understanding of the term doesn't limit articulation of ideas to verbal and graphic representations, neglecting the "crude reality of built works." Nor will this conception be useful if it prevents passage between times that are no longer, now, and not yet.

Despite the familiar metaphor, naturalized conceptions of temporal *flow*—from the past, through the present, toward the future—assume that very distinction insofar as the sequence is understood to be linear. Seconds tick away, one after another, minutes too, also hours, days, and years, each distinct, but all in line with one another, like the mile markers on a highway that measure a trip's progress, though the beginning and end are far less distinct than the middle, which is where or when one happens to be *at this moment*.

No matter how obvious it seems, that very sequence, linear and three-phased—before-now-later—obscures the reality of architecture in time. As long as the mediating intention of drawings assumes this sequence it, too, clouds the issue. The project cannot be defined by a drawing's dimensions, lines, and elements because it arises out of and persists through several articulations: verbal when discussed, visual when drawn, manual when modeled, material when constructed as enclosures and topographies, and then "naturalized" when seasoned, weathered, or ruined. When realized in the present it was prepared in the past in ways that only became known retrospectively, once construction had concluded and inhabitation begun. Still later, it will have become known differently though subsequent alterations that reprise the back and forth movements of before. Projects synchronize the entire spectrum of these "moments," despite their different degrees of remoteness, partiality, and indefiniteness.

Anyone who has worked on an architectural project will recall that going forward by going backward is common in design development. This also happens in building construction. Preliminary explorations often cause one to rethink and sometimes redefine the initial conception, for when visualized more concretely its problems become more apparent. When discussing the errors designers typically make, the Renaissance architect Leon Battista Alberti admitted that pleasing ideas he dreamed up in the evening were all too often discovered to be ill-considered when set down on paper the next morning.[3] Beginning again was the project's next step. At the same time, reversals pre-structure developments yet to come, turning the backward glance forward again, but with a different understanding of aims. Likewise, after the project has been built, it will inevitably be modified, sometimes renewed, through alternating periods of maintenance and neglect, addition and subtraction, conservation and reconstruction, and, more generally, admiration and indifference. But if the project's reality is not only what appears on the drawing, neither can it be the actual building at any given moment, for if that were true its most remarkable fact, singularity or self-sameness through time, would be forever lost.

In what follows I shall elaborate on the implications of these preliminary points by examining a single building, Rafael Moneo's *Museo Nacional de Arte Romano de Mérida*. Although my basic question concerns the temporal reality of the project, a number of related themes will also come into play: the reality of the historical past, the role of fiction in project making, and most importantly repetition, at the scale of the city, the building, and its elements. As indicated in the epigraph above, my approach to this last theme will be guided by Søren Kierkegaard.

Figure 4.2.2 Rafael Moneo, *National Museum of Roman Art*, Mérida, interior. Photograph David Leatherbarrow.

Figure 4.2.3 Rafael Moneo, *National Museum of Roman Art,* Mérida, ancient Mérida, bronze relief plan. Photograph David Leatherbarrow.

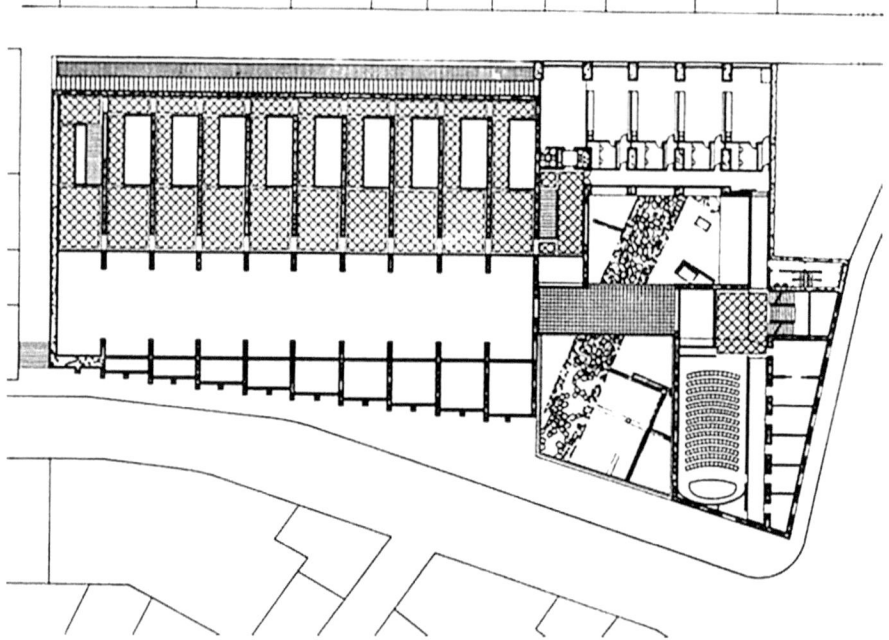

Figure 4.2.4 Rafael Moneo, *National Museum of Roman Art,* Mérida, ground plan. © Rafael Moneo.

Converging Parallels

The lineaments of Mérida's Roman Art Museum, like those of the contemporary city it transformed, elaborate traces of an ancient model, Augusta Emerita, which was no small or insignificant settlement in the first and second centuries of the common era. Often called the Rome of Spain, it was the capital city of Lusitania and grew to be the ninth largest city in the Empire in the fourth century, just prior to the arrival of the Visigoths, who were eventually defeated by the Moors in 711. Contemporary Mérida also contains vestiges of later Renaissance and Baroque cultures, mixed together with the typical outcomes of societal and technological modernization in the twentieth and twenty-first centuries.

The streets of the ancient town followed the typical Roman layout of parallels and perpendiculars, repeating the lines and angles of the *cardo* and *decumanus*, as they had been originally cut into the land. Although it adopted the checkerboard format used widely throughout the Empire, Augusta Emerita's primary axes were also coordinated with topographical geometries, particularly the lines of the pre-existing river, the Guadiana. It had no fixed edges; rivers, unlike canals, never do.[4] Yet, just where it was crossed by the bridge into the city, the river had been split into two parallel branches by a wide sandbar. Artifice imitated the outcome of natural processes. The *Cardo Maximus* was set out in alignment with the shore lines on both sides of the island. So, too, for all the parallel streets that followed, all the way across the breadth of the town in the first settlement and some of its extra-mural prolongations in subsequent reiterations. But likeness allowed difference, not in the geometry but the object of imitation: all of the parallels that were subsequently cut into the soil and constructed above it, including Moneo's, patterned themselves after lines that were not lines at all, only the variable margins of the river's flow, more like a zone than a line because of the bank's slight slope. Archaeological reconstructions of the early layout indicate that the bridge builders took advantage of mid-length dry ground to increase the structural stability of its nearly 800-meter length. I suppose the intelligence of that civil engineering partly explains its survival today as the longest ancient bridge in Europe.

The line that the bridge followed—perhaps it is better to say the line it *laid down*—perpendicular to the sandbar channels continued into the town as the *Decumanus Maximus*, edging the Temple of Diana which faced the *forum*, the *Cardo Maximus* to one side, and then extended to the opposite limit of the city, not terribly far from where the modern Museum would be sited twenty centuries later. The geometry thus inscribed seems to have played a more important role in the construction of Augusta Emerita than the axes and quadrants of the sky. The sun's path is approximately 45 degrees off the geometry of the grid. When judged according to precepts set out in myth,[5] the desired coordination or convergence of parallels and perpendiculars, coupling emblems of sky and soil, was only approximated, which, as the history of Roman city building shows, was often the case.

Construction during the subsequent Visigoth and Moorish periods, when the "Spanish" city developed, resulted in modifications to the pristine plan, partly through benign neglect, which is to say erosion and attrition, and partly through more violent changes, new streets sliced through the fabric and old ones widened or redirected toward new sacred sites, especially Christian temples and meeting houses, which had different ways of binding emblems of what is above and below, but required approach roads and clearings no less than Roman focal points. Despite localized modifications of this kind in subsequent centuries, a pattern of orthogonality can still be seen in the present urban form, as Moneo's analysis and design indicate.

The past that comes into visibility thanks to Moneo's project is thus a story told in a number of chapters: the ancient landform, the Roman settlement, the Gothic or Spanish modifications, and the developments that occurred in more recent centuries. Traces of each narrative invite interpretation, no less today than when Moneo developed his design thirty years ago, for every re-directed street, ruined arch, or broken torso both invites and limits understanding: it is obviously a man's head, but was he an aristocrat or artisan? The clearing in the urban fabric is sized to a sacred building, but did the Christian church seen today build anew on Roman temple foundations, and so on? One task of project making is to accomplish interpretations that answer questions like these, discovering communications or convergence between vestiges from different periods, overcoming confusion without expecting anything like full coincidence.

Moneo's basement-level (crypt) plan will make the problem of convergence clear in a preliminary way. Three distinct sets of parallel lines overlap in the part of the plan that shows where the building edges the pre-existing street, Calle José Ramón Mélida, and reveals a section of an ancient Roman road and nearby houses that have been exposed at the level of the crypt, in ruin of course. The parallels and perpendiculars of the ruins are not as regular as one might expect, nor do they consistently align with the road, which surely provided them with primary orientation; instead, slight inflections disturb the pattern, shifting the angle of a wall, for example, to make room for a doorway wide enough, pinching a corridor to meet the beginning of a short rise of steps, or centering a pool in its atrium not on the line that extends from the entry to the peristyle, and so on, all of which are adjustments that accommodated more perfectly the shape and style of specific domestic requirements than nicely regular forms would have done. Adjustments such as this were authorized by the principle of *decorum* or suitability, which was more important in domestic architecture than geometric regularity or *symmetry*, in the sense of proportionality that governed the layout of temples and civic buildings.[6] When centuries later Alberti, with Roman precedents in mind, discussed the plan forms of domestic and sacred buildings, he said that in houses, apartments, and villas geometric regularity "hardly matters"; much more important for residential plan-making is the appropriateness of the position, shape, and dimension of the several rooms (*fauces, atrium, tablinum, triclinium, peristylium, exedra*, etc.), with some positioned close to the street, others with the right degree of centrality or privacy, and still others properly arranged at the rear, around the garden, open to the sky, facing the family altar.[7]

Yet, when seen at the scale of urban blocks in archaeological surveys and reconstructions, the approximate conformity of the houses to the grid pattern of streets is clearly apparent. Even today, after centuries of adjustments and modifications that no doubt addressed all manner of practical contingencies, the initial urban configuration persists in the pattern of streets, blocks, and major public spaces. Insofar as this site's ensemble of domestic spaces was part of that whole, though extra-mural, one can say it recalls the ancient pattern.

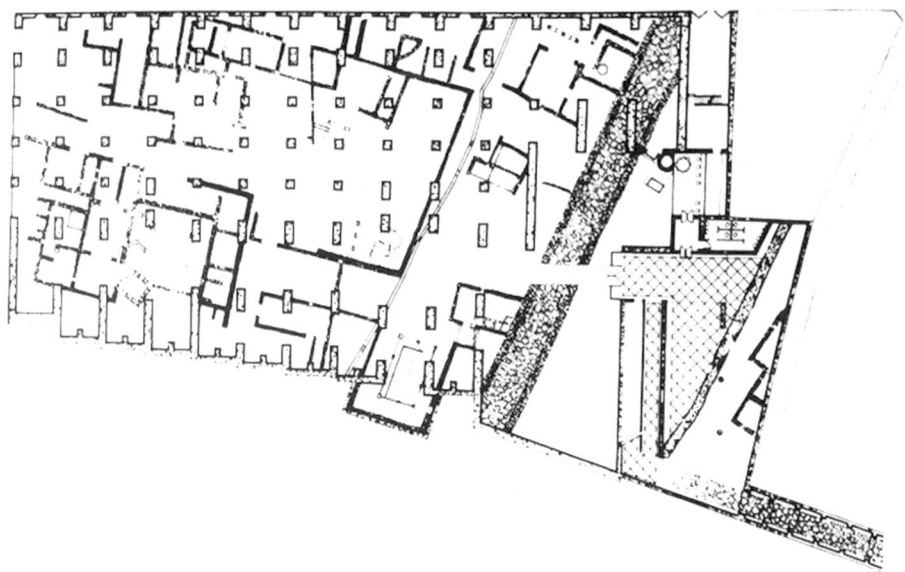

Figure 4.2.5 Rafael Moneo, *National Museum of Roman Art*, Mérida, partial basement plan. © Rafael Moneo.

Figure 4.2.6 Rafael Moneo, *National Museum of Roman Art*, Mérida, aerial view. Photograph David Leatherbarrow.

When compared to the ancient grid, the geometry of the modern town at this particular spot is rather unique. Calle José Ramón Mélida, at the top of which the Museum entry is located, neither aligns with the parallels that repeat the line of the ancient *Cardo Maximus*, nor exactly parallels the line of the nearby fortification wall, though it comes closer to that line, as defined in some archaeological reconstructions, such as the one shown on the Museum's entry door bronze relief. Yet, the angle is not isolated, for another grid of near parallels and perpendiculars extends the block pattern eastward, as if the extra-mural settlement repeated the intra-mural precedent, though misaligned. As a whole, the part of the town engaged by Moneo's "buttress wall" testifies to a history of adjustments, whereby the founding configuration was both repeated and altered, recalling a past that was never really present. One shouldn't conclude that adjusted geometries are inferior to their pristine antecedents simply because they came later, for they are no less a part of the town's past than the foundational moment. Perhaps they are even more vital today, though infrequent objects of tourist appreciation.

Proposing Precedents: Rafael Moneo's Museo Nacional de Arte Romano de Mérida

Figure 4.2.7 Rafael Moneo, *National Museum of Roman Art,* Mérida, bronze relief plan. Photograph David Leatherbarrow.

The Museum's buttress wall roughly parallels the line of façades on the opposite side of the non-Roman road, the Calle José Ramón Mélida, as I have said. The parallelism is approximated bay by bay, in what might be called saw-tooth fashion, along a southeasterly direction, toward the excavated ancient road that runs well below the current street level and extends the line of one of the ancient streets, beneath the location of the ancient fortifications and the modern Calle Mélida. The open court that allows one to view the sub-surface street and ruins is framed by a low wall that terminates the rhythm of bays, but in the absence of a concluding buttress, probably because the flanking wall around the corner offers sufficient resistance to the downward and lateral thrust of the roof at this point. Through the wall's running length, the verticals serve different purposes above and below the street, buttresses above and engaged piers below, each set resisting lateral forces but in opposite directions. These buttress-strengthened bays form the end walls of the Museum's *enfilade* of exhibition rooms—which Moneo somewhat oddly called "pavilions"—a line-up of offspring flanking the parent "pavilion" at the center, arched and sky-lit, a room that has also been called a nave, though Moneo characterized that notion as a "fiction."

The perfect regularity of the side bays, evident in the impressive rhythm of the buttresses and internal bays, is not matched by the lower level walls, however. On either side of the many arches, the walls have been cut down in length, many reduced to the size of piers, so as to trample as little as possible on the ruins, stepping unevenly but carefully through the spread of half walls, mosaic pavements, and pools, resting mostly in open spaces, which were in Roman times peristyles, gardens, alleys, and so on.

This sub-surface system of piers and arches is a second instance of adjustment to the plan's otherwise regular geometry of equally spaced parallel walls extending the ancient grid (the first instance of adjustment was shifting the saw-tooth wall off the right angle, so that it would nearly align with the Calle Mélida and maximize the plan area of the Museum). At the lower level, the basic pattern of parallel walls was modified to reflect two interpretations of the historical remnants: (1) Moneo's crypt walls approximate the regularity of the Roman pattern, perfecting to some degree the geometry of the houses and courtyards, more closely approximating the uniformity of the city plan and (2) they transform the monolithic walls above into a series of arched openings and random-width piers that tread cautiously through the ruins, conforming to their irregularities. Yet, the irregularity that results is neither random nor Piranesian, as has been sometimes said, still less picturesque; in fact, it is no less disciplined than the pattern of parallels above. The difference is that these elements are engaged with conditions that were not generated but revealed by the project, indeed measured by it. At street level, we've noted, there is the other adjustment, the dilation of the plan, bay by bay, to nearly parallel one of the city's non-Roman streets.

But maybe this use of the term *adjustment* badly phrases the sectional convergence of stratified parallels I've described, for that vocabulary takes for granted exactly what must be explained: how Moneo's design and construction disclosed conditions that had unintentionally prepared for their development. The divergence of the house geometry from the line of the exposed Roman road, for example, was unapparent until the piers and arches posed a framework of comparison. Nor would the misalignments between intra- and extra-mural grids have been so legible without Moneo's dilated plan, coinciding geometrically with the extra-mural system on one side and the Gothic street on the other. More surprisingly, perhaps, Moneo's arrangement of parallel walls, apparent in the buttress rhythm outside and the *enfilade* inside, exposed the *rectangularity* of the ancient grid.

Despite our casual use of the terms "grid" and "checkerboard" for ancient Roman plans like Augusta Emerita's, these blocks are not square. Reconstructions show that the sides of the ancient blocks that paralleled the *Cardo* were longer than those in line with the *Decumanus*. The same orientation can be seen in the geometry of the ancient city's two major public spaces. Moreover, the intervals between the parallels vary. Ostensibly a grid, the formal and tectonic principles of the Roman town seem to have been orthogonality and wall construction only, nothing more, notwithstanding the use of trabeation in the temple buildings, based on Greek precedents. My thesis is that these aspects of "the past" are apparent today thanks to Moneo's interpretation, not because the Museum he designed houses remnants but because its basic form reveals them, at the scale of the street, block, and town.

First Ernesto Rogers, then Vittorio Gregotti, spoke of the project's given site as a set of "pre-existing conditions," which, they argued, designs should acknowledge, even though they also transform them.[8] The notion will be unhelpful and distort the reality of project making if the implied sense of "givenness" assumes an obvious matter of fact, already existing in its own right, to which contemporary thinking can turn. Conditions such as those in Mérida were not matters of fact given to Moneo but newly exposed by him, or his project, having been previously overlooked, therefore unknown—perhaps never to be known. While extreme, perhaps, one can say that these dimensions of the past were produced by the project, for others could have been revealed and these ignored, left slumbering beneath the soil, or quietly lending a hand to some significant player in the modern life of the town—a "dance of dead things" as Sverre Fehn said of the ruins beneath his Museum at Hamar.[9] Layers of past building forms had sedimented themselves on the site and were waiting to be reactivated by a project. Prior to that moment, they were unobserved, as is so much of the past because we are much more commonly concerned with the present, inevitably so. Yet, the forward movement of design and construction had a retroactive effect on what preceded it, transforming it, showing it to be what it wasn't—now relevant—though it also appears to be exactly what it had been. Past and present co-determine one another in light of the project's anticipations. Moneo's work also brought to light a past more ancient than the Roman, the parallel river channels that once cut through the land.

All these parallels, the river banks, streets, blocks, and walls approximate the regularity the modern project has set out, despite the fact that their divergences also affected the new layout. Time after time, the past that seems to have prepared the project was revealed by it.

As long as pre-existing conditions are seen as categorically distinct from present circumstances, the doubly projective power of project making—disclosing its past and constructing its future—will remain obscure. The several periods I have noted, pre-Roman, Roman, Visigoth, Moorish, and modern, preceded the present; there's no doubt about that, those pasts had passed. Centuries of damage and erosion, through natural processes as well as human initiative or brutality, have left us with remains that show as much age, fatigue, and weariness as grandeur and beauty. Yet, while their times are no longer, the remnants from the several chapters of the city's history persist and are now visibly present because they were brought into relief by Moneo's project, thanks to which they can also be seen as pretexts, preparations, or first premises for its development. Cities of the past, like Augusta Emerita, remain present—the past is present—just not present in the same way as the cities in which we live currently. As an outgrowth of the present, the project reconfigures the landscape in which it finds its place, bringing into relief sedimented dimensions of earlier periods that obtain new relevance and unprecedented visibility thanks to that very reconfiguration.

Time and Again

Remnants from the past survive in two ways in the Mérida Museum: exposed and exhibited. Those that have been uncovered below street level survive as *in situ* remains, at rest in their home environment, though barely able to stand on their own. Those that are displayed above street level as archived fragments have been removed from the several sites in the city where they had resided, repatriated one might say, for their own good those in charge will argue, collected, organized, and exhibited on the walls, floors, and pedestals of the "pavilions," large and small. The second manner of survival takes advantage of the system of walls and arches, while the first qualifies it. Arches we learned in the crypt can increase in number and walls can be cut or lengthened to form irregularly sized piers. With these two manners of survival come two interpretations of the "Roman" walls. Above they are perfectly matched parallels, each opened by an identically sized and shaped arch and arrayed along a single centering line, under skylights and extending laterally as far as the site will allow. Below, the walls have been built as piers plus arches, the former varied in length, rather like the walls of the ruins themselves, which are also, we've seen, slightly misaligned with the road to which they were oriented.

In consideration of these two interpretations of the walls, a simple question presents itself: does the project present us with different styles of thought above and below the street level? Is there one kind of thinking at street level, within the great archive, and another below, where the arches spread themselves among the rubble walls, faded colors, and uneven soil? The contrast between sharply defined shadows above and indistinct

Proposing Precedents: Rafael Moneo's Museo Nacional de Arte Romano de Mérida 195

Figure 4.2.8 Rafael Moneo, *National Museum of Roman Art,* Mérida, museum interior. Photograph David Leatherbarrow.

shades below would also seem to suggest two ways of thinking about spatial character. Do the adjustments of the simple pattern to existing conditions below compromise the clarity, rationality, or radiance of the building above? Is the crypt landscape home to an architecture of exigency and chance, in which decisions are negotiable, methods pliant, and outcomes yielding? Would the first, the elevated architecture that limits its deployments to just a few elements and a set of simple rules, constitute the essence of the project, and the second, its lower antithesis, consist of a set of compromises and

Figure 4.2.9 Rafael Moneo, *National Museum of Roman Art,* Mérida, basement level. Photograph David Leatherbarrow.

distortions? Or is there a conception of project making that allows *variation within repetition*, making this not two projects but one?

"The dialectic of repetition is easy," Søren Kierkegaard observed, "for that which is repeated has been—otherwise it could not be repeated—but the very fact that it has been gives to repetition the character of novelty."[10] In this passage and more generally in his philosophical writings, he was not concerned with architecture, of course, but with ethical life, decisions, and conduct, especially among friends, but also among two people in love, married or not. "Does he actually love the girl, or is she not once again simply the occasion that sets his passions in motion? ... The split in him caused by his contact with her would be reconciled by his actually having returned to her."[11] The *return* the lover considers, the *once again* Kierkegaard asks about, is a surprisingly complex problem. Is a return even possible? Has she not changed? Him too? To whom (or in architecture what) would one return? Following what sort of prompt might a revisit occur, and with what kind of expectation? Every lover or friend knows that the mere repetition of a gesture is a very dull thing, an act without passion or commitment, essentially mechanical. Another sort, one wants to believe, can result in passionate engagement. But how? In marriage, the spouse returns to the same person time and again, daily and nightly, as the years pass. That unending return is an ethical act, fulfilling a commitment made long ago, no less binding if what was said then is now forgotten. Can pleasure, can aesthetic experience, also result from going back? Or do the desire and delight of a first love necessarily recede when revisited repeatedly? There is no doubt that what is sought has been lost, for an act that follows is never the same as the one that preceded it, though it is not wholly different either. If everything aimed at in repetition has been, then everything repeated has not. The difficulty is to know how a return, revisiting, or recounting can discover the engagement and passion that defined the initial act.

How can two or more elements in a building, or in buildings, be neither wholly the same nor entirely different? How can repetitive geometries or forms be instances of what was then and what is now, equally engaged and engaging, despite the fact that times are no longer what they once were?

Let's consider again the bays in Moneo's buttress wall, more specifically, each of the extended wall-ends and engaged piers. Obviously, they repeat themselves, but is each the same as all the others? Considering minute variations, one could equally well ask: are they different in each instance? Or, more sensibly, taking a customary view of things, are they merely similar?[12] Each element has been constructed again and again according to the dimensions and geometries that were set out on the drawings, which also intended specific construction procedures: piers of this plan shape and size, non-load bearing brick cladding over reinforced concrete, and so on. Each of the elements was to be the same, no matter whether it was built first or last. But again, is that what we have in fact? Is the first buttress at the lower end the same as the one that engages the wall around the lower-level court? In point of fact, there isn't one at the lower corner; the side wall at the top of the sidewalk steps turns 90 degrees onto Calle Mélida without a buttressing wall-end extension. We saw the same alteration at the opposite end, where the saw-tooth wall meets the enclosure of the sunken court. At each end, then, the run of buttresses begins at the mid-span of a bay. The first and last buttresses are unlike all those in-between. Illogical though it may seem, the desire to repeat makes this variation both plain and inevitable.

What about the verticals at the higher elevation: are they the same as those that rise from lower terrain? In plan yes, but in elevation certainly not. The lower are undeniably more robust, less "gothic," not so tall as those at the opposite end, farther up the slope, where they approach the entry. Topographical knowledge is the result: the varying height of the buttresses discloses a dimension of the pre-existing conditions that may

Figure 4.2.10 Rafael Moneo, *National Museum of Roman Art,* Mérida, external buttresses. Photograph David Leatherbarrow.

Figure 4.2.11 Rafael Moneo, *National Museum of Roman Art,* Mérida, terminal buttress and sunken court. Photograph David Leatherbarrow.

well have been overlooked, the fact that the Museum's entrance surmounts rising terrain. The varying pier widths in the crypt served an equivalent function, enhancing one's sense of the difference between private and public architecture in the ancient city.

Maybe the question concerning repetition becomes clearer if the phrase we've just used is abbreviated, not time and again, but simply again. Following Kierkegaard, we should replace reiteration with alteration; the series should allow *again and not-again*. The unexpected thesis is this: something repeated or done again is best or most perfect when it has something different about it, as is true for any occasion that's really unforgettable. The least memorable event is the one that went according to plan. The result of something unplanned or unexpected is not a reassuring, comforting sameness, but a rather more interesting or striking deviation from the norm. Do the crypt pier variations show neglect for the rules of the game, or does their "crude reality" catch the project's hidden essence that repetition requires variation thanks to the very discipline that defines it? Should we not say, following Kierkegaard, that *another* time is *an-other* time? The second never returns to the first, for that one is gone. The initial act, that first passionate encounter, occurred some time ago, then, which means now it can no longer be what it was. But nor can it have ended without leaving some trace, something to be uncovered, for then no relationship of any kind would be possible, let alone the sort of repetition that rekindles passion or refashions engagement. Might the architectural element that ostensibly repeats another always be different in some way, not the same, similar?

The word *again* has an instructive cognate, *against*. Contrariety is obvious in the second. Might it not also exist in the first? *Again* has the German *gegen* (opposite) in its word family, both are analogous to versus. Again and again should be understood as one repetitive element *versus* the next. Repetition exists in the Mérida Museum in two senses: serial arrangement of "identical" elements and doing again what was done before. In the first instance, one arch is designed to be the same as another nearby, but we've seen that's not true. In the second instance, each is equivalent to the one that came before. But Moneo's parallel walls are not the same as the orthogonal patterns that preceded his project, neither the Gothic nor the Roman. And what is true for the building's arches is also at play in the town's streets, not just in the ancient, but the subsequent urban forms, each of them built time and time again, now as before, but neither the same nor different. Perhaps one should regard variation as more rational than mechanical repetition, for it can be the way the project makes its principles of order apparent in given circumstances. After all efforts toward strict repetition have been made, surely the variations that are required to realize the work have a necessary part to play in the project, so do the unforeseen enrichments they may bring.

If this preliminary conclusion can be granted, the next question concerns the conditions that grant the passage from presumed sameness to similarity, somewhere short of difference. Is this passage granted by the design, or is it administered on the site, ruled by the hands of the builders and the physical properties of the soil and climate? No skilled builder seeks difference for its own sake, no matter whether it is arches or piers that are being made. Maybe the issue is otherwise with chairs and beds. In architecture, when individual sites are part of the work's "crude reality," skilled labor consists in approximating the same by means of the different, resulting, I've said, in elements that are similar, to varying degrees.

Is similarity so defined external to the project, the outcome of compromises one should have avoided? If so, we would once again be faced with the opposition between the design idea and the constructed fact, mediated by the drawing which I've said preserves the dichotomy we are trying to overcome. What must be understood is how every act of building is not deviation from the initial idea but its clarification.

No Longer and Not Yet

Apart from a few monuments, such as the theaters, aqueducts, and temple fragments, little of the Augusta Emerita the Romans knew is visible today, for the early settlement was buried under layers of subsequent development. Depending on your sense of project making, or more basically construction, the developments that followed the Roman can be seen as either elaborations or deviations. For my part, I'm not entirely sure the two are essentially distinct. Similarly, Moneo's initial, intuitive, architectonic conception is nowhere to be seen, unless one studies his drawings, for the lines and angles that appear there never show themselves in the built work; they are "buried" under layers of construction materials, the concrete, brick, glass, and steel of the finished building. Nevertheless, the project, like each Mérida that appeared after the Roman, was prepared by what preceded it.

Figure 4.2.12 Rafael Moneo, *National Museum of Roman Art,* Mérida, basement stair, ruins, and bridge. Photograph David Leatherbarrow.

Despite the foresight of its designers and builders, the outcome of construction must have been something of a surprise, surprisingly big for some residents, cavernous for archivists, or singular for the architect. I believe the wonder results from the fact that the pre-existing circumstances into which the project was placed had not been seen as its preparation until the construction brought their potential into visibility, generative though passive, a silent and secret pre-communication on which the work depended just as its articulations exceeded it. I've said above that the past has passed. While that is not wrong, it doesn't mean that it isn't also present in some way, for if not there would be nothing against which the presentness of the project could be judged. The past is present incompletely, as traces or remnants of once-vital conditions that have over time, through varying combinations of neglect and violence, deposited their patterns into the body of the landscape. Such a matrix was necessary for the project, but is insufficient to explain it. Its partiality opened the site to future possibilities that it could not have given in advance. The parallels of Moneo's project do, in fact, align those of the town, but they also compact them more closely together, improbably one can say, transforming a two-way grid into a system of bays that are suitable for archiving or warehousing. The town had prepared this "condensation," but did not expect it. What had been preserved was surpassed. Nevertheless, what it became revealed what it had been. More generally, the prospective dimension of projects brings the past into being. Projects crystalize conditions that had been previously unseen. Mérida believed it had a great Roman past, but what it understood was merely extrapolated from visible remnants; it lacked an intelligible and legible image of what once was. Such an image is what the project produced. Accordingly, projects do not "continue" the time that preceded them, but break from it, in order to show what the past actually had been.

Memory is dictated by human interests and therefore finds its origin in the present. Fragments had broken through the surface of the Mérida soil for centuries. Moneo's project unfolded in engagements with these fragments and others, torn rags of a fabric that no longer fit daily life. Implicit in them, misfits though they were, was an architectonic conception he felt was capable of clarifying the beauty and sense they once had, but only when compared with today's near equivalents.

4.3
Recalling Future Projects: Pezo von Ellrichshausen's Poli House

The now [is] the inmost image of what has been.
WALTER BENJAMIN, *THE ARCADES PROJECT*, c. 1930

The time of the project: what might this phrase mean? What phase or period defines the full temporal span of a design's development and conclusion? Is it the time of thinking, when basic premises are sought, discovered, and decided, or of drawing, when primary intentions are rendered visible, to the architect and others? If a choice seems unwise, maybe it is best to think of project time including both the first and the second. Then again, wouldn't the full span also include the time after the work gets built, possibly even all those years before it is torn down or falls to ruin? After all, it is only when construction has been concluded that the project's aims become palpably evident for everyone to see, in actual spaces and materials. Previously, we noted Rafael Moneo's unwillingness to neglect "the crude reality of built works" when defining the architectural project. That reality is, he said, the project's essence. Whatever its length—one, two, or three phases—the time of the project is surely *time to come*, for the word's stem, *projectum*, means something *thrown ahead*. Symmetrically opposite is the time before, into which a designer's thinking can sometimes be drawn regressively. But that sort of movement seems entirely misdirected; projects do not advance backward. Retreat's reward seems rarely if ever victory.

It is not only time's direction but duration that matters in project making, the weeks and months, sometimes years of growth and development in thinking, drawing, and building. But there is also the time of occupation or inhabitation. Might the decades that post-date construction likewise be included in project time, the phases of use and misuse, then renovation, restoration, or conservation, which variously but inevitably contend with initial impulses, even when their efforts, well intentioned though they may be, result in betrayal? Today's fast-track projects are different only in the sense that they unfold in shorter spans of time. They too advance through these same stages, eventually succeeding or failing in ways an architect can only partly foresee.

From Time to Time

Is there really no role for the thinking that preceded the project when its advance is designed or discussed, no yesterday in mind when tomorrow is imagined? Might the past persist implicitly? Could it play an important role without attracting notice? Initially, I have in mind something very simple, the use of familiar vocabulary in design discussions, language whose use doesn't require attention to its origins, despite the fact it has a history. Today we still speak of geometries, proportions, and composition when evaluating contemporary projects, reiterating terms and concepts that have been used by architects for centuries. Why is that? Is it a lazy habit of mind, or a way of quietly assuring ourselves that the work under consideration is not only contemporary but comparable to works from the past, which is to say, *architectural*? Could we assess the modernity of the modern without using the past as its frame of reference? When Louis I. Kahn famously asked "How'm I doing, Corbusier?"[1] he both assumed and affirmed his standing within a history that pre-dated his own work, a disciplinary inheritance that not only posed specifically architectural problems, but depended on the projects he was developing for its renewal.

Historical ground was there for Kahn—beneath his feet so to speak—but it was not something he felt he could take for granted.[2] Another of his aphorisms was emphatic on this point: "architecture," he said, "really does not exist. Only a work of architecture exists."[3] If not here today must it be imagined, can it be remembered? Does the second prompt the first? In design what role is played by traces of past architectures (built, photographed, or drawn)? Are they not the material equivalent to inherited language? I don't think Kahn ever doubted that the past had an important role to play in the drama of architecture's modernization. But it is also true to say that throughout his life he wondered what exactly that contribution might be. For him—no doubt for most moderns—the past was a foreign country.[4] Yet his imagination took him there, more than a few times, given the many reports in his essays and lectures, notes and sketches. Like all of us, he traveled in two worlds, material and imaginary, jumping through centuries each time. But his backward glances toward Rome, Egypt, or rural America opened onto no more than vestiges of civilizations, partially grasped fragments that were objects of desire as much as understanding, a past, I think one can say, that never existed, despite the intellectual force and hard definition of his travel drawings.

Architecture had to be rediscovered, he thought, first because it had been lost and second because it hadn't yet arrived. Along the line of time, symmetrical vectors extended from a mid-point understood as *architecture-not-at-this-moment*. One arrow pointed backward toward what once was and the other toward what was still to come. But what kind of line is this, composed of double vectors originating in a moment that was by definition uncertain, architecture's *not now*? More importantly, how could understanding or project making base itself on three uncertainties, architecture not

Figure 4.3.1 Louis I. Kahn, *Study for a Mural Based on Egyptian Motifs*, no. 1, 1951. Courtesy of Sue Ann Kahn/Art Resource, New York.

now, no longer, and not yet? These doubts about project time recall Saint Augustine's famous confession cited earlier: "What then is time? If nobody asks me, I know; if I must explain it to those who question me, I do not know."[5]

Linear thinking, the mental process that is commonly supposed to follow a line of development, seems out of place when starting points are unstable and both origins and ends are in principle unreachable. Might repetitions or cycles, movements that reactivate sedimented themes give us a better sense of what Kahn understood to be the project's fate and promise? What the philosopher Edmund Husserl said of himself—he was a perpetual beginner—can be said of an architect working projectively, pursuing *a quest without an object*. Kahn moved *towards* an architecture because in his judgment it didn't exist at the time. Yet he also felt that *an architecture* could only be imagined through specific buildings.

Defined in this way, the time of the project, the circling, synchronizes retreats with advances. What's more, each required a departure from the supposed present moment. Thus, it is not surprising that Kahn frequently addressed the issue of beginnings. Viewing inception as a task rather than a premise, he called the project's beginning a search for *volume zero* or *minus one*. Again, the ground seems to be slipping away. On the face of it, the effort seems ill-considered, adding by subtracting, or backing forward. Unfazed by the contradiction, his procedure was as follows: "The problem was a monastery. We began by assuming that no monastery existed ... We had to forget the word monk, the word refectory, the word chapel, the cell."[6] Methodologically, one wants to take him seriously, but that's not easy. The historical type he sought to renounce was obviously invoked in that very renunciation. The key point, though, is that the negation of terms and ideas from the past—more simply, the past as something negative: not now—who knows when—set the stage for design development. I suppose he believed that getting lost in language was a way of finding something previously unsaid. Each problem in Kahn's academic studio and professional office was an opportunity for students, teachers, and designers to reactivate the project by reversing the roles of the clear and the obscure, taking the second as the basis for achieving the first. What, they asked, is a room, a window, or a wall as if they didn't already know.

The wager seems to have been this: in the half-light of suspended certainties one can begin the serious and playful work of renewing primary premises. Here two senses of the word "primary" are implied, chiefly important and prior, interweaving ontological conditions with temporal dimensions. In the terms used earlier, moving forward required going backward, to the time before understanding was reduced to current assumptions, the time when more plausible premises might have existed. The unreachable destination of such a return could be called *a beginning of the beginning*.[7] While radically preliminary, it was a start that looked forward to its end. When seen together, the opposite directions functioned as *anticipated hindsight*. "I try to look at my work," Kahn said, "with a sense of what is forthcoming. The yet not said, yet not made," for that, he advised, is what "puts the sparks of life into you."[8]

Was he alone in following this path of non-linear double movement in project making? Can *retrograde headway* be seen in the drawings and writings of modernism's most famous proponent, the one against whom Kahn measured his own "progress?" Despite old stories about the single-mindedly progressive aims of architecture's *avant garde*,[9] Le Corbusier's advance out of the recent past into the modern world was always complemented by retreat toward the places and times of ancient even archaic culture, mythical though stories about them no doubt were. To confirm the claim, one need only cite the photos, sketches, and stories of the Capitoline Hill, Notre Dame, Pompeian houses, Parthenon, Turkish villages, and the Brittany shore that fill the pages of *Precisions* and *Towards an Architecture*, to say nothing of the sketchbooks.

Are his documentary findings credible, more so than Kahn's? Were they to him? Today, no one doubts that his buildings show the influence of his travels back in time,

Figure 4.3.2 Le Corbusier, *Parthenon*, sketch. © F.L.C./ADAGP, Paris/Artists Rights Society (ARS), New York 2019.

as do his paintings and prints, *Le Poème de l'Angle Droit*, for example.[10] The writings are particularly explicit about his retrospective habit of mind. In the published version of his South American lectures, *Precisions*, he admitted to turning away from the modern world's "unquiet life … of incessant anxieties" toward the architecture and cultures of the past. "I shall confess to you that I have had only one teacher: the past; only one education: the study of the past. Everything, for a long time, and still today: museums, travels, folk art … it is in the past that I found … the reasons for being of things."[11] Although this last phrase suggests that the retreat discovered solid ground, much of his study involved inference, surmise, and guesswork—also hyperbole, as is typical for him. Perhaps guesswork in this type of inquiry is inevitable. Insofar as his objects of study were remote in time, they were also fragmentary, in many cases mute—silent witnesses I've said. The foundation for project making thus provided was no less unstable than Kahn's. Could this be true for *avant garde* architecture generally, that it was and still is today an edifice built on the shifting soil of historical fiction?[12]

A third prominent modern, who followed a comparable curriculum, contributed corroborating evidence a few years earlier: "I am a modern architect," wrote Adolf Loos, "because I build in the manner of the ancient Viennese."[13] Less a confession than a claim, Loos made the statement in defense of his controversial project at the center of old Vienna. It seems the matter of history was inescapable in a design on Michaelerplatz, for the square had been disfigured, he argued, by imported-style architecture. Something different, something evidently contemporary was required. Yet, like Kahn and Le Corbusier, he sought to move modern architecture forward by simultaneously taking it backward, circling back, against the grain of the recent historicist inheritance, into more distant traditions that had been lost sight of, proceeding back through the ideas and work of Semper, Schinkel, and Schülter into the (fictional) ground on which they stood. But in his case, too, the grounds (reasons) that he reached were articulated in myth. He read some of the stories and invented others: "Let me take you to a rural scene."[14]

Although visions of this kind hardly seem progressive, still less *modern*, it was to the past that Loos, like Kahn and Le Corbusier, regularly turned, despite the latter's no less common advocacy of *l'Esprit Nouveau*. The sketches, surveys, and statements of these and other moderns speak for themselves and do so more loudly than the assertions of apologists for a progressive modernism, including the manifestos of the movement's protagonists.

Conversations with past architectures naturally extended in the opposite direction, into discussions of designs to be built. The back and forth was never *viva voce*, of course. The past, having passed, could not answer back. Ancient interlocutors, I've said, played the role of silent witnesses. Communication was not therefore ended, only strained.

Past forms had sedimented themselves in the soil on which (out of which) modern architecture was being built, present, one can say, but latent. Keeping the conversation going meant deciphering what was intended, struggling to grasp the sense of what had survived in traces. In this work, there was as much rewriting as reading, all of it a benevolent form of betrayal, as Aldo Rossi once said of forgetfulness.

There was also desire. Kahn's question to Le Corbusier was undeniably competitive, but it also expressed a longing for involvement in the larger project Le Corbusier had pursued. The same desire can be sensed in Kahn's self-comparisons with Palladio and Rome, a wish to take up their questions. For modern architects with non-dogmatic minds, history's reticence attracted passionate inquiry. Who among the moderns who still interest us today did not say both yes and no to work from the past, grounding their new architecture in anteceding examples, in history broadly conceived, the unexplored possibilities of which were discovered, developed, and surpassed by their own proposals? When one observes the continuity of the modern period from its beginnings to our present moment, one views a history that thoroughly absorbed pre-modern traditions. *Ground* in these instances is perhaps best thought of with the French not German equivalent in mind: not *grund* as reason, but *fond* as fund, reserve, or depth.

The architects whose work I will examine closely in this chapter have also had an ear for history's silent presence in today's architecture. In *Spatial Structure*, Mauricio Pezo and Sofia von Ellrichshausen describe the historical continuity of "architectonic culture" as more or less self-evident: "For sure there must be some ... ancient wisdom festered into every new building one can think of."[15] *Every new building*, by this do they mean there is a historical dimension in both the individual project and the discipline as a whole? The answer depends on how one understands the term *architectonic culture*. Surely that culture, an offspring of its more inclusive parent, is not defined by observable buildings only, historical or modern, for as Kahn said, project making is *a quest without an object*. Past architectures, these architects suggest, never play more than a tacit role in today's designs: "We assume the production of a new building as what it is; as the naïve attempt of inventing an original artifact, of bringing something new to our known world. Therefore, we have been explicit about our refusal to use any reference for what we do." Here we seem to be presented, yet again, with high-grade progressive modernism, a strategy and stance of renunciation.

But Pezo von Ellrichshausen have also observed that "there is an undeniable culture that infiltrates in what we see, in what we think and make." The decisive qualification follows next: that culture "is no more than a general background, an intellectual substratum, a kind of soft memory."[16] Direct references to the past are absent, but ancient wisdom has undeniable force, being neither fully present nor nothing. What can be said further about this "soft memory" and its force in project making? These questions take us, I believe, to the heart of project making, especially when it is understood as a dimension of building time.

Bloodlines

In *Joseph and His Brothers*, Thomas Mann described the moment when a father once saw his wife's face in their son's expression, a lovely sight in itself that was made more so because it appeared to him after she had died. Recognition of the likeness was granted by the moonlight, a source that was itself indebted. Unmistakable though it was, the resemblance couldn't be explained, rather like the son's past and future dream interpretations. Perhaps this instance of something deeply familiar though undeniably absent was anticipated in the novel's very first sentence: "Very deep is the well of the past. Should we not call it bottomless? … For the deeper we sound, the further down into the lower world of the past we probe and press, the more do we find that the earliest foundations of humanity, its history and culture, reveal themselves unfathomable."[17] Intensely personal though it was, Jacob's conversation with Rachel was in point of fact impossible, which is what makes Mann's story so beautifully puzzling.

A comparable sense of images that are strangely familiar can be discerned, I think, in the *soundings* that are attempted in all architectural projects, at least those that merit the name.[18] With whom from the past do architects converse? We've seen that Kahn, Le Corbusier, and Loos turned toward both masters and nameless builders. That's not all. They also talked to themselves. Problems that had bothered them for years always seemed to need still more discussion, thought, and work. Resumption of the inquiry was necessary because convincing answers hadn't yet been found and new problems were rather different from those that had come before. Self-doubt seems to have entered into the continuation of old tasks, also frank assessments of recent accomplishments and failures, and a willingness to abandon reliable premises for the sake of possible ways forward. It is interesting, though not primarily important, that a building they had designed for a site in Spain provided Pezo von Ellrichshausen with a key to solving a problem they faced again in their Guna House project: "[the] supporting podium in a single corner [of the Guna House] is the evolution of a previous house we built in Spain some years ago."[19] More significant than the similarity of the projects, I think, is the single theme the two designs addressed. It could be called

Recalling Future Projects: Pezo von Ellrichshausen's Poli House

Figure 4.3.3 Pezo von Ellrichshausen, *Casa Guna*, San Pedro, Chile. Courtesy of Pezo von Ellrichshausen.

Figure 4.3.4 Pezo von Ellrichshausen, *Casa Solo*, Cretas, Spain. Courtesy of Pezo von Ellrichshausen.

the podium problem. In brief, the question was this: should the incline of the site be structured (cut or capped) as one or a number of platforms, a single or several levels for entry, inhabitation, viewing the distance, surmounting the slope, and so on?[20]

Many, though not all the sites Pezo von Ellrichshausen have been given, were sloped. In response, their projects adopted either of two siting strategies: rising above the fall of the terrain, as did Lina Bo Bardi with the Casa de Vidro, or slicing into it, as did Mies van der Rohe with the Tugendhat Villa. The first way of working can be seen in the Sota, Abba, Guna, and Solo houses, for example, and the second in the Gago, Faro, Arco, Cien, Fosc, and Poli designs. Both approaches lead to the multiplication of platforms, below, within, or above the building's basic volume. Another way to think of this is to view each of these buildings as a very big stairway with each of its platforms (inside or out) serving the function of a landing, connected to others and the wider milieu by a few intermediate steps, so that the building-stairway continues the approach and extends the departure. The architects have suggested as much in a comment they offered about the Cien House: "Decisive coincidences such as the number of steps on a hill path nearby, an old cypress …, or even the elevation above sea level that defines [the] podium can explain this building's silhouette."[21] Well, at least partly. The stairway sense of the section, its continuity within and outside the building's proper limits, allows the work involvement with dimensions of the ambient surround that are not properly its own.

The role of this theme and others like it can be seen in the account the architects have given of the origins of their Casa Poli, 2005, located in Coliumo, Chile, the project on which I will chiefly focus. In an interview about the building from a few years ago, they explained that the remote site gave them "the sensation [they] could go as far back as possible to the roots of making architecture."[22] *As far back as possible to the roots*, when is that? And is it a prior or primary condition? Unlike the moderns I've mentioned, Pezo von Ellrichshausen rarely point to the ideas and buildings of their predecessors when describing their works. Nor do they dwell on origin myths, though they have cited the well-known Vitruvian tale.[23] Yet, a chain of references can be followed in their writing and work, linkages with the same double vectors we've seen in Kahn, Le Corbusier, and Loos. The connections are already evident in their understanding of architectonic culture: "Every case has led to the next." But again like Kahn, a circular not linear form can be traced. The symbol they chose to express the sequence is the windmill: "As soon as a blade [the single design] points down the next one appears, cancelling the previous one and dragging a seemingly lack of originality, perhaps protected by that very fact that seems to be our project."[24] Let us, then, follow the blades forward and backward, into the time of the project they call their own.

Recalling Future Projects: Pezo von Ellrichshausen's Poli House 213

Figure 4.3.5 Lina Bo Bardi, *Casa de Vidro*, São Paulo, Brazil. Photograph David Leatherbarrow.

Figure 4.3.6 Mies van der Rohe, *Villa Tugendhat*, Brno, Czech Republic. Photograph David Leatherbarrow.

Figure 4.3.7 Pezo von Ellrichshausen, *Poli House*, Coliumo, Chile, view from cliff. Photograph David Leatherbarrow.

Figure 4.3.8 Pezo von Ellrichshausen, *Poli House*, Coliumo, Chile, roof. Photograph David Leatherbarrow.

Intentions

There is no architectural project without an intention to act in the world of everyday life, sometimes acting within that world's familiar arrangements and forms, sometimes against them. Pezo von Ellrichshausen distinguish two types of intention, explicit and tacit, or consciously understood and unthinkingly assumed. These two types are developed within conditions or *grounds* that are correspondingly internal and external to the project.[25] Among the external conditions and pressures that shape architectural intentions are the many and varied contingencies of circumstance, the pressures of statics and aesthetics, they say, also physical and cultural loads. These conditions have the status of facts and the force of requirements, unavoidable in the first case, imposed in the second. For many people, in and outside architecture, this domain is named *reality*. Distinct from these types of conditions are those that are specific to architecture itself—one might say those of its own reality—not the problems buildings are designed to overcome, but architecture itself as a problem. These are the internal, disciplinary, or *architectonic* themes and questions that projects repeatedly address. Although clearly opposed, external and internal conditions, together with their associated intentions, are bound together in designs and buildings. But other questions must be addressed if the nature of *the architectonic project* so defined is to be properly understood, especially its peculiar temporality.

When it is said that a project's internal intentions are understood and assumed or made explicit in thought and allowed to remain tacit in action, two forms of thinking are distinguished: "deliberate" and "naïve." The sense Pezo von Ellrichshausen have given to the deliberate sort of intentions is not hard to grasp, they are the aims that one *has in mind*, that are *held in thought* and are *transparent* to oneself. And they are forward-looking: "It is obvious that there are no conceivable intentions for the past."[26] We've seen something like this already: projects, we said at the beginning, do not advance backward.

Separate from aims of this deliberative sort are intentions these architects have called naïve. They are not as easy to understand as the deliberative type. First, though no less forceful they are far less apparent. The relationship seems one of inverse

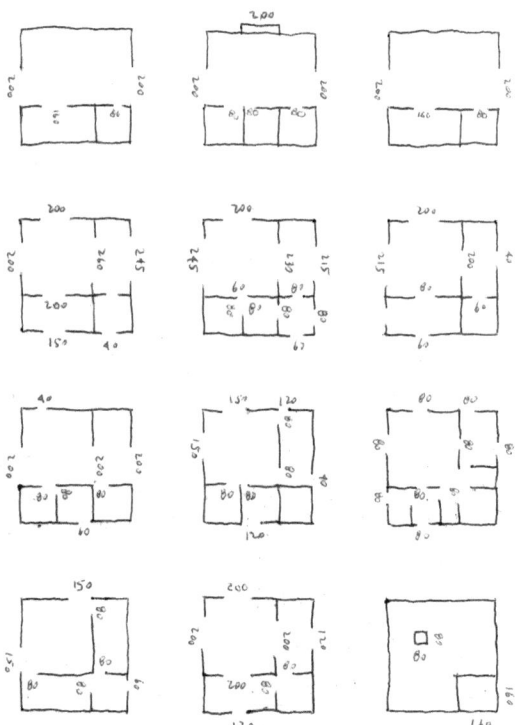

Figure 4.3.9 Pezo von Ellrichshausen, *Cien House*, Concepción, Chile, plan studies. Courtesy of Pezo von Ellrichshausen.

proportionality: the more obvious, the less consequential; the less evident, the more effective. Second, along the temporal register, naïve intentions exist prior to the design's beginning and are brought to it, having been previously shaped or formed through practice. A good comparison is with the acquisition of habits, which are not natural, having been formed, but over time come to seem so, which is why Aristotle called them second nature. What seems so natural hardly requires steady attention. Third, embodied knowledge of this kind is opaque to reflective thought. In *Spatial Structure*, the architects write of a "pre-linguistic" and "non-propositional" knowledge based on corporeal experience.[27] An example might be the kind of knowledge possessed by fingers on a keyboard, or by hands and arms that are good with a baseball bat or tennis racket. Embodied intentions accomplish their aims unreflectively, with neither premeditation nor focused regard, passively one can say. Much recent study in the sciences and philosophy traces the diffusion of knowledge into the body, providing us with many instances of what is typically called manual or motor intelligence.

Unremarkable in their performance, corporeal powers are known best after the fact of their exercise, in hindsight, through which, thankfully, they can be modified. Self-education takes this form, as does academic teaching. The outcome is rather like the *manners* described by sixteenth-century art theorists, in the sense of Leonardo's manner of drawing, when compared to Michelangelo's or Raphael's, or one's own handwriting style compared to a friend's. Each manner is accrued through repetitive practice, *sedimented* in muscles, that is by this means prepared for repeated use, rather like a fund or reserve upon which one can draw. In due course, tendencies develop into something like a settled disposition. In architecture, such a disposition shows itself as the inclination toward a certain kind of form. Kahn's fisted-pencil, for example, was inclined toward orthogonal geometries and bi-lateral symmetries. No doubt he thought about these preferences now and then, but certainly not all the time. If he spent all his time *deliberating* intentions, nothing would ever get done—not even started.

A third player also takes part in this naïve sort of work: the pencil and hand work together with the eye as a source of judgment—the mannerist *giudizio dell'occhio*—that is no less habituated than the fisted-pencil, nor necessarily deliberative, in the reflective sense of the word. When reviewing project documents, the drawings that look right to a trained architect often are, which is to say, discovered to make more and more sense when studied further. That initial judgment wasn't authorized by deliberative thought, but was decisive nonetheless. Moreover, its subsequent role in design and criticism will have been essential. By virtue of the passivity and anonymity of habituated practices and judgments, a dark spot impenetrable to reflective thought takes up residence within the office of project making. Although it might seem a "weakness" at the heart of design, naïve intentions always play a role in the beginning of the beginning. Insofar as it is through an architect's drawings that a disposition toward form is apparent, it is perhaps ironic that unthinking, non-deliberative, and anonymous practices define personal style. Freud said much the same thing about the basis for unintended (naively motivated) expressions, those slips of the tongue that reveal one's real inclinations.

Once acquired, naïve intentions operate with significant consequences in project making. Having their day outside the kingdom of sovereign thought, one might worry about negative consequences. The comparison with habit could suggest that non-deliberative, reflexive intentions lead to routine performances, still worse, mechanical repetition. A disposition toward form would then descend into formalism. But that only happens in degraded performances. Time and again, the resumption of an act— drawing a horizontal cut into a diagonal, positioning a podium on a steeply sloped, instead of a largely level site, for example—prompts adjustments to past solutions, changes that bring the practice into greater conformity with fundamental purposes. Naïve intentions can be both alert and adroit, which is to say attentive to changed conditions (the external contingencies) and nimble enough to adjust their course toward the given destination (the deliberative intention). Nevertheless, the iterations never quite coincide with themselves. At the time of the present design, the formative or preparatory antecedent is never quite right, missing some aspect or dimension that is now vitally important. There is, then, a double negation in naïve intentions: absence of self-awareness and lack of direct relevance. The truly significant consequence of this two-part lack is that it initiates the time in which the next iteration—today's project— can begin. Project time unfolds when a sequence of intentions develop their differences with one another, their non-coincidence within the temporal span.

Two as One

The podium problem to which I referred above was not the only topic of design that was revisited in Casa Poli. In their explanatory comments on the house, the architects explained that they had developed the idea of an "inhabited wall," which is to say a "double perimeter wall, with a service space of about a meter in between that contains all the specific and immobile functions of the house."[28] Here the architects are recalling but not naming a commonplace of post-war modern architecture, made most famous

Figure 4.3.10 Pezo von Ellrichshausen, *Poli House*, Coliumo, Chile, double wall. Photograph David Leatherbarrow.

perhaps by Kahn, in his distinction between served and serving spaces, with the latter often encased within parallel boundary walls. In their building, sited in a region that is far too frequently troubled by seismic activity, double walls make the house more likely to last in a place that may not. Feeling proud of itself for conquering the cliffs, the house's rather modest work-clothes are fitted out with quite a few square pockets, all empty, until filled with shadows or sun and wind. On the inside, environmental and structural roles are completed by spatial purposes. Nested forms between the inner and outer walls cluster co-dependent purposes: cupboards buttressing social spaces, for example, or closets in support of bedrooms. Quiet but ready, inner-wall provisionings wait to be consulted when the practices of dining, sleeping, conversing, or working need a little support—limiting their involvement to anticipations. Support such as this seems effortless. What is more, these configurations show impressive economy. I do not mean the tight-fisted, sparing sort, but the elegance that results from spaces sharing what commonly interests them. There is nothing like a corridor in the building, movement passes from room to room, across levels, and vertically by means of interstitial stairs. Adolf Loos would have understood and appreciated the economy of this spatial distribution, though when compared to his Villa Müller, with its orbital configuration of rooms, tied to a vertical core, but engaged with external opportunities, the Poli House is rather more open, interconnected, and fluid at its center, without compromising its wider involvements (with the sky, sea, and surrounding land). When circulation, storage, and service spaces are packed into wall thicknesses, the space of the Poli rooms is as generous as can be. The furniture that is not free-standing or centrally located is also admitted into wall depth (seating alcoves, benches, etc.), so that the movements of residing have the fewest constraints.

One suspects that economies such as these resulted from painstaking studies of intervals and alignments, worked and reworked until their number and variations were reduced to fullness. But the history of the topic exceeds the time span of this particular design, for the theme was visited in earlier, and revisited in later designs. Combinations of the forms at play in these projects have equivalents in a corresponding history of paintings. Projects, these two architects maintain, are at once single—Poli is not Ceno House—and linked, the first a "specific case" and the second part of a "continuous practice."[29]

The primary question concerning the time of the project is raised by this last term, *continuous practice*. Casa Poli's double perimeter wall supported informal interior spaces that were bound together orthogonally and diagonally, thanks to regular intervals and

Recalling Future Projects: Pezo von Ellrichshausen's Poli House   221

Figure 4.3.11 Pezo von Ellrichshausen, *Poli House*, Coliumo, Chile, plans. Courtesy of Pezo von Ellrichshausen.

Figure 4.3.12 Pezo von Ellrichshausen, *Poli House*, Coliumo, Chile, interior. Photograph David Leatherbarrow.

alignments in both plan and section, together with extra-large square apertures in both the exterior and interior walls. Thus configured, spaces and elements co-determined the qualities of the settings, as well as their interconnections with the surrounding landscape of stone and soil, shore and sea, sun and sky. The ambient conditions were specific to the project but could have been otherwise—and in due course will be, when other houses are built nearby, earth tremors unsettle the land, or the sea level rises. Nevertheless, the then-current conditions were matters of fact in the design that expressed their own temporalities: the steady pace of waves hitting the shore, the long hours of day and night, with shorter intervals of dawn and dusk in-between, seasonal change, so subtle in this part of the world, and the much slower alteration of the material surfaces, especially the sand, soil, and stone. Earlier, I called the sum total of these changes the time of the world. Every work that gets built finds itself caught up in these changes, welcoming some while resisting others, in synchronizations that are always imperfect.

Can the time of the project be absorbed into the time of the world by virtue of the work's physicality? The possibility is made plausible by the third phase of project time, the assembly and finishing of building materials. Once built, the work engages the cycles of site time. They cannot be escaped and always have their effect. The shutters housed in Casa Poli's double walls close the interiors against the cold night air and strong winds when they blow. This might be characterized as a mechanical form of synchronization. A different, material kind of interlapsing can be seen in the slower but steady absorption of the color of local vegetation and airborne deposits into its unpolished exterior surfaces, more on its shadow than sun sides.

But we've seen above that external and internal conditions have distinct temporalities. The time of the project includes each of them insofar as its full temporal span couples intentions with realizations. Insofar as the time of the project includes both, project and world time cannot be disassociated. But when seen more broadly, they can be distinguished, particularly when desires and intentions are developed through the course of not one but several projects, in a *continuous practice*, the architects have said.

What sort of time characterizes continuous practice? Certainly non-linear, given the reconsiderations and reactivations of recurring themes: again, the podium problem, now as then the inhabited wall, and so on. The time of *the architectonic project* is rather like the outer edge of the windmill the architects described. But the circular form it traces in the sky is never seen, only imagined, inferred, or implied by the path of the blades, one after another. Past positions are never as apparent as those in the present. Yet, individual works are always out of phase with regard to the imagined sweep, inclined one way or another, thus tangent, if only to a minor degree, infinitesimal perhaps, certainly no greater than what is required of particularity. The square apertures of Casa Poli are like those of Casa Gago, but obviously not the same: different frames, manner of operation, size, depth of surface, and so on. Casa Cien also has square windows, different again. Placed side by side, one can imagine the lines on the pages that guided builders on the site. One can also imagine the diagrams that preceded the drawings, perhaps also the thought about those diagrams, as well as the vocabulary of that thought, which long preceded the project, having been naturalized through repeated use, but learned in school, or before, after being formulated decades and centuries earlier, as part of an architectural topic that stays silent about its origin. Nor does anyone except the historian particularly care about the source(s) of a way of doing things or thinking about them. Although unstable, (unreasonable) ground such as this is capable of supporting what really matters, a new beginning. Like the philosopher or theorist who observes but doesn't take part, the historian steps onto the track after the race has been run. The relay runners have long since passed by, though each left behind a few traces of the run. On that basis the speeds and handoffs can be reconstructed, just as future races can be imagined, in part because the track takes a familiar form, circling without end.

Recollection Forward

I first saw Casa Poli several years after it had been built. By then it had accumulated traces of occupation and sedimentations of environmental influence. Corners had been chipped, revealing sub-surface aggregate, and the risers of some shade-side steps were being refinished with algae. Added to signs of post-construction history were evidences of the pre-occupancy construction process: specifically, the sequence of concrete pours, unmasked—therefore unlike the similar joints in Kahn's Parliament building in Dhaka, where marble tiles conceal the joints—and thus indicative of different mixes, aggregates, and skills. In an interview given a few years ago, the architects turned to the matter of ruins when describing the long history of their building.[30] Echoing Georg Simmel, they observed that the later stages of a building's life in time allow nature to reclaim what had been taken from it. The process is not, however, always only a matter or "moment of decay but as a sort of reconciliation between the two implicit forces, the natural and the human, one vector pulling down and the other up."[31] In its circularity, this departure and return are rather like the one we have observed in the pre-construction phases of project making, turning back to "the roots of making architecture," while advancing its unforeseen possibilities. Neither the individual design nor the continuous practice possesses full or complete autonomy, nor the a-temporal constancy that such autonomy might suggest. "We find it hard to believe," the architects observe, "that the architectonic dogma can only exist in a closed circuit, isolated from the everyday world."[32] Rather like the depredations suffered by the built work, human interests may be seen as an unfortunate but unavoidable obligation that results in the corruption of an ideal organization. But that is to take a narrow view of the project's nature and temporality. Without a judgment of what is right at this moment, in these circumstances, project making would loosen the anchorage that prevents it from drifting through the seas of time before and to come.

Figure 4.3.13 Pezo von Ellrichshausen, *Poli House,* Coliumo, Chile, concrete detail. Photograph David Leatherbarrow.

Recalling Future Projects: Pezo von Ellrichshausen's Poli House 225

Figure 4.3.14 Pezo von Ellrichshausen, *Poli House*, Coliumo, Chile, detail of steps. Photograph David Leatherbarrow.

4.4
Project Rhythms: Álvaro Siza's Swimming Pools at Leça da Palmeira

At every moment of the present there is always a hidden element whose emergence could alter everything: this is dizzy-making thought, but one which gives us comfort.
HUGO VON HOFMANNSTHAL, *BOOK OF FRIENDS*

Siza's project for the swimming pools at Leça de Palmeira took fourteen years to complete, 1959–73.[1] On the face of it, that would seem a rather long time for the design and construction of a building that looks so simple, even granting the fact that what we see now was built in phases. But maybe an even longer history should be considered when we seek to understand the character and quality of the project, the years before the first sketch was drawn and those after the last piece of copper was attached to the roof.

When do projects begin? Is it when mental images are rendered visible in the architect's first design drawing, or does the project start analytically, with the feasibility study, after the contract has been signed and the counting of hours and days commenced? Perhaps neither of these steps is truly inaugural, for nothing happens until the client decides to act on a previously inchoate desire: select the architect, obtain a site, and assemble the funds. What about the opposite end of the time line? What moment or event concludes the project? Is it when the drawings and specifications have been finished, stamped, and sealed? Or is that only phase one, to be followed by the months and years of site labor, without which there would be nothing to see or put to use? According to that conception, the project would end when the workers pack up their tools for the last time, the day

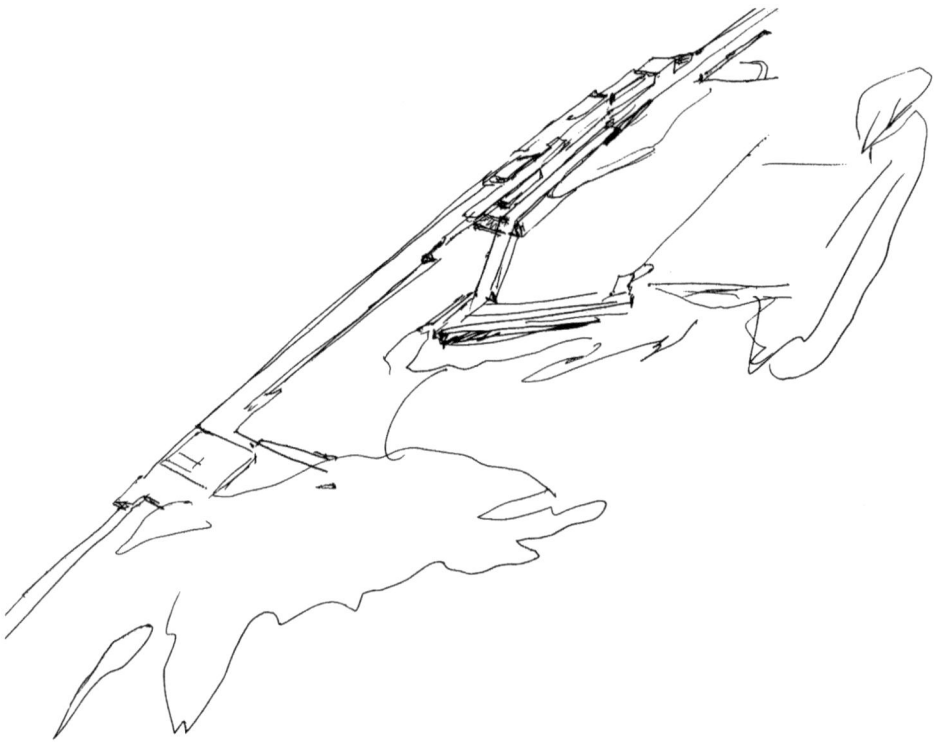

Figure 4.4.1 Álvaro Siza, *Leça da Palmeira Pools,* Porto, preliminary sketch. Courtesy of Álvaro Siza.

before occupation begins. But then one must ask about subsequent alterations and additions, by other architects in some cases, by Siza himself in the later phases of this one.

Perhaps it is our normal focus on the building itself—the physical object—that makes these determinations difficult. If we consider also the cultural, professional, and personal forces that typically bring designs into being and keep them relevant after completion, we might say that a project like Siza's preceded and followed itself, that the fourteen years abbreviate a longer history, that a work's professional period is only an intermediary episode, no more intelligible on its own than the middle of a three-act play. Accordingly, the surveying and sketching, the designing and detailing, and the fabricating that ostensibly define the built work are just a few of the many rhythms that compose the project's temporal field, a concert of anticipations, realizations, and consequences, whose players include earlier and later designs by Siza, comparable works within the discipline of architecture, and the material and cultural conditions of the project's location.

When the sketches, plans, and details themselves are considered, it is plain that previous ways of working were resumed at the start of the design process, but then surpassed as it progressed. It is also clear that designs Siza would develop in future were provisionally intimated in this one. There is no reason to assume that this wider spectrum was on Siza's mind during the several phases of design and construction. Most likely it wasn't. He admitted as much. Several times he confessed to the difficulty of saying where his ideas came from, despite the fact that in hindsight he could recognize them as his own. Nor has it been easy for Siza to see where his projects would lead. He observed that it is very hard to guess at any given moment what's ahead. If there is a logic in the development, it is one that created itself along the way. Yet, when seen retrospectively his later designs seem to have followed from those that came before, as if their sequel.

My opening suggestion is this: architectural projects never make sense culturally, professionally, or personally if their history is limited to the comparatively brief events of design and construction. This is to say they are what they are because of their relationships to what preceded and follows them. The linkages or relationships between former, future, and current concerns consist of both dependence and divergence, the first because projects proceed from what preceded them and the second because the developments that are truly significant cannot be deduced from their precedents. Although existing conditions cannot be said to cause design decisions, they do provide the context in which the merit of those choices will be decided. The strange thing about this context is that its dimensions and values are not evident until drawings and models bring them into relief, literally. While projects are by definition forward-looking, there is a corresponding retrograde movement, through which the past becomes the outcome of the present, not by choice but necessity, because what was is no longer, except for a few traces that require elaboration. Let us begin this concluding chapter's account of the time of project making with a review of the times and types of conditions that set the stage for Siza's work on this particular design: the location, the task he inherited, and his own way of developing designs. My premise is two-part: projects proceed from pre-conditions but cannot be comprehended on that basis alone.

Before the Beginning

"A site is valid for what it is," Siza once wrote, "and for what it could or wants to be—perhaps these are opposing things, but they are never unrelated."[2] Although one might think it would be obvious, the *validity* to which he refers is never easy to discern. In fact, catching the "what it is" of a design's location is one of the project's most demanding tasks. Obviously all built works engage *given conditions*. This is not simply because works that are built must be built somewhere, but also because that somewhere must be acknowledged and understood if the design is to make sense in common culture. Is it, then, the culture that *gives* the project its limits and resources, determines the site's validity? How is that—the validity of the gift—determined?

Were the characteristics of the location immediately apparent survey drawings and topographical models would be unnecessary. But the dimensions of the place that are pertinent to the project are not always, in fact rarely, observable directly. Much of what will become relevant to the project keeps itself hidden from pre-professional and preliminary views. Insofar as one wants to know what is particular to a place, the facts of the case, a significant degree of objectivity is required of survey drawings, as is expected of forensic investigation and expert testimony in judicial proceedings. Unopposed to the kind of objectivity that is proper to architecture, Siza often paced sites and annotated his drawings with the dimensions he determined. Getting the description right was his aim, retaining key aspects of what presented itself as itself, or was proper to the given situation. Obviously, not everything was documented—how could it be, and who would want that—only the distances and levels that attracted his eye or seemed significant, either because they helped him build an intelligible picture or because they suggested possibilities for intervention.

Another part of surveying is interpretative, for study drawings also express personal interests in the location and indicate how it might fulfill the topographical requirements of the project—this project, not another. After all, it was Siza himself who decided what to record and what to neglect in his sketches, and from the start he had swimming pools in mind, indefinite though his initial idea no doubt was. If his documentary drawings are said to be objective, it must be to a degree or of a kind that allows choice and judgment. A moment ago, I called this the right sort of objectivity.[3] His studies of given conditions sought to discern what was latent in the place, the risks it faced, its lateral engagements with other places, the memories that had been sedimented there, and most importantly its potential for change.

Should one therefore say the location thus described precipitated the project, that its lines and angles fell from the clouds or rose from the sand? Siza once said, "The idea lies in the 'place' more than in the mind—for those who are capable of seeing … it emerges at first sight."[4] Yet, he also equivocated on this point. Description, he noted, also discloses what the location *could be*, which is to say presents the conditions under which it might become what it hasn't been. At this precise moment, understanding yields to imagination. But perhaps inklings of new possibilities were already intuited in the first sketches, insofar as they brought salient dimensions into relief—those rocks, that infrastructure in the distance, and most importantly the sea wall, which appears on his drawings as a strong diagonal between the street and sea. If "God is in the details," that single line, appearing in several site sketches, is the tell-tale mark in this one. Nevertheless, seeing that line, together with the site's other primitive elements, meant not seeing other things. Once visual and manual choices were made on the page, preconditions became possibilities that didn't so much demand but enabled solutions. Constraints encourage: "The more you engage with the circumstances of your production, the more you are freed from it; 'voice' by being an impassive conductor of voices, is a measurement and not a limit in the search for perfection."[5] Preceding the project were premises of at least three different kinds: cultural, professional, and personal. I'll describe each in turn.

Before Siza arrived at what would become the swimming pool site, a beach was there. No doubt he'd walked the shore before, but not for the sake of project making. He knew the place as a boy, as did his friends and family, as well as all the other residents of Leça da Palmeira and the industrial harbor of Matosinhos, two neighboring suburbs north of Porto. To say the location consisted of water, sand, and sky is not wrong, but reductive. Even worse would be an account that focused on lines or levels, though they are there too. Physical things and geometries are the concerns of architects not swimmers, designers not fishermen, builders not sailors. Before the project, the shore was a place in the everyday world of the people who played or worked there, a spot that was familiar in Porto's culture, long established in its habits and prosaic traditions. For years, one imagines, children had tried to synchronize their steps with the approach and retreat of the waves. They performed their unscripted dance in front of parents, who sheltered themselves from too much sun under beach umbrellas, talking with friends about schools or shopping or some other pressing but passing concern. The ship workers in the harbor took less delight in the shore; departures and arrivals meant the welcomed end and inevitable resumption of work. The English tourists who arrived there would have thought they'd found paradise when they compared this beach to the shore at Brighton, but visitors from Rio maintained that Copacabana was much better. Strollers alongside the coastal road passed by slowly, traffic indifferently.

None of this—had it occurred—is particularly remarkable, actually just the reverse, entirely prosaic. Events of this kind made up something like a horizon of experience

Figure 4.4.2 Álvaro Siza, *Leça da Palmeira Pools,* Porto, aerial view. Courtesy of Álvaro Siza.

or topography of practices that defined the place well before any thought was given to an architectural project. Prosaic commonplaces wouldn't be worth summarizing except for the fact that they provided the project with some of its key resources: patterns of movement that could be extended, redirected, or ended, configurations that could be maintained or reshaped, and elements that could be recalled or rejected as emblems of one kind of place or another: a boat launch, goods warehouse, set of changing rooms, ball court, or café. As found, the beach was an ensemble of typical situations, micro institutions one could say, with and against which Siza could work out those of his project. Although their origins were uncertain and they were commonly taken for granted, one suspects that these situations, this culture, continued to effect the project's development well after Siza first put pencil to paper, through force of habit and the silent influence of unexamined premises.

The cultural pre-history that preceded the project had a parallel in what might be called its disciplinary context—another set of pre-dispositions and thus of beginnings. Siza was not only a resident of the region, he had practiced there as an architect, a professional whose training and knowledge prepared him for the work ahead. Among architects and landscape architects the swimming pool is a *type*. Topographical forms constitute one of its dimensions, likewise kinds of enclosure and boundary definition. These characteristics define its form, an abstract configuration that can be considered and interpreted independent of any particular program of use, which is to say a geometrical not functional type. The abstraction assumed in type intuition allows comparisons. In one of his explanations, Siza observed that he had designs by other architects in mind when he worked on this one, none of which, incidentally, were places to swim. Aalto's work seems to have had an influence; Siza also mentioned Frank Lloyd Wright, his Taliesin West in particular. Apparently, he had just bought a book on Wright's work: "When I began the project, I bought some publication about Frank Lloyd Wright's work, and [particular projects such] as the Desert House, had a positive influence on my own work … I remember that at the time, Wright was a kind of liberation for me."[6]

The Arizona desert is not the Portuguese seaside, nor is a house and studio a bathing facility, though there are pools at Taliesin. Still, the geometries and materials of Wright's work are part of the Leça project's pre-history, no less than Porto's everyday culture. One critic has emphasized the role of the diagonals in both projects, as they open orthogonal configurations toward distant views. Another writer turned from Wright to Aalto and described correspondences between fan-shaped elements.[7] No adjudication between these interpretations and source material is required for us to acknowledge a horizon of comparable works as an early chapter in the history of Siza's project, non-synchronous with his decades-long cultural predisposition. Considering works by Wright, Aalto, Távora, and others, the key is not how Siza adopted antecedents but the ways he transformed them.

No less important than formal precedents were the tools of his trade. I've noted already that Siza frequently dimensioned his survey drawings. Architects typically size up sites on orthographic views, which is to say plans or sections. Siza has done this on many occasions, but also, and a-typically, has noted lengths and widths on sketch perspectives, such as his survey drawings of the Cistercian Monastery Le Thoronet, where he designed a temporary installation in 2006. With or without dimensional notes, Siza uses perspective drawings to appropriate his sites, not so much to make them his own, but to assimilate them into an architectural way of seeing—as topographies, spaces, and distances. Of course, he did not invent this form of description, but he did use it in his own way for his own purposes—line drawings with little or no modeling, frequently from a raised, nearly aerial vantage, despite rather compressed foregrounds.

No perspective is innocent, nor do views of this type coordinate objects and backgrounds only; a third player is also required, the person taking the view, whose interests we have just acknowledged as architectural interests. What is shown or seen by means of perspective is something other than what would be experienced in prosaic

Figure 4.4.3 Álvaro Siza, *Le Thoronet*, survey sketch. Courtesy of Álvaro Siza.

or pre-professional experience. This fact is often overlooked because this particular optic has been thoroughly naturalized in and outside architecture. Nevertheless, every perspective view limits the perceptual field to something aimed at or intended. Siza's first sketch at the beach carved something unseen out of what had been obvious to his family, friends, and neighbors. But what he brought into relief was not only something formerly overlooked; it couldn't be found in the location's several situations. Perhaps it is too easy or quick to say that the world as lived was reduced in his sketches. A more modest and timely question would ask: what did Siza discover there, and how might what he found start the clock of his project, or been one of its several starts?

Certainly one can name all the things that appear on the page: the wall with its saddlebag steps, the rocks, the water's edge, and the distant horizon, with its cranes, pier, and so on. But together with the question concerning what is shown, one can profitably ask what has been left out. The fishermen who cast from the shore are not there, no hint of hope for an evening meal. Nor are the tourist-swimmers there, whose

Figure 4.4.4 Álvaro Siza, *Leça da Palmeira Pools,* Porto, preliminary sketch. Courtesy of Álvaro Siza.

memories of this stretch of sand and sea will make Brighton seem so dreary and Rio so good. Nor, again, are there parents and children, acting out the interplay of gossip and play. Instead of all of this and so much more, there are profiles, shadows, and surfaces. A hollow of special interests has been cut into the wide surroundings, a constructed view substituting something unseen for what was patently obvious, an artificial for natural space, professional possibilities for prosaic involvements. These substitutions suggest the world-as-lived had come to an end in the construction of a view.

Is That How Projects Begin, Destructively?

We shouldn't get ahead of ourselves. It would be premature to say that Siza's drawing shows forms and elements. They won't arrive till later. All that is rendered visible at this moment—something unseen by the fishermen, tourist-swimmers, or parents with children—is what an architect needed to begin the project, the distances, levels, and profiles. Projects begin when an architectural way of seeing is resumed, when the schedules and pace of prosaic life are substituted by the time of constructing another landscape, the first phase of which, the survey sketch, re-enacts a previously formed way of seeing. Two decades after his early work on the swimming pools, Siza returned to the role of site surveys in a project's beginning: "Much of what I have designed before (much of what others have designed) flows within the first sketch. In a disordered way. So much [so] that little appears of the site which is invoking it at all."[8]

Thus, the project's early history invokes yet another chronology, the past of Siza's preceding projects, and more exactly of his earlier surveys. This story is less disciplinary than personal. I've noted already that the swimming pool project was not Siza's first work at Leça da Palmeira. In 1963, he finished the Boa Nova Tea House, sited relatively close by, along the beach, not far from the lighthouse and a fourteenth-century church. He also worked on a comprehensive plan for the entire waterfront between Leça and Boa Nova. As with the swimming pools, he saw the need to take possession of the primary structure of the place with this earlier project: "Where to 'place' the building had to be decided with great care, so that once it was there it would not be possible to imagine its not being there. It was not a case of imagining however but of understanding."[9] In this case, *understanding* led toward a high degree of conformity between what was given and what was made, the two—land and building—were similarly irregular.[10] This is not the case with the white walls, which contrast strongly with the stone, soil, and sea; rather, with the building's upper profile, the way it recalls the outline of the rocks, likewise with the plan's non-orthogonality. Congruent though they were, the forms were too abundant, he later observed. Thus, at the pools, and the houses at Maia, also designed at this time, there is evidence of a sort of corrective simplification: "eliminating anything that was not necessary."[11]

Within an architect's body of work, projects can be said to proceed from one another, but less by repetition than differentiation, or what I earlier called divergence. Dissimilar conditions and unrelated tasks contribute to this type of change, but also, and more largely in this case, self-criticism and a sense of new possibilities. Despite the fact that similarities exist between examples, each is its own chapter in the longer text: "The design of one house is almost the same as the design of another: walls, windows, doors, roof. And yet it is unique."[12]

Habits of both representation and perception are especially evident in Siza's drawings of works by other architects and of places that attracted his attention, even if he wasn't sizing the spot up for a project.[13] He made the work of others his own in the same way that he appropriated sites for future construction, perspective sketches with a particular style of spatial representation: the page seems to tip forward and background figures hover over those that are close by, despite the fact that line weights remain the same no matter what or whose profile they trace. His explanations give one the sense of an impersonal process: "Suddenly my pencil or biro starts putting down images, faces in the foreground, subdued profiles or luminous details, the hands which draw them."[14] Hands and eyes discover the world by describing it, or, more narrowly and architecturally, structuring space as much as recording it. Siza's sight seems strengthened by weakening his hold on things. The settings themselves move his pencil across the page, secretly preparing him for future work: "Liberated to the point of drunkenness … [the wandering eye and obedient hand] learn hugely and what we learn reappears, dissolved in the lines which we later draw."[15]

Design topics acquired in this way persist through reformulation. I've alluded to the insistent diagonal against which approximate parallels and non-orthogonals can be contrasted, to give both continuity and variety to extended stretches of terrain. In the case of the pools, the knife-like slanting line, which marks the top edge of the sea wall, cuts and couples urban and shoreline geometries. Similarly, compressed space, in so many of the sketches, reappears in the tight enclosures and layered passages of the Leça changing rooms and showers. And third, the continuity of profiles one sees in all the drawings, which seems to neglect differences in material makeup, can be seen in the non-distinction between the pool's walls of rock and concrete. Insofar

Figure 4.4.5 Álvaro Siza, Macchu Picchu travel sketch. Courtesy of Álvaro Siza.

as topics such as these have their unchronicled beginnings in the travel drawings, and their re-emergence in later design sketches, we have located yet another starting point for the project.

Like any habit, drawing is a pre-disposition absorbed through time into practices that unfold unreflectively or without premeditation. Perhaps we are too quick to think mechanism when describing the enactment of a *habit*, for the resumption of an act in the context of changed circumstances always prompts an adjustment of the norm, slight thought it may be, to achieve the desired end or bring the performance into closer proximity to the underlying aim or idea than the past performance would have done. Habit is by definition a settled disposition. But when practiced, it is also a kind of behavior, tendency, or inclination that is in principle mutable, through unforeseen, unending, and generally minor innovations. Laws of the limbs are also aims and ideas in action. Every settled disposition is a tendency that couples inertia with spontaneity. Hence Siza's beautiful characterization of drawing, partly cited already: "First timid strokes of the pencil, captive, imprecise, then obstinately analytical, here and there giddily definitive, liberated to the point of drunkenness; then tired and gradually irrelevant."[16]

A common metaphor for project making, also used by Siza, is movement along a *path*. In his account of the "bumpy road," Siza never suggested his project making followed anything like a straight line or linear sequence of steps, nor was he particularly clear on its points of departure and arrival, as we have seen. Our opening comments on the difficulties of saying when projects begin and end hinted at this very uncertainty. Thus far we've uncovered not one but several points of departure. What more can be said about the movement, about its pace and speed, not direction, also the interruptions and pauses that seem rather common, as well as the reversals and renewals to which, we will see, he also referred? That advance was progressive seems clear. Commenting on the role of rapid sketches in the initial stages of project development, Siza observed: "They help establish a permanent dialectical relationship between intuition and precise examination, in a progressive process of full understanding and visualization."[17]

Progress along the path of this process reaches behind and ahead of itself, arising out of past experiences and encouraged by a sense of likely consequences. One cannot move forward in the absence of some confidence that the aims will be realized, but the grounds for that conviction are unstable. Siza observed that no project develops with

Figure 4.4.6 Álvaro Siza, *Leça da Palmeira Pools,* Porto, sketch of site. Courtesy of Álvaro Siza.

consistency in the absence of belief that the right path has been taken: closely packing parallels to the sea wall at Leça, opening the space of the terraces and pools alongside a diagonal that diverges from the initial cluster, and so on. That these premises were provisional cannot be denied, though the line of development he took was not the only one that was possible. But without such a *projective cast*, no development would have been possible.[18] He saw the cards on the able, had a hunch about the outcome of his hand, and placed the bet.

The path is not only uneven, he said, it is also indirect. What about the timing of design practice? "Jobs proceed," Siza observed, "in alternate phases; at times they shoot ahead, at other they proceed slowly or wait their turn … where the tempo is made up of different elements."[19] Modulating this tempo are alternating phases of intensely focused concentration and marginal awareness. These vary in duration of course, the first can be no more than a few hours or as long as several days and the second can extend much longer. "Dead time" also contributes to project rhythm, the hours spent traveling to a distant site, waiting for a meeting or conversation, or simply being distracted. Even if these moments cannot be said to have yielded this or that insight or conclusion, they play a role in the history, rather like the pauses that end and begin a dancer's movements. There are also the times of reconsideration, in which the sequence folds back on itself, together with those of expectation, when hoped-for developments exist in sketchy profile only. When seen in sequence retrospectively, design drawings attest to daily doubts, small advances, and mistakes; sometimes configurations that held promise before are abandoned as misdirected; other times a pattern or form intended as one solution provides a key to another, seized for what it suggests, though the steps that will follow are no more certain to arrive at a convincing answer than the first. If a path, it is always meandering or roundabout. The temporality of this kind of thought and work is non-compartmental: ancient habits of thinking and seeing cross into understandings and skills being acquired as the work progresses.

Siza's hands have their strengths, but drawings are not buildings; other hands and strengths are required for that. The many vocations involved in the process also modulate its rhythms. Working with others, he once observed, is a lot like working on one's own, except that one's capacity for both analysis and invention is greatly multiplied by the contributions from other designers and from engineers who possess one form of expertise or another. Again a bumpy road: their criticisms can slow or reverse forward momentum, just as their suggestions can accelerate it. "Each person's discoveries, each hypothesis launched into the flow, generate further hypotheses and further discoveries ... at a giddy rate."[20] But that's only the best version of team work. He also admitted that today one finds not a chorus, whose voices acknowledge the work's measure, but dissonant and ill-timed notes, improvisations on a non-existent score.

What, then, sets the measure or determines the project's tempo? Surprisingly, perhaps, Siza does not turn from the chorus to the solo voice when suggesting an answer to this last, most basic question. One of the most remarkable premises of his thinking about project making is his insistence on the broader cultural context (with which we began) as the framework for creative work. Project making is, we've seen, at once forward and backward looking; it unfolds in movements that are simultaneously prospective and retrospective; the outcome is a world that hasn't been seen before. The most obvious indication of a project's advance is seen in the progressive articulation of the solution in the sequence of drawings lined up in hindsight.

But Siza also noted another kind of advance, movement away from the individual we see as the work's radical source, the architect him or herself. In a wonderful text called "Educational Journeys," Siza returned to the theme of architecture's shared and social purpose, defining its basic task as the revelation of "the hazily latent collective desire."[21]

Words might achieve this for an author, but for the architect other media come into play: "collective desire manifests itself in every stone and in every pore."[22] The truly striking thing about this revelation is that it involves a kind of de-personalization. That might seem an outrageous claim for career-minded architects. Nevertheless, that's Siza's position. Next, he observes that architecture is a risk, the wager to which I referred above. And the risk so defined seeks impersonal desire and anonymity, which is to

Figure 4.4.7 Álvaro Siza, travel sketch. Courtesy of Álvaro Siza.

say the target of a project's bet is a set of concerns and longings felt by many, those of a given cultural context, Porto in his case. Hence the two-part conclusion that seems so untimely in today's architecture: "In the last analysis [architecture requires] a progressive distancing of the I."[23] And further: "Nowhere is a desert. I can always be one of the inhabitants."[24] If this thesis represents "thoughts out of season" it is, nevertheless, still a memory and a hope for more than a few today, lingering and emerging at the margins of the present moment.

Notes

Chapter 1.1

1   This definition of architecture, now rather commonplace, originated with Louis I. Kahn. See Louis I. Kahn, *Louis I. Kahn: Talks with Students Architecture at Rice 26* (Houston: Rice University, 1969). The phrase has also been used in one of the most insightful books on Kahn to be published in recent years: Michael Merrill, *Louis Kahn on the Thoughtful Making of Spaces: The Dominican Motherhouse* (Zurich: Lars Müller, 2010). I am grateful to Michael Benedikt for his advice on this opening observation.

2   A good recent study of this topic is: Hilary Sample, *Maintenance Architecture* (Cambridge, MA: MIT, 2016).

3   Georg Simmel, "The Ruin," [1911] in Kurt H. Wolff, ed., *Essays on Sociology, Philosophy and Aesthetics* (New York: Harper & Row, 1965), 259–66.

4   I allude to this type of change in David Leatherbarrow, *Uncommon Ground: Architecture, Technology, and Topography* (Cambridge, MA: MIT, 2000) and cite Aris Konstantinidis' beautiful account of Easter whitewashing in Greece; see Aris Konstantinidis, *Elements for Self-Knowledge* (Athens: Agra, 1975), 305.

5   Kengo Kuma, "Breaking Down into Particles," in Hiroshi Watanabe, trans., *Anti-Object: The Dissolution and Disintegration of Architecture* (London: Architectural Association, 2008), 98–120.

6   This observation is central to the thesis argued in: David Leatherbarrow and Mohsen Mostafavi, *On Weathering: The Life of Buildings in Time* (Cambridge, MA: MIT, 1993).

7   William Faulkner, *The Sound and the Fury* [1929] and *As I Lay Dying* (New York: Random House, 1946), 104.

8   These terms paraphrase Maurice Merleau-Ponty, "Temporality," [1945], *Phenomenology of Perception*, trans. Colin Smith (New York: Humanities, 1962), 410–33.

9   I have developed this set of observations about "qualification" in a text called "Necessary Qualifications: Design before, during, and after Construction," in A. Dutoit, J. Odgers, and A. Sharr, eds., *Quality Out of Control: Standards for Measuring Architecture* (London: Routledge, 2010), 105–18.

10 He introduces these terms and makes this distinction in Aldo Rossi, *The Architecture of the City*, trans. Diane Ghirardo and Joan Ockman (Cambridge, MA: MIT, 1982).

11 August Schmarsow, "The Essence of Architectural Creation," [1893], cited in Harry Mallgrave and Eleftherios Ikonomou, eds., *Empathy, Form, Space: Problems in German Aesthetics, 1873–1893* (Santa Monica: Getty Center for the History of Art and the Humanities, 1994), 295.

12 An excellent study of types of spatial movement from which I have benefited greatly is: John Dixon Hunt, "'Lordship of the Feet': Toward a Poetics of Movement in the Garden," in M. Conan, ed., *Landscape Design and the Experience of Motion* (Washington, DC: Dumbarton Oaks, 2003), 187–213.

13 Although his accent is on spatial conditions, something like "folds of time" is *implied* throughout Gilles Deleuze, *The Fold: Leibniz and the Baroque*, trans. Tom Conley (Minneapolis: University of Minnesota Press, 1993).

14 Johann Wolfgang von Goethe, *Goethe on Art*, edited and translated by John Gage (Berkeley: University of California Press, 1980), 196. This passage is used again as an epigraph to chapter 3.1.

15 See the recent text on this theme in Le Corbusier's work: J. L. Cohen and S. Ahrenberg, eds., *Le Corbusier's Secret Laboratory: From Painting to Architecture* (Ostfildern: Hatje Cantz, 2013).

16 A useful collection of essays arguing this thesis is Robin W. Winks, ed., *The Historian as Detective: Essays on Evidence* (New York: Harper Colophon, 1969).

17 This point is made in the classic study by Carlo Ginzburg, "Clues: Roots of an Evidential Paradigm," in John and Anne Tedeschi, trans., *Clues, Myths, and the Historical Method* (Baltimore: Johns Hopkins, 1989), 96–125. More recently, this topic has received philosophical interpretation in Paul Ricoeur, "Documentary Proof," in Kathleen Blamey and David Pellauer, trans., *Memory, History, Forgetting*, (Chicago: University of Chicago, 2004), 176–81. These two authors also show similar methods in medicine, a doctor's reading of symptoms, and in psychoanalysis, Freud's interpretations of gestures and dreams. For the bearing this line of thinking has on architecture, see Joseph Rykwert, "A Healthy Mind in a Healthy Body," in *History in, of, and for Architecture*, J.E. Hancock, ed. (Cincinnati: University of Cincinnati, 1981), 44–8.

Chapter 2.1

1 Paul Ricoeur, "Architecture and Narrative," in Pietro Derossi, ed., *Identità i Differenze*, vol. 1, The 19th Triennale di Milano, 1996, 64–72.

2 Peter Zumthor, "A Way of Looking at Things" [1988], in *Thinking Architecture* (Baden: Lars Müller, 1998), 24–5. The subsection of the paper from which this citation has been taken is called "Melancholy Perceptions."

3 The background walls of other interiors painted by Menzel are similarly indefinite or ambiguous; see, for example, *Living Room with Sister*, *Interior with Justice Minister Maercker*, or *Children Reading*.

4 Michael Fried, *Menzel's Realism: Art and Embodiment in Nineteenth-Century Berlin* (New Haven: Yale University Press, 2002), 84.

5   Claude Keisch, in Claude Keisch and Marie Ursula Riemann-Reyher, eds., *Adolph Menzel, 1815-1905: Between Romanticism and Impressionism* (New Haven: Yale University Press, 1996), 186.

6   Mario Praz, *An Illustrated History of Interior Decoration: From Pompeii to Art Nouveau*, trans. William Weaver (London: Thames and Hudson, 1982), 334.

7   Rainer Maria Rilke, *The Notebooks of Malte Laurids Brigge*, trans. M.D. Herter Norton (New York: W. W. Norton, 1949), 48.

Chapter 2.2

1   Eileen Gray and Jean Badovici, "*E 1027 Maison en bord de mer*," [1929], *L'Architecture Vivante* (Automne-Hiver: Albert Morancé, 1929): 17–38; published in translation in Caroline Constant, *Eileen Gray* (London: Phaidon, 2000), 241. Constant's book has been my guide through the history and ideas of Gray's work.

2   So far as I can tell, this line (from the corner of the bed to the beginning of the arc) also runs in a direction that is very close to—if not exactly—west to east. Gray did not, however, label it in this way; *lever* not *est* was her concern.

3   All of this adopts a pre-Copernican view; one that the philosopher Edmund Husserl described as our "natural attitude" in his famous observation that "the earth does not move" (in our everyday experience of the world). Husserl's phrase, "*Die Erde bewegt sich nicht*," can be found in his late text *Grundlegende Untersuchungen zum phänomenologischen Ursprung der Räumlichkeit der Natur* (1934). See Edumnd Husserl, "Foundational Investigations of the Phenomenological Origin of the Spatiality of Nature," in Martin Farber, ed., *Philosophical Essays in Memory of Edmund Husserl* (Cambridge, MA: Harvard University Press, 1940), 307–25.

4   For ρυθμός (*rhythmos*) as "pose," see J.J. Pollitt, *The Ancient View of Greek Art: Criticism, History, and Terminology* (New Haven: Yale University Press, 1974), 218–33. See also Curt Sachs, *Rhythm and Tempo* (New York: Columbia University Press, 1953).

5   I will return to this theme and elaborate its implications for architecture more fully later in this book; see chapter 2.4.

6   The deeper philosophical and wider historical context of this distinction is set out in: Hans Blumenberg, *Lebenszeit und Weltzeit* (Frankfurt: Suhrkamp, 1986).

7   The intertwining of what Aldo van Eyck called "place and occasion" is proposed in the explanation of topography and the topographical arts I set out in *Topographical Stories: Studies in Landscape and Architecture* (Philadelphia: University of Pennsylvania Press, 2004).

8   Constant, 241.

9   Gray and Badovici, "From Eclecticism to Doubt," in Constant, 242. Here she is again describing E. 1027, not Tempe à Pailla.

10 I put this hyphenated term in quotation marks in deference to Reyner Banham's widely read book, even though the apology he makes for mechanized instruments of environmental control would not have been made by Eileen Gray—just the reverse. See Reyner Banham, *The Architecture of the Well-Tempered Environment* (Chicago: University of Chicago, 1969).

11 See Giacomo Marramao, *Kairós: Towards an Ontology of "Due Time,"* trans. Philip Larrey and Silvia Cattaneo (Aurora, CO: Davies Group, 2007). Equally relevant and very interesting for its spatial or architectural implications is Phillip Sipiora and James S. Baumlin, eds., *Rhetoric and Kairós: Essays in History, Theory, and Praxis* (Albany: State University of New York, 2002).

12 Caroline Constant made this observation; see Constant, 148.

13 This is the argument set forth in Peter Adam, *Eileen Gray: Architect/Designer* (New York: Harry N. Abrams, 2000), 288–9.

14 Miguel de Cervantes, *Don Quixote*, vol. 1, bk. iii, ch. vi.

Chapter 2.3

1 Sverre Fehn, "An Architectural Autobiography," in Marja-Ritti Norri and Maija Kärkkäinen eds., *Sverre Fehn: The Poetry of the Straight Line* (Helsinki: Museum of Finish Architecture, 1992), 48.

2 With the term "footprints in the sand," I invoke the ancient example of "traces on the Rhodian shore," to which Vitruvius referred in the prologue to his second book, as did many writers who followed. For the initial reference see Vitruvius, *Ten Books on Architecture*, ed. Ingrid Rowland (Cambridge: Cambridge University, 1999), 75. The implications this story had for the subsequent history of conceptions of art and nature are set out in Clarence Glacken, *Traces on the Rhodian Shore: Nature and Culture in Western Thought from Ancient Times to the End of the Eighteenth Century* (Berkeley: University of California, 1967). More recent and helpful on what Aristippus discovered at the shore, and how he got there in the first place, is: Hans Blumenberg, *Shipwreck with Spectator: Paradigm of a Metaphor for Existence*, trans. Steven Rendall (Cambridge, MA: MIT, 1997). The idea that tracings made by men are ephemeral was amplified by Michel Foucault in his account of nothing less than the erasure of man: "As the archaeology of our thought easily shows, man is an invention of recent date. And one perhaps nearing its end … some event of which we can at the moment do no more than sense the possibility … [yet we might] wager that man would be erased, like a face drawn in sand at the edge of the sea." Michel Foucault, *The Order of Things: An Archaeology of the Human Sciences* (London: Tavistock, 1970), 387. Fehn's "footprints," Vitruvius' "geometric diagrams," and Foucault's "face" are obviously different kinds of marks. The arguments that follow will elaborate these very differences.

3 Here is the relevant passage: "Now to remember what is future is not possible—that is an object of opinion or expectation … nor is there memory of what is present, but only sense-perception … memory relates to what is past." Aristotle, "On Memory," 449b 10–13, *The Complete Works of Aristotle*, vol. 1 (Princeton: Princeton University Press, 1984), 714.

4 As I've noted in this book's Introduction, the use of "clues" in hunting, police work, and historical study—the hermeneutics of suspicion—is helpfully described in Carlo Ginsburg, *Clues, Myths, and the Historical Method* (Baltimore: Johns Hopkins, 1989). A comparison to psychoanalytic methods

is also relevant: what traces were to Sherlock Holmes (Sir Arthur Conan Doyle), symptoms were to Sigmund Freud. Very useful on the philosophical dimensions of this issue is: Paul Ricoeur, *Memory, History, Forgetting* (Chicago: University of Chicago Press, 2004), 170. Ricoeur observed: "There exist traces that are not 'written testimonies' and that are equally open to historical observation, namely, 'vestiges of the past,' which are the favorite target of archaeology: urns, tools, coins, painted or sculpted images, funerary objects, the remains of buildings, and so forth."

5   Sverre Fehn, "Villa Busk," in Marja-Ritti Norri and Maija Kärkkäinen eds., *Sverre Fehn: The Poetry of the Straight Line* (Helsinki: Museum of Finish Architecture, 1992), 6–7; first published in *Arkitektguiden*, no. 2 (February 1990): 14–47.

6   Fehn once observed: "The dimensions of the tree … have functioned as an inspiration for constructions of use to human beings." Further, the tree's existence was defined by a "dramatic confrontation between earth and sky." The trunk, which he also called the tree's "horizon," was the place where it gathered "all its strength and reached its maximum constructive size"—column-like. See Sverre Fehn, "The Dream of Great Construction," in Marja-Ritti Norri and Maija Kärkkäinen eds., *Sverre Fehn: The Poetry of the Straight Line* (Helsinki: Museum of Finish Architecture, 1992), 34.

7   Fehn, "Villa Busk," 6.

8   Le Corbusier was fond of bragging about the plants in his garden. In one of several notes about the garden he wrote as follows: "1940 Disaster! Exodus! Paris is deserted. The garden roof … has been left to its own devices. Heat waves in 1940 and 42, winter, rain, and snow … the abandoned garden does not die but instead responds to these conditions. Wind, birds, and insects fill it with seeds … nature has reclaimed its rights." I cite this and the other passages in: David Leatherbarrow, "Gardens and the Larger Landscape," in John Dixon Hunt, ed. *A Cultural History of Gardens in the Modern Age* (London: Bloomsbury, 2013), 181–206. This particular quotation from Le Corbusier can be found in "*Reportage sur un toit-jardin*," *Oeuvre Complète 1938–1946* (Zürich: Girsberger, 1946), 140.

9   Thomas Mann, *The Holy Sinner*, trans. H. T. Lowe-Porter (New York: Alfred A. Knopf, 1951), 244 and 246. The "sinner" was saved—at least nurtured—by the unexpected fecundity of otherwise unyielding stone.

10 The distinction between life and living is given ethical valence in: Georg Simmel, *The View of Life Four Metaphysical Essays with Journal Aphorisms* (Chicago: University of Chicago Press, 2010), particularly in his account of the human "act" in chapter 4, "The Law of the Individual."

11 Fehn, "Villa Busk," 6.

12 This aversion was explained to me by Per Olaf Fjeld, Fehn's friend and collaborator for so many years, who is also the leading authority on Fehn's architecture and thought.

13 Fehn, "Villa Busk," 7.

14 The analogy between plot and plan elaborates etymology, for they are cognate words (as are plane, plank, plat, place, and many other terms common in architecture). The stem behind the Greek and Latin variants seems to be the Indo European *pla*, meaning flat or broad. The linkage between plan (design), plat (ground), and plot (scheme) was beautifully set out by Ben Jonson in the sixteenth century, when the connections between these terms, influenced by the French *complót*, were fluid. In a text called *Explorata*, he used the following comparison to explain the unity and proportionality of a well-composed "fable or plot": "If a man would build a house,

he would first appoint a place to build it in, which he would define within certain bounds. So in the constitution of a poem, the action is aimed at by the poet, which answers place in a building, and that action hath his largeness, compass, and proportion." Ben Jonson, *Explorata (Timber): or Discoveries*, lines 3323–30. For a recent commentary on this and related ideas in Elizabethan literature, see Roy Eriksen, *The Building in the Text: Alberti to Shakespeare and Milton* (State College: Penn State University Press, 2000).

15 Fehn, "Villa Busk," 6.

16 Michel Tournier, *Friday*, trans. Norman Denny (New York: Pantheon, 1969), 100–2.

17 Fehn, "Villa Busk," 7.

18 If the intervals can be called bays, the bedroom is three, the open-air deck also three, the dining room two, the narrow kitchen three again, the entry hall two, and the living room four. It is interesting that the fireplace extends beyond this measure (less than a fifth bay), while the bath falls short of it (less than a fourth), ending and beginning the sequence with intervals that were comparable but a-typical.

19 Formwork was reused for interior wall cladding in the building studied later; see 4.3 From Time to Time.

20 This last term is redundant: trait, like character, results from drawing across or cutting into a surface; if the surface is land, the mark is called a track; if the lines are on paper, a tract. Obviously, trait, track, and tract are cognate with trace, although etymologists divide the terms into two groups. The Latin stem is *trahere*, meaning to pull or draw. Here, too, movement is implied, as in trek, indicating both the journey and its path.

21 Leonardo da Vinci offered a wonderful definition of force that clarifies this double sense of "rest." Force is "an incorporeal agency [or] invisible power" diffused within bodies, according to which each maintains an active life and the capacity to move while "[hastening] furiously to its desired death," which it achieves and shows in rest. Leonardo de Vinci, *The Notebooks of Leonardo da Vinci*, ed. E. McCurdy (New York: Renyal & Hitchcock, 1956), 530. For an account of different conceptions of force, see Max Jammer, *Concepts of Force: A Study in the Foundations of Dynamics* (New York: Harper, 1957). Jammer cites and discusses Leonardo's conception on pages 95–7.

22 This observation is developed at greater length later in this book, see 2.4 World Rhythms

23 Consideration of this topic (staining) opens the study that has served as the foundation for the present investigation: David Leatherbarrow and Mohsen Mostafavi, *On Weathering: The Life of Buildings in Time* (Cambridge, MA: MIT, 1993).

24 See Pollitt, *The Ancient View of Greek Art*, 14–22.

Chapter 2.4

1 Álvaro Siza, "Every year, with the spring tides ..." [1980], in *Piscina na Praia de Leça*, Michael Toussaint and Maria Melo, eds. (Lisbon: A + A Books, 2016), 9. The original is: *Todos os anos, nas mares vivas, o mar leva o que não é essencial*. Here is the full text in translation:

Every year, with the spring tides, the sea takes away what is not essential. In that place, a rocky massif cuts through the three parallel lines: where the sea meets the sky, where the beach meets the sea, the long retaining wall of the street.

Someone thought to protect a depression in that mass of solid rock and use it as a tidal pool. Only the Atlantic is not the Mediterranean, nor is it easy to build a swimming pool where not many are made: water treatment, difficult collection, strict regulations, approval dependent on a number of entities. "Best to bring in an architect." Nothing deeply changed.

The changing rooms' building is anchored like a boat to the street wall. It is not going anywhere. Concrete walls sustain the pine and copper roof and support the access paths to the pool. These paths were there (on hard ground, one knows where to put their feet), the pool was there, the walls run parallel to the granite street wall, from which they just stand out. Here and there small interventions consolidate the natural platforms. Not much has changed.

In the first spring tides the sea took away a piece of the wall, correcting what was not right. For seven years still, as Jacob, the architect studied the outer limits, to the north and to the south, where it was hard to deliver what was made to what was. As luck would have it, from that, a plan for the seafront was made, and delivered, and for it he was paid. But it was all deemed useless: easy to understand that the architect merely chose where to put his feet and where not to go, fearful of the dangers and of the sea rocks. And someone said, "anyone will know where to put their feet, the architect is supposed to put his different places than everyone else." And soon enough he was dismissed.

2   Tide and time are cognate words; the first means the *time of high water*, but also, when used metaphorically, refers to the right or due time (*kairós*) for other kinds of increase: *high time* means the moment to act, *evening tide* means (or once meant) time to rest, and *high tide* once designated the time of a festival, hence holiday tidings.

3   Le Corbusier argued similarly: "How much deeper is my feeling for the admirable clock that is the sea, with its tides, its equinoxes, its daily variations according to the most implacable of laws, but also the most imperceptible, the most hidden law that exists." Le Corbusier, *Modulor 2* (Cambridge, MA: MIT, 1955), 27.

4   Paul Ricoeur, *Time and Narrative*, vol. 1, trans. Kathleen McLaughlin and David Pellauer (Chicago: University of Chicago, 1984). The thesis is introduced on the first page of the book, page 3, and then developed throughout.

5   Francis Ponge, *The Voice of Things*, ed. Beth Archer (New York: McGraw Hill, 1972), 74.

6   Resilience is something different. Much discussed today, partly in response to recent seaside disasters and widely attributed to climate change, it suggests something different from endurance: a capacity to recover quickly from difficulties, the ability to spring back into previous shape or form—as if the impact had not occurred. Siza has a different kind of erasure in mind, not of history but of incorrect insertions.

7   Ponge, ibid.

8   This observation begins a wonderful text on the several meanings of waiting in contemporary culture; see Andrea Köhler, *Passing Time: An Essay on Waiting*, trans. Michael Eskin (New York: Upper West Side Philosophers, 2011), 17.

9   This term has obtained great currency in contemporary philosophy, thanks in a large part to the writings of Giorgio Agamben, whose arguments provide orientation for mine.

10 Werner Jaeger, *Paideia: The Ideals of Greek Culture*, vol. 1, trans. Gilbert Highet (Oxford: Oxford University Press, 1945), 125–7.

11 See Pollitt, *The Ancient View of Greek Art*, 227. Pollitt's phrasing is beautifully precise: "suggesting to the viewer both the fact of the backswing and the potentiality of the forward swing."

12 These phases are set out in an authoritative and definitive text by Christian Gänshirt, "Swimming Pool on the Beach at Leça da Palmeira: The Presence of the Atlantic Ocean," in D. Leatherbarrow and A. Eisenschmidt, eds., *Companions to the History of Architecture: Twentieth-Century Architecture*, vol. 4 (New York: Wiley, 2017).

Chapter 3.1

1 Two texts by Martha Hollander have helped me understand the structure and meanings of this painting. See Martha Hollander, "The Divided House of Nicolaes Maes," *Word and Image*, vol. 10, no. 2 (April–June 1994): 138–55; and Martha Hollander, *An Entrance for the Eyes: Space and Meaning in Seventeenth-Century Dutch Art* (Berkeley: University of California Press, 2002).

2 With the term "episode," I refer to Aristotle's critique of plots in which incidents simply follow one another in sequence, without any intelligible or dramatic order of unfolding. See *Poetics*, as well as the interpretation by Paul Ricoeur in *Time and Narrative*.

3 This is Hollander's term, usefully spatial. My task in this chapter is to clarify the corresponding temporal order.

4 In point of fact, the relationship between the kitchen and lover's hallway is ambiguous: is the red floor on the other side of the foreground right doorway also within reach of the level on which the lovers stand? For that to occur they would need to be standing next to another run of steps, which would be very awkward.

5 The upper landing could turn on itself and give way to a run of steps up to another floor, bedrooms would be likely. But this image shows no evidence of that.

Chapter 3.2

1 Although published many decades ago, the study undertaken by Fritz Saxl is still very useful, indicating very clearly the range of interpretations the phrase has allowed and sustained. See Fritz Saxl, "Veritas Filia Temporis," in R. Klibansky and H.J. Paton, eds., *Philosophy and History: Essays Presented to Ernst Cassirer* (Oxford: Clarendon, 1936), 197–222. Also useful is the paper by Saxl's University of Hamburg colleague Erwin Panofsky: see Erwin Panofsky, "Father Time," *Studies in Iconology: Humanistic Themes in the Art of the Renaissance* [1939] (New York: Harper & Row, 1962), 69–94.

2 August Schmarsow, "The Essence of Architectural Creation," in H.F. Mallgrave and Eleftherios Ikonomou, eds., *Empathy, Form, and Space* (Sant Monica: Getty Center for the History of Art and the Humanities, 1994), 295.

3   These definitions are from the *Oxford English Dictionary*.

4   A short but very helpful text on the possibilities of grasping moments in time as the same—as opposed to different or similar—is Paul Ricoeur, *The Reality of the Historical Past* (Milwaukee: Marquette University Press, 1984).

5   My thinking about this temporal double has benefited greatly from Anne Carson, *Eros the Bittersweet* (Princeton: Princeton University Press, 1986).

6   Hence the famous lines from Alexander Pope: "Let not each beauty everywhere be spied, Where half the skill is decently to hide. He gains all points, who pleasingly confounds, Surprises, varies, and conceals the bounds." Alexander Pope, "Epistle to Richard Boyle, Earl of Burlington," lines 51–5.

7   For elaboration of this point, see Aron Gurwitsch, *Marginal Consciousness*, ed. Lester Embree (Athens: Ohio University Press, 1985).

8   Jacques Derrida, *Writing and Difference*, trans. Alan Bass (Chicago: University of Chicago Press, 1978), especially chapter 2.

9   I've examined this design in another text, David Leatherbarrow, "From Pedestal to Place," in Penny Florence, ed., *Thinking the Sculpture Garden* (London: Routledge, 2019), 101–24. For present purposes, I have not modified the historiographic information and analysis published there. But while that study used the Louisiana Museum to exemplify the *spatial questions* involved in siting sculpture (platforms, places, and pedestals), this one considers the *temporal structuring* of the landscape (still and passing moments).

10 This heading is from a classic text: André Malraux, *Museum without Walls* (Garden City: Doubleday, 1967). Malraux argued that the distinctive aspect of the Museum was the dislocation of its objects, the fact that they had been removed from the spatial, material, and functional environments that had originally contributed to their meanings. Once removed from their native settings, they ceased to function in the ways their makers and patrons intended—practically, politically, or religiously. Portraits that were removed from family estates to museums, Malraux said, became *pictures*. Votive carvings and talismans came to be classed as examples of the minor arts, *handicrafts*.

11 The basic sources on the Museum's history and holdings are the following texts: Michael Sheridan, *Louisiana: Architecture and Landscape* (Humlebaek: Louisiana Museum of Modern Art, 2017); Helle Crenzien, *The Louisiana Sculpture Park* (Humlebaek: Louisiana Museum of Modern Art, 2008); John Pardey, *Louisiana and Beyond: The Work of Vilhelm Wohlert* (Hellerup: Bløndal, 2007); and Knud W. Jensen, et al., *Louisiana: samling og bygninger* (Humlebaek: Louisiana Museum of Modern Art, 1992). Also interesting, though indirectly, is Jean Nouvel, et al., *Louisiana Manifesto* (Humlebaek: Louisiana Museum of Modern Art, 2008).

12 Pardey, *Louisiana and Beyond*, 46.

13 Paul Valéry, "The Problem of Museums," in *Degas, Manet, Morisot: The Collected Works of Paul Valéry*, D. Paul, trans., vol. 12 (New York: Pantheon, 1960), 205.

14 Knud W. Jensen, *Mit Louisiana liv* (Copenhagen: Gyldendal, 1993), 128.

15 I've made the same observation about a more recent project, the Lewis Glucksman Gallery in Cork, Ireland, designed by O'Donnell and Tuomey. See David Leatherbarrow, "Landings and Crossings," in *Architecture Oriented Otherwise* (New York: Princeton Architectural Press, 2009), 221–41.

16 A number of the points I've made here restate and elaborate observations made in Maurice Merleau-Ponty, *The Phenomenology of Perception* (New York: Humanities Press, 1962), 302. On viewing distance, see also José Ortega y Gasset, *The Dehumanization of Art and Other Essays on Art, Culture, and Literature*, trans. Willard R. Trask (Princeton, NJ: Princeton University Press, 1968).

17 David Summers, "Real Metaphor: Towards a Redefinition of the 'Conceptual' Image," in N. Bryson, et al., eds., *Visual Theory: Painting and Interpretation* (London: Polity Press, 1991), 231–59. See pp. 246 ff.

18 See Jean-Luc Marion, *Being Given: Toward a Phenomenology of Givenness*, trans. Jeffrey L. Kosky (Stanford: Stanford University Press, 2002), esp. Bk. 1, section 6.

19 This type of encounter is described very beautifully and helpfully in Ananda Coomaraswamy, "The Meeting of Eyes," in R.E. Lipsey, ed., *Traditional Art and Symbolism: Selected Papers*, vol. 1 (Princeton: Princeton University Press, 1977), 233–40.

Chapter 3.3

1 Wang Shu, "Build a World to Resemble Nature," in Mark Cousins and Chen Wei, eds., *Architecture Studies 2: Topography and Mental Space* (Beijing: China Architecture & Building Press, 2012), 198. The heaviness he noted may well have been cultural—not only physical but metaphorical. If it is true that he named the hill, this project augmented its cultural sense.

2 Rather than introduce a general definition of this highly contested term at the beginning of this chapter, I will gradually elaborate what I believe is Wang Shu's sense of the term "image" by citing his writings and interpreting his buildings. My study of this building, together with the role of landscape paintings in its design and visualization, has been guided by a recent Ph.D. dissertation. See Linfan Liu, *A Pictorial Vision of Space: Looking at Modern Architecture in China through Landscape Painting*, University of Pennsylvania, 2018.

3 Here I allude to the Renaissance interpretation (distortion) of the Aristotelian principle of "unity of action" in tragic drama, which is to say plot construction. While Aristotle insisted on unity of action, in which parts are organically integrated into a whole, as in the makeup of an animal, Renaissance writers, especially in France and Italy, extended his *description* of typical limits on time and place into *prescriptions*, like those he required of action, hence, the so-called three unities.

4 George Rowley, in *Principles of Chinese Painting*, 2nd ed. (Princeton: Princeton University Press, 1959), 61, observed, "A scroll painting must be experienced in time like music or literature. Our attention is carried along laterally from right to left, being restricted at any one moment to a short passage which can be conveniently perused." Perspective space in European art also extended beyond the limits of the painting or fresco's frame, in baroque and rococo art especially. For a good account of the latter, see Karsten Harries, *The Broken Frame: Three Lectures* (Washington, DC: Catholic University of America Press, 1989).

5 Leonardo da Vinci had made similar observations in his account of the "thick air" that results from rising vapors and mists in the space between the eye and a distant mountain.

6   Shu, "Build a World to Resemble Nature."

7   Ibid.

8   Ibid.

9   Guo Xi, *An Essay on Landscape Painting*, trans. Shio Sakanishi (London: John Murray, 1935), 37.

10 No sense of defeat is implied here. An instructive parallel may be the "negative capability" John Keats attributed to Shakespeare, the type of demeanor in which a person is "capable of being in uncertainties. Mysteries, doubts, without any irritable reaching after fact and reason." Keats to his Brother, December 21, 1817.

11 Wang Shu, "A Picturesque House," in *Imagining the House* (Lars Müller: Zürich, 2012), np.

12 Wang Shu, "A House as Sleep," in *Imagining the House* (Lars Müller: Zürich, 2012), 1.2.

13 Rowley observed: "In the T'ang period [Chinese artists] reworked the early principles of time and suggested a space through which one might wander and a space which implied more space beyond the picture frame ... They practiced the principle of the moving focus, by which the eye could wander while the spectator also wandered in imagination through the landscape." *Principles*, 61–2.

14 Wang Shu, *Imagining the House*, 201.

15 Two older but still fundamental texts on this subject are: Miriam Schild Bunim, *Space in Medieval Painting and the Forerunners of Perspective* (New York: Columbia University Press, 1940); and Fritz Novotny, *Cézanne und das Ende der Wissenschaftlichen Perspektive* (Vienna: Anton Schroll, 1938). Together they nicely bracket the five centuries of the perspective tradition, indicating the limits of its historical reign: first single then multiple points of convergence, later theatrical and anamorphic perspective, and then to perspectives of emotions and atmospheres, much discussed today.

16 One point of contention in the interpretation of traditional Chinese landscape paintings is the use of the term "picture plane," which seems so obvious when one's point of departure is from within the history and culture of European painting. A number of scholars have questioned the validity of this premise when interpreting non-European art, particularly Chinese landscape paintings. One of the older but still relevant texts to argue this thesis, Wilfrid H. Wells, *Perspective in Early Chinese Painting* (London: Edward Goldston, 1935). Wells opened his study as follows:

> We are so accustomed to the practice of breaking through the surface to attain an effect of depth in painting that we are apt to forget that this presupposes the conception of the surface as a geometrical plane, and that this in turn presupposes considerable abstractness of thought. Both are premises which we cannot assume in early Chinese art. A great deal of what we regard as an attitude of mind towards the surface was an attitude of mind towards the edges ... in early Chinese painting ... [t]here simply is no [picture] plane (p. 11).

A broad, insightful, and more recent study of this problem is set out in David Summers, *Real Spaces: World Art History and the Rise of Western Modernism* (London: Phaidon, 2003), esp. sections 6.11. and 6.23.

17 The difficult and important vocabulary of distance and depth is explained clearly in Liu, *A Pictorial Vision of Space*. See Definitions, sections 1-3, and chapter 1, section 3.

18 Wang Shu, "A House as Sleep," *Imaging the House*, n. p.

19 Again, a reference to pre-perspective or early perspective European painting is useful, the so-called continuous narrative paintings of the early Italian Renaissance; specifically, the works of figures like Giotto, Masaccio, and Lippi. A very helpful study of this theme is Lew Andrews, *Story and Space in Renaissance Art: The Rebirth of Continuous Narrative* (Cambridge: Cambridge University Press, 1995). Especially relevant to the arguments I've been making is Andrews' chapter "By the Ocean of Time." The use of the term "rebirth" in the book's subtitle acknowledges the fact that painters long before the Renaissance period took up the theme of "narrative." For a good account of the very early history of this theme in Western art, which also takes up the problem of viewing images on a roll rather than framed canvas or parchment, see Kurt Weitzmann, *Illustrations in Roll and Codex: A Study of the Origin and Method of Text Illustration*, 2nd ed. (Princeton: Princeton University Press, 1970).

20 Recently, Wen C. Fong connected the early practice of structuring depth through the layering of mountain peaks to its "ideographic counterpart, *shan* comprising three peaks, a 'host' mountain flanked by two 'guests.'" See Wen C. Fong, "Building the Vocabulary," in *Images of the Mind* (Princeton: Princeton University Press, 1984), 22.

21 Guo Xi in *Lofty Aims in Forests and Streams* (*c.* 1117) differentiated the three as follows: "The bottom of the mountain looking up toward the top, this is called the 'high distance'. From the front of the mountain peering toward the back of the mountain, this is called the 'deep distance'. From a nearby mountain looking past distant mountains, this is called the 'level distance.'"

22 A good account of the "situated" character of non- or a-metric dimensioning begins Witold Kula, *Measures and Men*, trans. R. Szreter (Princeton: Princeton University Press, 1986).

23 Xi, *An Essay on Landscape Painting*, 32.

24 Cited in Susan Bush, *The Chinese Literati on Painting: Su Shih (1037–1101) to Tung Ch'i-Ch'ang (1555–1636)*, 2nd ed. (Hong Kong: Hong Kong University Press, 2012), 32. For an introduction to the European understanding of the relationships between painting and poetry, see Rensselaer Lee, *Ut Pictura Poesis: The Humanistic Theory of Painting* (New York: W. W. Norton, 1967).

Chapter 3.4

1 St. Augustine, *Confessions*, XI, 14.17.

2 As noted above in 3.2, clarification of the peculiar temporality of *now then* can be found in Anne Carson, "Now Then," in *Eros the Bittersweet: An Essay* (Princeton: Princeton University Press, 1986), 117–22.

3 Álvaro Siza, "Every year, with the spring tides …" (1980), in *Piscina na Praia de Leça*, Michael Toussaint and Maria Melo, eds. (Lisbon: A A Books, 2016), 9.

4 Aldo Rossi, *The Architecture of the City* (Cambridge, MA: MIT Press, 1982), 57–61.

5   Here is intended the ancient understanding of rhythm (*rhythmos*) explained above in chapter 2.4, which was approximately synonymous with pose, that moment and stance in a sequence or passage that both summarizes past and initiates future movement.

6   A half a century ago, the great French linguist Emile Benveniste explained the early history of *tempus* by relating it to *kairós* (due time) rather than *chronos* (sequential time) because both imply mixing, the meaning of which survives in the English *temper*: to temper one's emotions or a composite metal. Weather, no matter what the temperature, is similarly composite. For Benveniste's arguments, see Emile Benveniste, "Latin *tempus*," in *Mélanges de philologie, de littérature et d'histoire anciennes offerts à Ernout* (Paris, 1940), 11–16. As noted above, this study has been amplified recently in Giacomo Marramao, *Kairós* (Aurora, CO: Davies Group, 2007), esp., 69–72.

7   I use this term in the sense Le Corbusier gave it in his account of "human-limb objects." See Le Corbusier, "Type-Needs Type-Furniture," in James I. Dunnett, trans., *The Decorative Art of Today*, (Cambridge, MA: MIT Press, 1987), 69–79.

8   Le Corbusier, *Poem of the Right Angle*, A2 (Paris: Fondation Le Corbusier/Editions Connivences, 1989), np.

9   Plato, *The Collected Dialogues*, Edith Hamilton and Huntington Cairns, eds., Princeton: Princeton University Press, 1961), 1167.

10 Although Vitruvius reported that Aristippus was delighted to find geometrical signs in the sand of the Rhodian shore—because the marks indicated the shipwrecked sailor was among civilized people—the "signs" also required interpretation. What was seen implied more than was apparent. For a recent study of this story, see Hans Blumenberg, *Shipwreck with Spectator* (Cambridge, MA: MIT, 1997).

Chapter 4.1

1   Vittorio Gregotti, *Inside Architecture*, trans. Peter Wong and Francesca Zaccheo (Cambridge, MA: MIT, 1996), 67.

2   Gregotti, 17.

3   Paul Klee, *Pedagogical Sketchbook* [1925] (New York: Praeger, 1953), 16.

4   Le Corbusier, *The Final Testament of Père Corbu: A Translation and Interpretation of Mise au point* [1966], trans. Ivan Žaknić (New Haven: Yale University Press, 1997), 144: *Rien hors de la règle! Sinon je n'ai plus de raison d'exister. Là est le clef. Raison d'exister: jouer le jeu.*

5   Alison and Peter Smithson, "The 'As Found' and 'The Found,'" in David Robbins, ed., *The Independent Group: Postwar Britain and the Aesthetics of Plenty* (Cambridge, MA: MIT, 1990), 201–2; cited in David Leatherbarrow and Mohsen Mostafavi, *Surface Architecture* (Cambridge, MA: MIT, 2002), 177. The ancient Greek concept of *mêtis* was described by Marcel Detienne and Jean-Pierre Vernant as follows: "Two antagonistic forces confront each other. Over this fraught and unstable time of the *agôn mêtis* gives one a hold without which one would be at a loss. During the struggle, the man of *mêtis*—compared to his opponent—displays at the same

time a greater grip of the present where nothing escapes him, more awareness of the future, several aspects of which he has already manipulated, and richer experience accumulated from the past." See *Cunning Intelligence in Greek Culture and Society*, trans. Janet Lloyd (Chicago: University of Chicago Press, 1991), 14 and elsewhere throughout.

6 Useful here for this point and a number of those to follow is: Alexander Nagel and Christopher S. Wood, *Anachronic Renaissance* (New York: Zone Books, 2010), especially chapter 24 "Anti-Architecture."

Chapter 4.2

1 "[I]n the crude reality of built works one can see clearly the essence of a project, the consistency of ideas." Rafael Moneo, *The Solitude of Buildings*. The Kenzo Tange Lecture, March 9, 1985 (Cambridge MA: Harvard University, 1986), 12.

2 See in particular the interview with Rafael Moneo, "The Idea of the Lasting," *Perspecta*, vol. 24 (1988): 146–57.

3 Leon Battista Alberti, *On the Art of Building in Ten Books*, trans. J. Rykwert, N. Leach, and R. Tavernor (Cambridge, MA: MIT Press, 1988), especially chapter 9.

4 The river banks and shore lines that served projective purposes—orthogonality—required both abstraction for drawings and imposition for construction. This point is essential to Dilip da Cunha's *Invention of Rivers: Alexander's Eye and Ganga's Descent* (Philadelphia: University of Pennsylvania Press, 2018).

5 Joseph Rykwert, *The Idea of a Town: The Anthropology of Urban Form in Rome, Italy and the Ancient World* (London: Faber and Faber, 1976).

6 See J.J. Pollitt, "Symmetry," in *The Ancient View of Greek Art* (New Haven: Yale University. Press, 1974), 218–28.

7 Alberti, *On the Art of Building in Ten Books*, book 6, chapter 5. I discuss this passage and idea in *The Roots of Architectural Invention: Site, Enclosure, Materials* (Cambridge: Cambridge University Press, 1993), 94–6.

8 Ernesto Nathan Rogers, "Preexisting Conditions and Issues of Contemporary Building Practice," in J. Ockman and E. Eigen, eds., *Architecture Culture 1943–1968* (New York: Rizzoli, 1993), 200–4, and Vittorio Gregotti, "On Modification," in *Inside Architecture* (Cambridge, MA: MIT Press, 1996), 67–73.

9 Sverre Fehn, "The Dance Round Dead Things," in Marja-Ritta Norri and Maija Kärkkäinen, eds., *Poetry of the Straight Line* (Helsinki: Museum of Finnish Architecture, 1992), 4–5.

10 Søren Kierkegaard, *Fear and Trembling & Repetition*, eds. Howard V. Hong and Edna H. Hong (Princeton: Princeton University Press, 1983), 149.

11 Kierkegaard, *Fear and Trembling & Repetition*, 185.

12 What follows has been informed by Paul Ricoeur, *The Reality of the Historical Past* (Milwaukee: Marquette University Press, 1984).

Chapter 4.3

1. Patricia McLaughlin, "'How'm I Doing, Corbusier?': An Interview with Louis Kahn," *Pennsylvania Gazette*, vol. 71, no. 3 (1972): 18–26.

2. *Historical Ground* is the title of a marvelous book by John Dixon Hunt, which discusses the presence of the past in landscape architecture. See John Dixon Hunt, *Historical Ground: The Role of History in Contemporary Landscape Architecture* (London: Routledge, 2014).

3. Louis Kahn, in *Louis Kahn: Writings, Lectures, Interviews*, ed. Alessandra Latour (New York: Rizzoli International Publications, 1991), 168.

4. Here I cite the title of a book that has been useful to me in this study: David Lowenthal, *The Past Is a Foreign Country* (Cambridge: Cambridge University Press, 1985).

5. St. Augustine, *Confessions*, XI, 14.17.

6. Louis I. Kahn, in Alessandra Latour, ed., *Louis I. Kahn: Writings, Lectures, Interviews* (New York: Rizzoli, 1991), 221.

7. I've addressed the line of thinking in Kahn's design practice in a text with this title: David Leatherbarrow, "The Beginning of the Beginning: Louis I. Kahn's Site Sketches at the Salk Institute," forthcoming in Michael Merrill, *Louis Kahn: Drawing, Thinking, Architecture* (Zurich: Lars Müller, 2019), 30 pp. ms.

8. Louis I. Kahn, "I Love Beginnings," in Richard Saul Wurman, ed., *What Will Be Has Always Been: The Words of Louis I. Kahn* (New York: Rizzoli, 1991), 177.

9. I mean the early histories of modern architecture, by figures like Nikolaus Pevsner, Sigfried Giedion, and Henry-Russell Hitchcock, and their predecessors among the moderns themselves, Walter Curt Behrendt, Adolf Behne, Karel Teige, and so on.

10. A good recent study of this theme is Maiken Umbach and Bernd Hüppauf, *Vernacular Modernism: Heimat, Globalization, and the Built Environment* (Stanford: Stanford University Press, 2005).

11. Le Corbusier, "To Free Oneself Entirely of Academic Thinking," in *Precisions on the Present State of Architecture and City Planning*, trans. Edith Schreiber Aujame (Cambridge, MA: MIT, 1991), 33.

12. Outside of architecture, in philosophy, a brief but useful account of this possibility is: Paul Ricoeur, "The Function of Fiction in Shaping Reality," in M. Valdés, ed., *A Ricoeur Reader: Reflection and Imagination* (Toronto: University of Toronto Press, 1991), 117–36.

13. Adolf Loos, "Eine zuschrift," in *Trotzdem, 1900–1930* (Vienna: Georg Prachner, 1982), 110–11 See p. 111.

14. Adolf Loos, "Architectur," in *Trotzdem, 1900–1930* (Vienna: Georg Prachner, 1982), 90–104. A comparable story was offered by an even more prominent modern, Frank Lloyd Wright. He narrated cave origins in *The Living City*. "Go back far enough in time," he said, "Mankind was divided into cave-dwelling agrarians and wandering tribes of hunter-warriors." The first group sheltered themselves in the "shadow-of-the-wall," while the second enjoyed life under the sun, resting now and then under a bower of trees or a

tent. See Frank Lloyd Wright, "The Shadow-of-the-Wall—Primitive Instincts Still Alive," in *The Living City* (New York: Horizon Press, 1958), 21–4. This story is cited and discussed in David Leatherbarrow, "Nature and Artifice in the Architecture of Sverre Fehn," in Christophe Girot and Albert Kirchengast, eds., *Landscript* vol. 4 (2017): 103–23.

15 Pezo von Ellrichshausen, *Spatial Structure* (Copenhagen: Arkitekturforlaget B, 2016), 31.

16 Aaron Paterson, "Interview: Pezo von Ellrichshausen," *architecturenow.co.nz/articles/*Pezo-von-Ellrichshausen.

17 Thomas Mann, *Joseph and His Brothers*, trans. H.T. Lowe-Porter (London: Penguin, 1978), 3.

18 "Strangely familiar" is the term John Tuomey used to describe what he hoped will be the sense of buildings he and Sheila O'Donnell had designed. See John Tuomey, *Architecture, Craft, and Culture: Reflections on the Work of O'Donnell + Tuomey* (Cork: Gandon, 2008).

19 Aaron Paterson, "Interview: Pezo von Ellrichshausen," *architecturenow.co.nz/articles/*Pezo-von-Ellrichshausen.

20 The significance of this "problem" in architecture is argued in Pier Vittorio Aureli, *The Project of Autonomy: Politics and Architecture Within and Against Capitalism* (New York: Princeton Architectural Press, 2012).

21 Maurizio Pezo and Sofia von Ellrichshausen, "Cien House," *Harvard Design Magazine*, vol. 34 (2011): 110–13. See p. 110.

22 Pezo von Ellrichshausen, "'Singular, without Claiming Any Singular Feature': An Interview with Mauricio Pezo and Sofia von Ellrichshausen," in *Casa Poli* (Amsterdam: The Architecture Observer, 2013), 148.

23 "This text [*Spatial Structure*] … has not so much been a focus on trying to return to the origin, as it has been a force trying to approximate the focus to the center of a disciplinary matter." Pezo von Ellrichshausen, *Spatial Structure*, 10. They do, however, attend to the Vitruvian account, which in their assessment is still the "most accurate" origin story. Pezo von Ellrichshausen, *Spatial Structure*, 21.

24 Pezo von Ellrichshausen, *Spatial Structure*, 58.

25 While this distinction is apparent in a number of their texts, Pezo von Ellrichshausen discuss the two most fully in *Naïve Intention* (Chicago: IITAC Press and New York: Actar, 2018), 8 ff.

26 *Naïve Intention*, 22.

27 Pezo von Ellrichshausen, *Spatial Structure*, 147.

28 Pezo von Ellrichshausen, "'Singular, without Claiming Any Singular Feature,'" 149.

29 Ibid., 151

30 Aaron Peterson, "Interview: Pezo von Ellrichshausen," *architecturenow.co.nz/articles/***Pezo-von-Ellrichshausen**.

31 Ibid.

32 Pezo von Ellrichshausen, *Spatial Structure*, 255.

Chapter 4.4

1. Siza gives the dates 1961–6 as the time of the project; but this is only one phase of the work. Of the many studies that have studied the chronology, narrated the history, and interpreted the significance of this project, most helpful to me has been Christian Gänshirt, "Swimming Pool on the Beach at Leça de Palmeira: The Presence of the Atlantic Ocean," in D. Leatherbarrow and A. Eisenschmidt, eds., *The Companions to the History of Architecture: Twentieth Century Architecture*, vol. 4 (New York: John Wiley & Sons, 2017), 525–38. See, too, an earlier version of this text in: Luiz Trigueiros, ed., *Álvaro Siza: Leça de Palmeira, 1959–1973* (Lisbon: Editorial Blau, 2004). Also useful, for its description and references, is Kenneth Frampton, *Álvaro Siza: Complete Works* (London: Phaidon, 2000).

2. Álvaro Siza, "Eight Points," in A. Angelillo, ed., *Siza: Architecture Writings* (Milan: Skira, 1997), 204.

3. With this qualification, I am invoking an important argument made by Paul Ricoeur about the kinds or degrees of objectivity in cultural studies. See Paul Ricoeur, "Objectivity and Subjectivity in History," in C.A. Kelbley, trans., *History and Truth* (Evanston: Northwestern University Press, 1965), 21–40. Also useful to me has been Ernst Cassirer, *The Logic of the Cultural Sciences: Five Studies* (New Haven: Yale, 2000).

4. Álvaro Siza, "He Was Called an Architect," in A. Angelillo, ed., *Siza: Architecture Writings* (Milan: Skira, 1997), 175.

5. Álvaro Siza, "Post-Modern," in A. Angelillo, ed., *Siza: Architecture Writings* (Milan: Skira, 1997), 38.

6. Álvaro Siza, "Fragments of an Experience," in Pedro de Llano and Carlos Castanheira, eds., *Álvaro Siza: Works and Projects* (Madrid: Electa, 1995), 32–3.

7. See Luiz Trigueiros, ed., *Álvaro Siza: Leça de Palmeira, 1959–1973* (Lisbon: Editorial Blau, 2004), 65–6.

8. Siza, "Eight Points," 204.

9. Álvaro Siza, "Restaurant at Boa Nova," in *Siza: Architecture Writings* (Milan: Skira, 1997), 149.

10. Ibid.

11. Ibid., 151.

12. Álvaro Siza, "Building a House," in A. Angelillo, ed., *Siza: Architecture Writings* (Milan: Skira, 1997), 51.

13. With respect to drawings of places of interest, two publications should be consulted; one new, the other old: Álvaro Siza and Giovanni Chiaramonte, *Measure of the West: A Representation of Travel* (Montreal: McGill-Queen's University Press, 2018); and Álvaro Siza, *Álvaro Siza: Esquissos de viagem* (Porto: Documentos de Arquitectura, 1988).

14. Alvaro Siza, "Travel Sketches," in A. Angelillo, ed., *Siza: Architecture Writings* (Milan: Skira, 1997), 113.

15 Ibid.

16 Ibid.

17 Álvaro Siza, "The Initial Procedure," in A. Angelillo, ed., *Siza: Architecture Writings* (Milan: Skira, 1997), 25.

18 With this italicized term, I allude to the wonderful title by Robin Evans, whose reflections on drawing have played a role in these arguments, despite the fact that project making in the narrow sense I'm considering was not his focus. See Robin Evans, *The Projective Cast: Architecture and Its Three Geometries* (Cambridge, MA: MIT, 1995).

19 Álvaro Siza, "Design as Experience," *Domus,* vol. 746 (February 1993): 28.

20 Álvaro Siza, "On Working in a Team," in *Siza: Architecture Writings* (Milan: Skira, 1997), 27.

21 Álvaro Siza, "Educational Journeys," in *Siza: Architecture Writings* (Milan: Skira, 1997), 30.

22 Ibid.

23 Álvaro Siza, "Educational Journeys," in *Siza: Architecture Writings* (Milan: Skira, 1997), 30.

24 Álvaro Siza, "Eight Points," in *Siza: Architecture Writings* (Milan: Skira, 1997), 204.

Bibliography

Adam, Peter, *Eileen Gray: Architect/Designer*, New York: Harry N. Abrams, 2000.
Alberti, Leon Battista, *On the Art of Building in Ten Books*, translated by J. Rykwert, N. Leach and R. Tavernor, Cambridge, MA: MIT Press, 1988.
Agacinski, Sylvane, *Time Passing Modernity and Nostalgia*, New York: Columbia University Press, 2003.
Andrews, Lew, *Story and Space in Renaissance Art: The Rebirth of Continuous Narrative*, Cambridge: Cambridge University Press, 1995.
Aristotle, "On Memory," 449b 10–13, *The Complete Works of Aristotle*, vol. 1, Princeton: Princeton University Press, 1984.
Aureli, Pier Vittorio, *The Project of Autonomy: Politics and Architecture Within and Against Capitalism*, New York: Princeton Architectural Press, 2012.
Bachelard, Gaston, *Intuition of the Instant*, Evanston: Northwestern University, 2013.
Banham, Reyner, *The Architecture of the Well-Tempered Environment*, Chicago: University of Chicago, 1969.
Benveniste, Emile, "Latin *tempus*," in *Mélanges de philologie, de littérature et d'histoire anciennes offerts à Ernout*, Paris: Klincksieck, 1940.
Blumenberg, Hans, *Lebenszeit und Weltzeit*, Frankfurt: Suhrkamp, 1986.
Blumenberg, Hans, *Shipwreck with Spectator: Paradigm of a Metaphor for Existence*, translated by Steven Rendall, Cambridge, MA: MIT, 1997.
Blundell Jones, Peter and Meagher, Mark, *Architecture and Movement: The Dynamic Experience of Buildings and Landscapes*, London: Routledge, 2015.
Brilliant, Richard and Kinney, Dale, *Reuse Value* Spolia *and Appropriation in Art and Architecture from Constantine to Sherrie Levine*, Farnham: Ashgate, 2011.
Burke, Peter, *Eyewitnessing: The Uses of Images as Historical Evidence*, Ithaca: Cornell University Press, 2001.
Bush, Susan, *The Chinese Literati on Painting: Su Shih (1037–1101) to Tung Ch'i-Ch'ang (1555–1636)*, 2nd ed., Hong Kong: Hong Kong University Press, 2012.
Cairns, Stephen and Jacobs, Jane M., *Buildings Must Die: A Perverse View of Architecture*, Cambridge, MA: MIT Press, 2014.
Carl, Peter, "Architecture and Time," *AA Files*, vol. 22 (1991): 48–65.
Carson, Anne, *Eros the Bittersweet*, Princeton: Princeton University Press, 1986.
Cassirer, Ernst, *The Logic of the Cultural Sciences: Five Studies*, New Haven: Yale, 2000.
Cervantes, Miguel de, *Don Quixote*, vol. 1, translated by Edith Grossman, New York: HarperCollins, 2005, bk. iii, ch. vi.
Cohen, J. H. and Ahrenberg, S., eds., *Le Corbusier's Secret Laboratory: From Painting to Architecture*, Ostfildern: Hatje Cantz, 2013.
Constant, Caroline, *Eileen Gray*, London: Phaidon, 2000.

Coomaraswamy, Ananda, "The Meeting of Eyes," in *Traditional Art and Symbolism: Selected Papers*, vol. 1, edited by R.E. Lipsey, Princeton: Princeton University Press, 1977.

Corona-Martínez, Alfonso, *The Architectural Project*, College Station, TX: Texas A&M Press, 2003.

Crenzien, Helle, *The Louisiana Sculpture Park*, Humlebaek: Louisiana Museum of Modern Art, 2008.

da Cunha, Dilip, *Invention of Rivers: Alexander's Eye and Ganga's Descent*, Philadelphia: University of Pennsylvania Press, 2018.

Deleuze, Gilles, *The Fold: Leibniz and the Baroque*, translated by Tom Conley, Minneapolis: University of Minnesota Press, 1993.

Derrida, Jacques, *Writing and Difference*, translated by Alan Bass, Chicago: University of Chicago Press, 1978.

Detienne, Marcel and Vernant, Jean-Pierre, *Cunning Intelligence in Greek Culture and Society*, translated by Janet Lloyd, Chicago: University of Chicago Press, 1991.

Eriksen, Roy, *The Building in the Text: Alberti to Shakespeare and Milton*, State College: Penn State University Press, 2000.

Evans, Robin, *The Projective Cast: Architecture and Its Three Geometries*, Cambridge, MA: MIT, 1995.

Faulkner, William, *The Sound and the Fury, & As I Lay Dying*, New York: Random House, 1946.

Fehn, Sverre, "An Architectural Autobiography," in Marja-Ritti Norri and Maija Kärkkäinen eds., *Sverre Fehn: The Poetry of the Straight Line*, Helsinki: Museum of Finish Architecture, 1992.

Fehn, Sverre, "The Dance Round Dead Things," in *Poetry of the Straight Line* in Marja-Ritti Norri and Maija Kärkkäinen eds., Helsinki: Museum of Finnish Architecture, 1992.

Fehn, Sverre, "Villa Busk," in Marja-Ritti Norri and Maija Kärkkäinen eds., *Sverre Fehn: The Poetry of the Straight Line*, Helsinki: Museum of Finish Architecture, 1992, first published in *Arkitektguiden*, no. 2 (February 1990), 14–47.

Fong, Wen C., "Building the Vocabulary," in *Images of the Mind*, Princeton: Princeton University Press, 1984.

Foucault, Michel, *The Order of Things: An Archaeology of the Human Sciences*, London: Tavistock, 1970.

Frampton, Kenneth, *Álvaro Siza: Complete Works*, London: Phaidon, 2000.

Fraser, J.T., *Time: The Familiar Stranger*, Amherst: University of Massachusetts, 1987.

Fried, Michael, *Menzel's Realism: Art and Embodiment in Nineteenth-Century Berlin*, New Haven: Yale University Press, 2002.

Gänshirt, Christian, "Swimming Pool on the Beach at Leça da Palmeira: The Presence of the Atlantic Ocean," in *Companions to the History of Architecture: Twentieth-Century Architecture*, vol. 4, edited by David Leatherbarrow and Alexander Eisenschmidt, New York: Wiley, 2017.

Ginzburg, Carlo, *Clues, Myths, and the Historical Method*, translated by John and Anne Tedeschi, Baltimore: Johns Hopkins, 1989.

Glacken, Clarence, *Traces on the Rhodian Shore: Nature and Culture in Western Thought from Ancient Times to the End of the Eighteenth Century*, Berkeley: University of California, 1967.

Goethe, Johann Wolfgang von, *Goethe on Art*, edited and translated by John Gage, Berkeley, CA: University of California Press, 1980.

Gray, Eileen and Badovici, Jean, "*E 1027 Maison en bord de mer*," *L'Architecture Vivante* (Automne-Hiver 1929): 17–38.

Gregotti, Vittorio, *Inside Architecture*, translated by Peter Wong and Francesca Zaccheo, Cambridge, MA: MIT, 1996.

Gros, Frédéric, *A Philosophy of Walking*, London: Verso, 2014.

Gubster, Michael, *Time's Visible Surface Alois Riegl and the Discourse on History and Temporality in Fin-de-Siècle Vienna*, Detroit: Wayne Statue University Press, 2006.

Guo Xi, *An Essay on Landscape Painting*, translated by Shio Sakanishi, London: John Murray, 1935.
Gurwitsch, Aron, *Marginal Consciousness*, edited by Lester Embree, Athens: Ohio University Press, 1985.
Harries, Karsten, *The Broken Frame: Three Lectures*, Washington, DC: Catholic University of America Press, 1989.
Harris, Jonatnh Gil, *Untimely Matter in the Time of Shakespeare*, Philadelphia: University of Pennsylvania Press, 2009.
Hartog, Francois, *Regimes of Historicity Presentism and Experiences of Time*, translated by Saskia Brown, New York: Columbia University Press, 2015.
Hobsbawn, Eric, *On History*, New York: The New Press, 1997.
Hollander, Martha, "The Divided House of Nicolaes Maes," *Word and Image*, vol. 10, no. 2 (April–June 1994): 138–55.
Hollander, Martha, *An Entrance for the Eyes: Space and Meaning in Seventeenth-Century Dutch Art*, Berkeley: University of California Press, 2002.
Hunt, John Dixon, "'Lordship of the Feet': Toward a Poetics of Movement in the Garden," in *Landscape Design and the Experience of Motion*, M. Conan, ed., Washington DC: Dumbarton Oaks, 2003.
Hunt, John Dixon, *Historical Ground: The Role of History in Contemporary Landscape Architecture*, London: Routledge, 2014.
Husserl, Edmund, "Foundational Investigations of the Phenomenological Origin of the Spatiality of Nature," in *Philosophical Essays in Memory of Edmund Husserl*, edited by Martin Farber, Cambridge, MA: Harvard University Press, 1940.
Jakob, Michael, *Paysage et Temps*, Gollion, Infolio, 2007.
Jaeger, Werner, *Paideia: The Ideals of Greek Culture*, vol. 1, translated by Gilbert Highet, Oxford: Oxford University Press, 1945.
Jammer, Max, *Concepts of Force: A Study in the Foundations of Dynamics*, New York: Harper, 1957.
Jensen, Knud W., et al., *Louisiana: samling og bygninger*, Humlebaek: Louisiana Museum of Modern Art, 1992.
Jensen, Knud W., *Mit Louisiana liv*, Copenhagen: Gyldendal, 1993.
Jonson, Ben, *The Complete Poems*, edited by George Parfitt, London: Penguin Books, 1975.
Kahn, Louis I., *Louis I. Kahn: Talks with Students Architecture at Rice 26*, Houston: Rice University, 1969.
Kahn, Louis I., "I Love Beginnings," in *What Will Be Has Always Been: The Words of Louis I. Kahn*, edited by Richard Saul Wurman, New York: Rizzoli, 1991.
Kahn, Louis I., *Louis Kahn: Writings, Lectures, Interviews*, edited by Alessandra Latour, New York: Rizzoli International Publications, 1991.
Keats, John, "Letters, to his Brother," December 21, 1817.
Keisch, Claude and Riemann-Reyher, Marie Ursula, eds., *Adolph Menzel, 1815–1905: Between Romanticism and Impressionism*, New Haven: Yale University Press, 1996.
Kermode, Frank, *The Sense of an Ending Studies in the Theory of Fiction*, New York: Oxford University Press, 1967.
Kierkegaard, Søren, *Fear and Trembling & Repetition*, edited by Howard V. Hong and Edna H. Hong, Princeton: Princeton University Press, 1983.
Klee, Paul, *Pedagogical Sketchbook*, New York: Praeger, 1953.
Köhler, Andrea, *Passing Time: An Essay on Waiting*, translated by Michael Eskin, New York: Upper West Side Philosophers, 2011.
Konstantinidis, Aris, *Elements for Self-Knowledge*, Athens: Agra, 1975.
Krackauer, Siegfried, *History: The Last Things before the Last*, completed by Paul Oskar Kristeller, Oxford: Oxford University Press, 1969.

Kristeva, Julia, *Time and Sense Proust and the Experience of Literature*, translated by Ross Guberman, New York: Columbia University Press, 1996.
Kubler, George, *The Shape of Time Remarks on the History of Things*, New Haven: Yale University Press, 1962.
Kula, Witold, *Measures and Men*, translated by R. Szreter, Princeton: Princeton University Press, 1986.
Kuma, Kengo, "Breaking Down into Particles," *Anti-Object: The Dissolution and Disintegration of Architecture*, translated by Hiroshi Watanabe, London: Architectural Association, 2008.
Kwinter, Sanford, *Architectures of Time: Toward a Theory of the Event in Modernist Culture*, Cambridge, MA: MIT Press, 2002.
Le Corbusier, "*Reportage sur un toit-jardin*," *Oeuvre Complète 1938–1946*, Zürich: Girsberger, 1946.
Le Corbusier, "Type-Needs Type-Furniture," in *The Decorative Art of Today*, translated by James I. Dunnett, Cambridge, MA: MIT Press, 1987.
Le Corbusier, *The Final Testament of Père Corbu: A Translation and Interpretation* of Mise au point, translated by Ivan Žaknić, New Haven: Yale University Press, 1997.
Le Corbusier, "To Free Oneself Entirely of Academic Thinking," in *Precisions on the Present State of Architecture and City Planning*, translated by Edith Schreiber Aujame, Cambridge, MA: MIT, 1991.
Leatherbarrow, David, *Uncommon Ground: Architecture, Technology, and Topography*, Cambridge, MA: MIT, 2000.
Leatherbarrow, David, *Topographical Stories: Studies in Landscape and Architecture*, Philadelphia: University of Pennsylvania Press, 2004.
Leatherbarrow, David, "Landings and Crossings," in *Architecture Oriented Otherwise*, New York: Princeton Architectural Press, 2009.
Leatherbarrow, David, "Necessary Qualifications: Design before, during, and after Construction," in *Quality Out of Control: Standards for Measuring Architecture*, edited by A. Dutoit, J. Odgers and A. Sharr, London: Routledge, 2010, 105–18.
Leatherbarrow, David, "Gardens and the Larger Landscape," in *A Cultural History of Gardens in the Modern Age*, edited by John Dixon Hunt, London: Bloomsbury, 2013.
Leatherbarrow, David, "Nature and Artifice in the Architecture of Sverre Fehn," in Christophe Girot and Albert Kirchengast, eds., *Landscript*, no. 4 (2017): 103–23.
Leatherbarrow, David, "From Pedestal to Place," in *Thinking the Sculpture Garden*, edited by Penny Florence, London: Routledge, 2020.
Leatherbarrow, David and Mostafavi, Mohsen, *On Weathering: The Life of Buildings in Time* Cambridge, MA: MIT, 1993.
Leatherbarrow, David and Mostafavi, Mohsen, *Surface Architecture*, Cambridge, MA: MIT, 2002.
Leatherbarrow, David, "The Beginning of the Beginning: Louis I. Kahn's Site Sketches at the Salk Institute," in *Louis Kahn: Drawing, Thinking, Architecture*, edited by Michael Merrill, Zurich: Lars Müller, 2020.
Lee, Rensselaer, *Ut Pictura Poesis: The Humanistic Theory of Painting*, New York: W. W. Norton, 1967.
Leonardo de Vinci, *The Notebooks of Leonardo da Vinci*, edited by E. McCurdy, New York: Renyal & Hitchcock, 1956.
Liu, Linfan, *A Pictorial Vision of Space: Looking at Modern Architecture in China through Landscape Painting*, University of Pennsylvania, 2018.
Loos, Adolf, "Eine zuschrift," and "Architectur," in *Trotzdem, 1900–1930*, Vienna: Georg Prachner, 1982.
Lowenthal, David, *The Past Is a Foreign Country*, Cambridge: Cambridge University Press, 1985.
Luiz Trigueiros, ed., *Álvaro Siza: Leça de Palmeira*, 1959–1973 Lisbon: Editorial Blau, 2004.

Lynch, Kevin, *What Time Is This Place*, Cambridge, MA: MIT Press, 1972.
Malraux, André, *Museum without Walls*, Garden City: Doubleday, 1967.
Mann, Thomas, *The Holy Sinner*, translated by H.T. Lowe-Porter, New York: Alfred A. Knopf, 1951.
Mann, Thomas, *Joseph and His Brothers*, translated by H.T. Lowe-Porter, London: Penguin, 1978.
Marion, Jean-Luc, *Being Given: Toward a Phenomenology of Givenness*, translated by Jeffrey L. Kosky, Stanford: Stanford University Press, 2002.
Marramao, Giacomo, *Kairós: Towards an Ontology of "Due Time,"* translated by Philip Larrey and Silvia Cattaneo, Aurora, Colorado: Davies Group, 2007.
McLaughlin, Patricia, "'How'm I Doing, Corbusier?': An Interview with Louis Kahn," *Pennsylvania Gazette*, vol. 71, no. 3 (1972): 18–26.
Merleau-Ponty, Maurice, *The Phenomenology of Perception*, New York: Humanities Press, 1962.
Merrill, Michael, *Louis Kahn on the Thoughtful Making of Spaces: The Dominican Motherhouse*, Zurich: Lars Müller, 2010.
Moneo, Rafael, "The Idea of the Lasting," *Perspecta*, vol. 24 (1988): 146–57.
Moxey, Keith, *Visual Time: The Image in History*, Durham: Duke University Press, 2013.
Muldoon, Mark S., *Tricks of Time Bergson, Merleau-Ponty and Ricoeur in Search of Time, Self and Meaning*, Pittsburgh: Duquesne University Press, 2006.
Nagel, Alexander and Wood, Christopher S., *Anachronic Renaissance*, New York: Zone Books, 2010.
Nouvel, Jean, et al., *Louisiana Manifesto*, Humlebaek: Louisiana Museum of Modern Art, 2008.
Novotny, Fritz, *Cézanne und das Ende der Wissenschaftlichen Perspektive*, Vienna: Anton Schroll, 1938.
Ortega y Gasset, José, *The Dehumanization of Art and Other Essays on Art, Culture, and Literature*, translated by Willard R. Trask, Princeton, NJ: Princeton University Press, 1968.
Panofsky, Erwin, "Father Time," in *Studies in Iconology: Humanistic Themes in the Art of the Renaissance*, New York: Harper & Row, 1962.
Pardey, John, *Louisiana and Beyond: The Work of Vilhelm Wohlert*, Hellerup: Bløndal, 2007.
Paterson, Aaron, "Interview: Pezo von Ellrichshausen," *architecturenow.co.nz/articles/***Pezo-von-Ellrichshausen***.
Pezo von Ellrichshausen, "'Singular, without Claiming Any Singular Feature': An Interview with Mauricio Pezo and Sofia von Ellrichshausen," in *Casa Poli*, Amsterdam: The Architecture Observer, 2013.
Pezo von Ellrichshausen, *Spatial Structure*, Copenhagen: Arkitekturforlaget B, 2016.
Pezo von Ellrichshausen, *Naïve Intention*, Chicago: IITAC Press and New York: Actar, 2018.
Pezo, Maurizio and Ellrichshausen, Sofia von, "Cien House," *Harvard Design Magazine*, vol. 34 (2011): 110–13.
Plato, *The Collected Dialogues*, edited by Edith Hamilton and Huntington Cairns, Princeton: Princeton University Press, 1961.
Pollitt, J.J., *The Ancient View of Greek Art: Criticism, History, and Terminology*, New Haven: Yale University Press, 1974.
Ponge, Francis, *The Voice of Things*, edited by Beth Archer, New York: McGraw Hill, 1972.
Poulet, Georges, *Studies in Human Time*, New York: Harper Torchbooks, 1959.
Pope, Alexander, "Epistle to Richard Boyle, Earl of Burlington," lines 51–5.
Praz, Mario, *An Illustrated History of Interior Decoration: From Pompeii to Art Nouveau*, translated by William Weaver, London: Thames and Hudson, 1982.
Quinones, Ricardo J., *The Renaissance Discovery of Time*, Cambridge, MA: Harvard University Press, 1972.
Ricoeur, Paul, "Objectivity and Subjectivity in History," in *History and Truth*, translated by C.A. Kelbley, Evanston: Northwestern University Press, 1965.

Ricoeur, Paul, *The Reality of the Historical Past*, Milwaukee: Marquette University Press, 1984.
Ricoeur, Paul, *Time and Narrative*, vol. 1, translated by Kathleen McLaughlin and David Pellauer, Chicago: University of Chicago, 1984.
Ricoeur, Paul, "The Function of Fiction in Shaping Reality," in *A Ricoeur Reader: Reflection and Imagination*, edited by M. Valdés, Toronto: University of Toronto Press, 1991.
Ricoeur, Paul, "Architecture and Narrative," in Pietro Derossi, ed., *Identità i Differenze*, vol. 1, The 19th Triennale di Milano, 1996, 64–72.
Ricoeur, Paul, "Documentary Proof," in *Memory, History, Forgetting*, translated by Kathleen Blamey and David Pellauer, Chicago: University of Chicago, 2004.
Rilke, Rainer Maria, *The Notebooks of Malte Laurids Brigge*, translated by M.D. Herter Norton, New York: W. W. Norton, 1949.
Rogers, Ernesto Nathan, "Preexisting Conditions and Issues of Contemporary Building Practice," in *Architecture Culture 1943–1968*, edited by J. Ockman and E. Eigen, New York: Rizzoli, 1993.
Rossi, Aldo, *The Architecture of the City*, translated by Diane Ghirardo and Joan Ockman, Cambridge, MA: MIT, 1982.
Rowley, George, *Principles of Chinese Painting*, 2nd ed., Princeton: Princeton University Press, 1959.
Rykwert, Joseph, *The Idea of a Town: The Anthropology of Urban Form in Rome, Italy and the Ancient World*, London: Faber and Faber, 1976.
Rykwert, Joseph, "A Healthy Mind in a Healthy Body," in *History in, of, and for Architecture*, edited by J.E. Hancock, Cincinnati: University of Cincinnati, 1981.
Sachs, Curt, *Rhythm and Tempo*, New York: Columbia University Press, 1953.
Sample, Hilary, *Maintenance Architecture*, Cambridge, MA: MIT, 2016.
Saxl, Fritz, *Veritas Filia Temporis*, in *Philosophy and History: Essays Presented to Ernst Cassirer*, edited by R. Klibansky and H.J. Paton, Oxford: Clarendon, 1936.
Schild Bunim, Miriam, *Space in Medieval Painting and the Forerunners of Perspective*, New York: Columbia University Press, 1940.
Schmarsow, August, "The Essence of Architectural Creation," 1893. Reprinted in *Empathy, Form, Space: Problems in German Aesthetics, 1873–1893*, edited by Harry Mallgrave and Eleftherios Ikonomou, Santa Monica: Getty Center for the History of Art and the Humanities, 1994.
Schorske, Carl E., *Thinking with History Explanations in the Passage to Modernism*, Princeton: Princeton University Press, 1998.
Sheridan, Michael, *Louisiana: Architecture and Landscape*, Humlebaek: Louisiana Museum of Modern Art, 2017.
Simmel, Georg, "The Ruin," 1911. Reprinted in *Essays on Sociology, Philosophy and Aesthetics*, edited by Kurt H. Wolff, New York: Harper & Row, 1965, 259–66.
Simmel, Georg, *The View of Life: Four Metaphysical Essays with Journal Aphorisms*, Chicago: University of Chicago Press, 2010.
Sipiora, Phillip and Baumlin, James S., eds., *Rhetoric and Kairós: Essays in History, Theory, and Praxis*, Albany: State University of New York, 2002.
Siza, Álvaro, *Álvaro Siza: Esquissos de viagem*, Porto: Documentos de Arquitectura, 1988.
Siza, Álvaro, "Design as Experience," *Domus*, vol. 746 (February 1993): 28.
Siza, Álvaro, "Fragments of an Experience," in *Álvaro Siza: Works and Projects*, edited by Pedro de Llano and Carlos Castanheira, Madrid: Electa, 1995.
Siza, Álvaro, "Eight Points," in *Siza: Architecture Writings*, edited by A. Angelillo, Milan: Skira, 1997.
Siza, Álvaro, "Every Year, with the Spring Tides" (1980), in *Piscina na Praia de Leça*, edited by Michael Toussaint and Maria Melo, Lisbon: A + A Books, 2016.
Siza, Álvaro and Chiaramonte, Giovanni, *Measure of the West: A Representation of Travel*, Montreal: McGill-Queen's University Press, 2018.

Smithson, Alison and Peter, "The 'As Found' and 'The Found,'" in *The Independent Group: Postwar Britain and the Aesthetics of Plenty*, edited by David Robbins, Cambridge, MA: MIT, 1990.

Sorabji, Richard, *Time, Creation, and the Continuum Theories in Antiquity and the Early Middle Ages*, Ithaca: Cornell University Press, 1983.

St. Augustine, *Confessions*, XI, 14.17.

Summers, David, "Real Metaphor: Towards a Redefinition of the 'Conceptual' Image," in *Visual Theory: Painting and Interpretation*, edited by N. Bryson, et al, London: Polity Press, 1991.

Summers, David, *Real Spaces: World Art History and the Rise of Western Modernism*, London: Phaidon, 2003.

Sypher, Wylie, *The Ethic of Time Structures of Experience in Shakespeare*, New York: Seabury Press, 1976.

Tournier, Michel, *Friday*, translated by Norman Denny, New York: Pantheon, 1969.

Trachtenberg, Marvin, *Building-in-Time from Giotto to Alberti and Modern Oblivion*, New Haven: Yale University Press, 2010.

Treib, Marc, ed., *Spatial Recall Memory in Architecture and Landscape*, New York: Routledge, 2009.

Trigueiros, Luiz, ed., *Álvaro Siza: Leça de Palmeira, 1959–1973*, Lisbon: Editorial Blau, 2004.

Tuomey, John, *Architecture, Craft, and Culture: Reflections on the Work of O'Donnell + Tuomey*, Cork: Gandon, 2008.

Umbach, Maiken and Hüppauf, Bernd, *Vernacular Modernism: Heimat, Globalization, and the Built Environment*, Stanford: Stanford University Press, 2005.

Valéry, Paul, "The Problem of Museums," in *Degas, Manet, Morisot: The Collected Works of Paul Valéry*, vol. 12, translated by D. Paul, New York: Pantheon, 1960.

Vitruvius, *Ten Books on Architecture*, edited by Ingrid Rowland, Cambridge: Cambridge University, 1999.

Wang Shu, "Build a World to Resemble Nature," in Mark Cousins and Chen Wei, eds., *Architecture Studies 2: Topography and Mental Space*, Beijing: China Architecture & Building Press, 2012.

Weitzmann, Kurt, *Illustrations in Roll and Codex: A Study of the Origin and Method of Text Illustration*, 2nd ed., Princeton: Princeton University Press, 1970.

Wells, Wilfrid H., *Perspective in Early Chinese Painting*, London: Edward Goldston, 1935.

Wilcox, Donald J., *The Measure of Times Past Pre-Newtonian Chronologies and the Rhetoric of Relative Time*, Chicago: University of Chicago Press, 1987.

Winks, Robin W., ed., *The Historian as Detective: Essays on Evidence*, New York: Harper Colophon, 1969.

Wright, Frank Lloyd, "The Shadow-of-the-Wall—Primitive Instincts Still Alive," in *The Living City*, New York: Horizon Press, 1958.

Yourcenar, Marguerite, *That Mighty Sculptor, Time*, 1954 and 1983 reprint, translated by Walter Kaiser, New York: Noonday Press, 1992.

Zumthor, Peter, "A Way of Looking at Things," in *Thinking Architecture*, Baden: Lars Müller, 1998, 24–5.

Index

Aalto, Alvar 23
adjustment 41, 43—4, 189—92, 195, 218, 238
Aion 102, 162
Alberti, Leon Battista 184, 189
   On the Art of Building 49
   On Painting 23
ambient conditions 6, 13, 26, 28, 30, 41, 64, 222
Aristotle 51, 82—3, 95, 101, 146, 217
   De Anima
   Physics
Auerbach, Erich 20

Bacon, Francis 101
Badovici, Jean 31
Benjamin, Walter 203
Bill, Max 114
Bo, Jørgen and Wohlert, Vilhelm 101—2, 106, 113, 115—17, 119, 121
   Louisiana Museum of Modern Art, Copenhagen Figs. 3.2.1—3, 3.2.6—10, 3.2.13—15
Bo Bardi, Lina
   Casa del Vidro, São Paulo 212, Fig. 4.3.5
Breuer, Marcel
   De Bijenkorf Department Store, Amsterdam 6, 9, Fig. 1.1.5
Brinkman Johannes and Leendert van der Vlugt
   Van Nelle Chocolate Factory, Rotterdam 44

Calder, Alexander 115
Cezanne, Paul 29, 135
Chareau, Pierre 37
Chronos 102, 162
close reading 19—20
concurrency 3, 9, 34, 36, 48, 49, 97—8, 151—2, 183

Conrad, Joseph
   Mirror of the Sea 149
contrapposto 84, 175—6

Dahl, Johan Christian 55
days, diurnal cycles 3, 14, 23, 35, 39
depth 18, 96, 104—5, 115, 119—20, 157, 162, 209
   deferred, recursive, and abrupt 140—146
   pictorial 18, 73, 93, 98, 135—46, 179
   of thought 133
   of topography 14, 57, 131
   urban 162
   vertical 162—5
   of walls 220, 223
dishing of treads 6, 12, 67—8
distance 38, 96—97, 105, 157
   defect of 112
   level, deep, and high 136—146
   pictorial 135—6, 138—40
   viewing 111—112
Derrida, Jacques 105
Dickinson, Emily
   Forever—is composed of nows 138
Doesburg, Theo van 118
Dubuffet, Jean 114
Duccio 135
duration, endurance 3, 23, 48, 74, 82, 97, 119, 137, 140, 151, 162, 169, 204, 239

event 10, 18—9, 29, 35, 38, 41, 47—8, 51, 55—7, 64, 67, 73—4, 93—7, 125, 134, 146, 169, 173, 175—9, 199, 227, 229—31
   episodic 77, 93—5, 228
experience 18, 30, 37, 51, 80, 84, 122, 123, 140, 150
   aesthetic 110, 197

architectural 102, 151, 157
  bodily 15, 83, 103, 217
  perceptual 14, 67, 105, 115, 126, 134, 136
  prosaic 104, 138, 149, 231—4

Faulkner, William 10
Fehn, Sverre 49—74, 193
  Archbishopric Museum, Hamar Fig. 2.3.1
  National Museum of Architecture, Oslo Fig. 2.3.2
  Villa Busk, Bamble Figs. 2.3.3—16
Ferrara Cathedral 11, Fig. 1.1.6
finishing 10, 71, 80, 170, 222
  re-finishing 3, 56, 67, 170
forces 6, 25, 223, 228
  of allowing and resisting 27—8, 30, 41, 43, 67—8, 78, 222
  ambient 6, 23, 53, 88
  in equilibrium 82, 84
  of nature 26—9, 55, 65, 7—6, 88, 129, 151, 215
Freud, Sigmund 218

Giacometti, Alberto 107, 119—21
  Giacometti Room, Louisiana Museum, Copenhagen Figs 3.2.14—15
Giotto 135
given conditions 49, 170—1, 193, 202, 230
Goethe, Johann Wolfgang von 15
  Palladio Architecture 93
Gray, Eileen 31—48
  Tempe à Pailla, Castellar, France Figs. 2.2.1—7
Gregotti, Vittorio 193
Guo Xi 129—30, 140

Heraclitus 138
Hesiod 48
Hofmannsthal, Hugo von
  Book of Friends 227
Holmes, Sherlock 20, 51
Homer 48
Horace 18, 49, 144
horizon 36, 43, 78, 84, 110, 125—6, 135, 145, 149, 151, 154, 156, 158—65, 234
  temporal 10, 13, 30, 231
Husserl, Edmund 206

Jaeger, Werner 83
Jensen, Knud 106, 108—11, 113, 116

Joyce, James
  Working notes for Ulysses 169

Kahn, Louis I. 6, 204—12, 217, 220, 223
  Dominican Mother House 17, Fig. 1.1.9
  National Parliament House, Dhaka 223
  Salk Institute, La Jolla, California 6, 8, Fig. 1.1.3
  Study for a Mural Based on Egyptian Motifs Fig. 4.3.1
Kahlo, Frida 46
Kierkegaard, Søren 185
  Repetition 181, 196–200
Klee, Paul 172
Klimt, Gustav 135
Kuma, Kengo
  Hiroshigi Museum of Art, Bato Nakagawa Fig. 1.1.4

Le Corbusier 65, 118, 159, 173, 204, 207–12
  Parthenon sketch Fig. 4.3.2
  Porte Molitor Apartment, Paris 54
  Swiss Pavilion, Paris 14—5, Fig. 1.1.8
Leonardo da Vinci 101, 217
  Adoration of the Magi 173—9, Fig. 4.1.1
Loos, Adolf 208—12, 220
  Looshaus on Michaelerplatz, Vienna 208
  Villa Müller, Prague 220

Maes, Nicolaes 93—9
  Eavesdropper Fig. 3.1.1
maintenance 5, 68, 185, 122
Mann, Thomas 54, 210
Martini, Simone 135
materials 6, 27, 52, 55—6, 64
  finishing of 10, 80, 170, 222
  labor of 28, 68
  smart 6
  temperature of 44–5
  time of 10, 80, 223
Matisse, Henri 135
memory 4, 5, 51, 135, 151, 202
  cultural 130, 209—10, 242
  recollection 5, 18, 105, 135, 137, 183, 202, 223
Menzel, Adolf
  Balcony Room 23—30, Fig. 2.1.1
Michelangelo 84, 174—5, 217
Mies van der Rohe 118, 212—13
  Villa Tugendhat, Brno, Czech Republic Fig. 4.3.6

Miró, Joan 116, 118
  Personage, Louisiana Museum of Modern Art Fig. 3.2.12
modification 5–6, 64, 160, 170—2, 181, 188—9
Moneo, Rafael, 181—2, 185—95, 197, 199, 201—3
  Museo Nacional de Arte Romano de Mérida Figs. 4.2.1—4.2.12
Moore, Henry 110, 116—117
  Three Piece Reclining Figure-Draped, Louisiana Museum of Modern Art Fig. 3.2.11
movement
  bodily 3, 14—5, 18, 36, 97—8, 102—5, 133—4, 137, 151—7
  meandering 14, 238
  patterns of 23, 88, 151, 232
  of the eye 126, 133—5, 136—7, 140, 237
  of natural elements 25, 36, 88
  schedules of 23, 34, 41, 48
Myron of Eleutherae 83—4
  Discobolus Fig. 2.4.4

Neutra, Richard
  Desert House, Palm Springs 44
Niemeyer, Oscar
  Ministry of Education, Rio de Janeiro Fig 1.1.7
Nietzsche, Friedrich 75, 83
Noack, Astrid 113, 114
  Kneeling Figure: Young Man Planting a Tree Standing Woman
Nørgård, Ole and Edith 108—9
  Garden rooms, Louisiana Museum of Modern Art, Copenhagen Figs. 3.2.4—5

Palazzo Ragione, Padova 11
Palladio, Andrea 15, 53—5, 209
Parthenon, Athens 207
passivity 82, 217
  active 68, 80, 82
permanence 3—5, 10—12, 17—8, 48, 126, 152
persistence 18
Pezo von Ellrichshausen 209—25
  Casa Guna, San Pedro, Chile 210—12, Fig. 4.3.3
  Casa Solo, Cretas, Spain 211—12, Fig. 4.3.4
  Cien House, Concepción, Chile 212, Fig. 4.3.9
  Poli House, Coliumo, Chile 212, 214—15, 218—25, Figs. 4.3.7—8,
  Spatial Structure 209, 217

Plato 31, 73, 162
  Laws 101
Ponge, Francis 77
potential, or capacity 82—4, 88—9
  material 82
product, production 16, 171—2
project, projection 16, 28, 171—3, 179, 181—5, 188, 193, 200—4, 216—9, 227—8
  as drawings 183—4, 201, 217—8, 230, 233, 236—40

Quintilian 31

Raphael 217
recollection 5, 18, 105, 135, 137, 183, 202, 223
repetition 55, 98–99, 143, 157, 181, 185, 196—02
rhythm 14, 16, 23, 38, 46, 61—2, 83—9, 111, 157—8, 160, 239—40
Ricoeur, Paul 23, 77
Rilke, Rainer Maria 28
Rivera, Diego 46
Rodin, Auguste 84, 174
Rogers, Ernesto 193
Rossi, Aldo 10, 11, 152, 209

St. Augustine 150, 206
Schmarsow, August 12, 103
seasons, seasonality 3, 14, 23, 28, 30, 39
sedimentation, saturation 6, 13, 28, 65, 68, 193, 209, 217, 222
shadows 13, 29, 34, 37, 82, 89, 136, 157—62, 220
Simmel, Georg 6, 223
Siza, Álvaro 17, 75—89, 150—66, 227—42
  Swimming Pools at Leça da Palmeira, Porto Figs. 1.1.1, 2.4.1—2.4.3, 2.4.5—2.4.8, 3.4.1—14
Smithson, Alison and Peter 173
Spitzer, Leo 20
stories 23, 57, 70, 74, 207
  topographical 55—6, 65, 77, 96, 188
Su, Shi 123, 144
Summers, David 112
synchronicity 17, 41, 48, 184, 206, 222
  non- 12, 34, 38, 43—4, 96, 135

Távora, Fernando 233
Temples of Sun and Moon, Teotihuacan, Mexico 46
testimony 20, 23, 28—30, 51, 67, 209
time
    anachronistic 173—9
    clock 10, 13, 46, 98, 137, 149—50
    cyclical 56, 64, 75, 135, 206, 212, 223
    of daily life 55, 64, 146, 215, 231—3, 236
    delayed 16, 42, 105, 140, 163—5
    flowing 69, 184
    future anterior 73, 223
    historical 10, 23, 101, 204
    of a journey 110, 116, 126—7, 135, 139
    linear 150, 173, 184, 206, 212
    momentary 95, 114, 137, 150, 169, 184
    of natural elements 37, 96, 146, 222
    no longer-not yet 10, 98, 103—4, 137, 165, 178, 183, 201—2, 206
    opportune 44, 46—7, 157—61
    periodic 69, 76, 88, 96
    pre-figured 10, 16, 48, 68, 70—3, 172, 193
    sequential 57
    simultaneity 98, 134, 143
    still passing 103—5, 121—2
    unity of 125, 134
topography 38–39, 54, 108, 131, 149, 231–232
    and disorientation 144, 157
Tournier, Michel 60
traces 4, 12–13, 20, 23, 28, 30, 49, 51, 55, 64—7, 187—8, 202, 209, 223

Valery, Paul 106
Vignola 98

Wang, Shu 18, 123—4, 127, 129—36, 140—8
    Guest House, China Academy of Art, Hangzhou Figs. 3.3.1, 3.3.5—17
    Wenzheng College, Suzhou 126—9, Figs. 3.3.2—4

Wells Cathedral Fig. 1.1.2
Wright, Frank Lloyd 137, 233

Xenophon 73

Zumthor, Peter 23